Command Performance

TO JANE ALEXANDER WITH BEST WISHES – KEVIN SIERS

Jane Alexander

COMMAND PERFORMANCE

AN ACTRESS IN THE THEATER OF POLITICS

PublicAffairs
NEW YORK

Copyright © 2000 by Jane Alexander.

Published in the United States by PublicAffairs™, a member of the Perseus Books Group.

All rights reserved.

Printed in the United States of America.

No part of this book may be reproduced in any manner whatsoever without written permission except in the case of brief quotations embodied in critical articles and reviews. For information, address PublicAffairs, 250 W. 57th Street, Suite 1321, New York, NY 10107.

Book design by Jenny Dossin.

Library of Congress Cataloging-in-Publication Data

Alexander, Jane, 1939-

Command performance: an actress in the theater of politics / Jane Alexander.

p. cm.

Includes index.

ISBN 1–891620–06–1

1. Alexander, Jane, 1939-

2. Arts administrators—United States—Biography.

3. Actresses—United States—Biography.

4. National Endowment for the Arts.

I.   Title.

NX768.A43 A3 2000

792'.028'092—dc21

[B]

00–023375

FIRST EDITION

10 9 8 7 6 5 4 3 2 1

Contents

This book is dedicated to the staff of the National Endowment for the Arts.

Acknowledgments

The process of producing a book is different from that of presenting a play, but neither endeavor is accomplished alone. I would like to acknowledge the fine people who made this book possible.

My literary agent, Owen Laster, introduced me to publisher Peter Osnos and editor Lisa Kaufman at PublicAffairs, which provided the perfect home for me. Lisa gave invaluable advice and criticism every step of the way. All writers should have such a thoughtful editor.

My assistant Rosemarie Rogers organized many boxes of papers and photos and cheerfully aided me in additional research.

Jane Fritsch was originally going to be my co-writer, and though I decided to write the book on my own, I am grateful for her initial suggestions and for the title. My friends Jane Milliken, Gretchen Dow Simpson, and Clare Weaver read the first draft, offering encouraging comments, as did Alexander Crary and Margaret Sherin with the second draft. Keith Donohue put aside the writing of his own book to spend time on mine. He wrote copious notes and urged me to become friendly with the comma. He also reminded me that the cast of characters might view the events depicted in my book in a different light: "As the Irishman said to his wife on their wedding night, 'Brace yourself, Bridget.'"

My son, Jace Alexander, and my daughter-in-law, Madeleine Corman, gave constant support even as they were producing their own main event, baby Isabelle Moon Alexander.

I would like to thank my computer and Windows 98. I am sorry to contribute to the demise of erasers in the world, but "cut and paste" is a lot of fun and the entire computer world is a miracle.

Another miracle is my husband, Ed Sherin, who makes life joyous and who made sure that I carried out the first ergonomic principle of writing: the juxtaposition of the seat of my pants with the seat of a chair.

Prologue

"You gonna fund pornography?" the senator barked at me across the vast expanse of government desk, made all the more intimidating by his diminutive size, or perhaps I was the one who was shrinking in my chair. Strom Thurmond had been South Carolina's senator for forty years. Over and over again he had been returned to office. He had a reputation for getting things done for his constituents, whether it was a tobacco issue or defense or a local favor. Call Strom—he'll take care of it.

As I sat before this taut, leathery gnome of a man with hair a color not found in nature, I couldn't help but admire his fortitude. At ninety he was still donning jogging shorts and doing a daily turn around Capitol Hill. He was a survivor, and now he was going for the gold. He was determined to be the oldest sitting senator in the history of that august body. His one-hundredth birthday was just around the corner, and neither infirmity nor inability was going to stop him. *The Guinness Book of World Records* was waiting.

"You gonna fund pornography?" His question to me was flung out like a glove slapping the ground. I rose weakly to the challenge and responded that the National Endowment for the Arts did not fund obscenity, that obscenity was considered unprotected speech. He said he didn't care what the Endowment did, he wanted to know what *I* thought.

I said, somewhat grandly, that I was an artist, that as an artist nothing human was alien to me. It was a phrase I had pondered a lot in the past, a phrase originally attributed to the Roman playwright Terence in 350 B.C. As I said it, images of the fall of the Roman Empire arose in my mind.

"Aren't you a moral woman?" Thurmond shot back.

Well, *that* was a question no one had ever asked me. It took me by surprise, and I had to think a minute. All the roles I ever played flashed before my eyes: mothers, daughters, lovers, wives; murderers, lawyers, judges, and drunks; lesbians, nurses, saints, and sinners. I had to love them when I played them; I had to love something about every character, and moral judgment never came into it. As for my own life, had I been guilty about things? Sure. Had there been regrets? Of course. But overall I didn't think in absolutes.

I replied, "Yes, I'm a moral woman." And then I began to descend the slippery slope. I felt compelled to defend the artist in me and all the artists who had ever existed, knowing full well that controversy and political expediency had been entwined from time immemorial to the present day. Hadn't the pope in the 1500s asked Michelangelo to put a fig leaf on the private parts of his statue of David? And as I have been writing this, didn't New York's Mayor Rudolph Guiliani threaten to close the Brooklyn Museum because of a painting he thought was sacrilegious? I forged ahead anyway.

"First Amendment rights protect free speech," I said.

This elicited instantaneous disgust. The senator was almost apoplectic. "Ach," he spat out, "First Amendment rights are an excuse for people to do things they shouldn't be doing!"

Whoops. There goes two hundred years of jurisprudence, I thought.

I made one last try to rescue this disastrous interview.

"The Endowment doesn't fund pornography," I repeated. And not wishing to alienate this venerable institution of the South any further, I beat a hasty retreat out of his office and down the marble halls of Congress.

I was shaken, and scared out of my wits. Was this the U.S. Senate? Was this what a senator of the United States actually believed? What had happened to the Constitution? Hadn't all the battles been fought already by the Continental Congress when they hammered out their brilliant document on the nature of democracy and a civil society? I knew the answer in my heart; I knew these precepts had to be defended over and over again with each generation, but it was a tough first visit to the Hill. And I hadn't even been confirmed as NEA chairman yet. Things would only get worse as it became clear that the arts and the

National Endowment for the Arts in particular were flashpoints for many of the issues troubling society in the late twentieth century. My journey through the minefield of the next four years would change my thinking considerably about politics, the arts, and the government's role. My visit to Strom Thurmond was only the opening salvo in the ensuing war for the NEA.

Command Performance

CHAPTER ONE

Early Training

My life was never without drama. If the daily events of girlhood failed to arouse the requisite emotions of passion, sadness, or delight, I would provoke them with stories, spun endlessly in my mind. I don't remember ever being bored. Like many other little girls my age, I put myself center stage as a cowgirl, a ballerina, or a nurse, but my imagination drew me more often to the realm of the fantastic. Trees and flowers were animate beings that housed magical creatures at the base of their roots, elves and fairies who tended to the world at night and made things right. I kept a fairy in a Kleenex box and watched her comings and goings on my windowsill with as much conviction as one would watch a bird. And I acted out the dramas of the natural world as I observed it at three feet high. The flutter of a moth entangled in the filaments of a web as the spider stealthily advanced would first scare and then excite me as I played the role of victim and then conqueror. The eternal mysteries of birth, death, and love ignited my curiosity at an early age.

My mother didn't know what she had in me, but she tolerated the interminable whirling to Strauss waltzes and the rudimentary rhymes on subjects as banal as a leaf or as monumental as the birth of a baby sister. She listened with appreciative awe to my fairy tales as I recounted them. All her friends knew that their unwanted clothes had a home in my closet for "dress-up," an after-school event I engaged in with regularity when I wasn't climbing trees. And my mother guided me in wonderland by naming the animals and plants and revealing the worlds to be found under rocks or in the hearts of flowers.

My mother, Ruth Pearson, was the daughter of a farm girl from Nova Scotia and a widowed streetcar conductor, and she grew up in South Boston scrapping for every opportunity. Her good looks and good mind took her from that impoverished background to the highest echelons of nursing, scrubbing for neurosurgeons in the operating room. Mother knew nothing of the worlds of painting, literature, music, and theater but was embarrassed sufficiently by the Nova Scotian handicrafts of knitting and crocheting, which my grandmother practiced so deftly, that she disavowed them completely. My grandmother sold white wool socks for fifty cents a pair back in the 1940s, and her unschooled English was peppered with more "ain'ts" and "dese" and "dose" than my upwardly mobile mother could bear. When my mother met my father in the corridors of a New York hospital where he was doing his residency, she thought him cultured and urbane and fell swiftly in love.

My father *was* cultured—by education, not inheritance. Growing up in North Platte, Nebraska, there was not much to see but corn, cattle, and vast train yards. His maternal grandfather had emigrated from Germany, crossed the plains in a covered wagon, and assumed a management position with the Union Pacific railway, which terminated in North Platte in 1867. There is a photograph of my grandmother, tambourine in hand, surrounded by other members of a teenage musical ensemble a hundred years ago. I imagine it is this grandmother who dreamed of larger horizons, harking back to the museums and concert halls of her own mother's German youth. She sent her only son, my father, away to Harvard on scholarship at the tender age of sixteen. Bart Quigley never returned to live in the West again.

The study of medicine was the natural route for my father to take. My grandfather, born of Irish immigrants, was a pioneer in the use of radium to treat cancer and of vitamins as nutritional supplements. He also wrote of the dangers of white flour and sugar forty years before such information became common knowledge in the 1960s. He rarely left Nebraska, but my grandfather's impact on medicine west of the Mississippi is well documented. One of his patients was the Wild West showman Buffalo Bill Cody, whose ranch, Scout's Rest, was a few miles from my grandparents' home. I still have many stop-action photos he

took of cowboys and Indians on horseback engaged in the mock war-
fare that Buffalo Bill directed. My grandfather loved his Kodak cameras
and passed his love of photography to my father, who in turn passed it
on to my brother and me.

My father's inquisitiveness, which consumed him throughout his
life, was satisfied at Harvard with its limitless possibilities of study. Dad
was a gifted child who excelled in every course he ever took. He had a
prodigious vocabulary and kept a standing bet with us until the day he
died that we could not stump him on a word in *Webster's Standard Dic-
tionary*. I collected the five-dollar reward only twice in three decades.
He was also a man of wit and silliness, which made our childhood with
him either great good fun or deeply embarrassing. He was not above
slathering swarthy makeup on his face, toweling his head in a turban,
and greeting my blind date at the door with, "Avast ye mate!" The poor
boy would cower before him, not knowing whether he should laugh or
whether Dr. Quigley was genuinely mad.

April Fool's was Dad's favorite day of the year. He'd go to work at the
hospital with a faucet on his forehead or a spool of thread inside his
breast pocket with the end flauntingly dangled on the outside of his
dark jacket. An unsuspecting stranger would go to pick off the offending thread only to keep pulling and pulling it with no end in sight.
Dad's mirth would bubble over.

I was the eldest, my brother Tom was born nineteen months later,
and my sister Pam arrived eight years after him. We grew up in a
comfortable clapboard house in Brookline, Massachusetts, in a neighborhood called Pill Hill because so many doctors lived there. Fortunately—because my mother did not learn to drive until well after I
did—the neighborhood was only a few blocks from the Boston border
and from public busses and trolleys. Pill Hill was bordered on the east
by Whiskey Point and on the west by The Farm, two less privileged
neighborhoods where scruffy youngsters sometimes took us on,
whirling baseball bats over our heads in their displeasure or screaming
words my father never used.

But for the most part my childhood was contained in the one short
block of Hawthorn Road where twelve families lived. We children
climbed trees together, sledded the tiny hills, and played kick-the-can

on hot summer nights until it was too dark to see the can and the cicadas had begun their nightly drumming. At the end of the street lived the only African American family in the neighborhood. It was not easy for them, and they kept to themselves despite the fact that Roland Hayes was one of the great concert singers in America at the time. My mother had an open, generous way with people and befriended Mrs. Hayes. Occasionally their only child, Africa, and I played together. She was a few years older, but I was grateful for her attention. I heard her father sing a spiritual hymn once, the sonorous tones so much more emotional than the Protestant hymns I was used to. The world had greater variety to offer than our little block. Still there was comfort in the fact that we were all known to Pat, the red-faced Irish cop on our beat, and that when a homeless man knocked on our back door my mother would invite him into the kitchen and give him a meal. Life was simpler then.

One summer of the early 1950s brought tragedy to our happy idyll. My friend Sally was diagnosed with polio and taken to Children's Hospital one June morning. The rest of us were quarantined for the next three months lest we too were carriers. We anxiously awaited word of our little friend's daily progress and sensed that things were not going well when our parents said less and less. We continued our games, made up plays and puppet theater, and leaped over whirring sprinklers in the sweltering heat.

Sally died of spinal meningitis one August afternoon. It had not been polio at all. We knew of the dangers of infantile paralysis, and each of us had school chums who had been afflicted, but spinal meningitis was altogether new to us. In our grief we sought to keep her memory alive by creating a fund in her name. Eight of us preteens went door to door with a basket and raised twenty-four dollars for Sally that first day. We gave it to the hospital for spinal meningitis research.

The horror of her death obscured the horror of the misdiagnosis. All of my parents' friends were doctors, and many of them were in the forefront of medicine at that time. My mother's obstetrician, and the man who delivered me in 1939, was John Rock, one of the inventors of the birth control pill. Others were doing the first kidney transplants or specializing in brain surgery, and my own father, who was the doctor for the Harvard football team, helped found the field of sports medicine. Doctors were gods, and I rarely heard a word against them. They were authority figures whom one did not cross or question. But even then, in my eleven-year-old mind, as I lay in bed crying for my friend Sally, I wondered about that misdiagnosis. I never fully trusted the word of authorities again.

My parents insisted that I go to a girls' school, Beaver Country Day, several miles away, rather than attend the Brookline public schools. Given how smitten I was with boys from the age of five, it was probably a wise decision. I cannot remember a time when I was not madly in love. In kindergarten there was a fellow who snapped gum when the teacher's back was turned, delighting us all with his boldness as she searched in vain for the culprit. When he graced me with his cocky smile, I melted. The feeling was so good that I sought to re-create it again and again as one love replaced another through the years. This thing called love was a total mystery to me, but the vagaries of passion and despair that accompanied each devotion kept my life in high drama.

My love of performing was first realized in a school production of *Treasure Island* in the fifth grade. I played a wily Long John Silver to the delight of my classmates. Their laughter and applause hooked me, and I decided to pursue theater from then on. I performed in school plays, in community theater, and in summer stock productions until I graduated in 1957. Our drama teacher, Mrs. Smith, suggested that I was good enough to make acting a career. Beaver also introduced me to painting, ceramics, woodworking, and choral singing. I made a cradle for my baby sister and vases for my mother and was lucky enough to sing Handel's *Messiah* in Boston's Symphony Hall with other high school choruses.

Headmaster Crosby Hodgman had strong feelings about education based on the teachings of John Dewey. We rigorously studied the traditional fields of history, languages, and the sciences, but the arts were also part of the curriculum and tapped areas in each of us that might otherwise have remained unearthed. Some of my classmates went on to become painters, writers, and singers, while others excelled in business, education, and science.

Boston was a fine city to grow up in. The public transportation was excellent, and there was always plenty to do, from Red Sox baseball games (where my father was often consulted for injuries) to the Science Museum, or the Peabody Museum at Harvard where the collection of glass flowers never failed to tantalize. But perhaps more than anything Boston represented the cradle of liberty. It was here that tea was dumped in the harbor by disgruntled taxpayers, and it was close by in Lexington and Concord that a citizen militia first stood their ground against the forces of the British crown. Our family would sometimes take Sunday outings to the graveyards along the Freedom Trail and marvel at the famous names etched in the stones, each with a story that had contributed to the building of our nation. Our school education was steeped in the pride of early patriotism. The contributions of Benjamin Franklin, Tom Paine, and Nathan Hale were as much a part of my youth as Disney's *Snow White* and *Dumbo*. (Although Nathan Hale's declaration "I only regret I have but one life to lose for my country" was fixed in my mind forever the way my dad chose to remember it: "I only regret I have but one wife and live in the country.") We grew up well versed in the accomplishments of our revolutionary heroes, proud of what our democracy stood for, and idealistic in our political beliefs.

I played a small role in politics at school. It was hard for me not to be the boss in group situations. I did not enjoy being in large groups generally, but since we were all thrust into them daily, being the leader seemed the least frustrating option. My classmates must also have felt that it was best for me to lead because they elected me president of the class almost every year. We numbered only fifty-seven girls, but I enjoyed being the liaison between them and the faculty and delegating committees for everything from the prom to social work. I had no aspiration for higher office, such as head of the student council, and never once considered a career in politics. My ten years at Beaver were insular and secure and rewarded me with lifelong friendships and a sense that I could accomplish anything I set out to do.

As much as I wanted to forgo college and head straight to New York to become an actress, my father said that all knowledge would serve me and that the more I knew the more I could bring to my work. He was supportive of my hope to become an actress eventually. In the late 1920s Dad had been a member of the University Players, a summer theater group on Cape Cod that had included Henry Fonda and James Stewart, among other fledgling actors. Although my father opted for medicine, his love of theater never abated, and he gave me his utmost support.

He suggested, however, that I have "an ace in the hole" in case acting did not work out. I went to Sarah Lawrence College in Bronxville, New York, because it was close to New York City and its arts program had a fine reputation. I took mathematics as well as theater with the idea of becoming an IBM programmer should I fail at an acting career. Math was always exciting for me; it was the language that got us to the stars and created the giant computers that were making their debut in the late 1950s. A single computer could fill an entire room and took days to compute what is accomplished now in less than a second by a hand-held PC. Programming the huge IBMs forty years ago seemed like a glamorous and exciting job. My math teachers throughout school had been exceptional, and although I was never very good at it, I loved the subject. Still, my heart was set on the theater.

The atmosphere at Sarah Lawrence was intense. We women saw plenty of men on the weekends when we rock-and-rolled to Jerry Lee Lewis and Chuck Berry, but from Monday to Friday we roamed the campus in black tights and leotards debating Kierkegaard and Martin Buber. Harold Taylor, the dynamic president of the college, was an exemplary role model and a kind and gentle man. He was deeply committed to the educational system that Sarah Lawrence espoused—a system grounded, like Beaver's, in the philosophy of John Dewey. With the exception of a few lecture classes such as those of the popular Joseph Campbell, we students sat at round tables with our teachers and discussed the subject at hand collectively in seminars. We were required to write extensive papers in all areas of study. This was very difficult work for undergraduates but sharply honed our skills in reading, research, synthesizing, and writing.

I flourished in the theater department, playing many roles in contemporary and classic plays. I even directed the first effort of the playwright Tina Howe, a futuristic piece called *Closing Time*. Sarah Lawrence was known for its modern dance program under the leadership of the great Bessie Schonberg. I took up the rear of the class watching longingly as Lucinda Childs and Meredith Monk leapt like gazelles across the polished wood. My future would never be in dance, but theater seemed more and more promising.

One rainy evening during sophomore year my roommate and best friend, Nona Evans, was hit by a car; she died five days later. I was bereft and confused. It was incomprehensible to me that my young, vivacious friend could be robbed of her life at the age of nineteen. I made it through the rest of the year in a daze and decided that since most of my friends were graduating seniors, and since Harold Taylor was stepping down as president, I too would leave Sarah Lawrence.

My junior year was spent at one of the oldest universities in Europe, the University of Edinburgh in Scotland. It was the first time I had attended classes with members of the opposite sex since kindergarten, and the result was predictable. I didn't get much work done. Within a few weeks I was part of a high-spirited group of students who hailed from Sweden, Hungary, Poland, Norway, Britain, Africa, and North America. The Swedish girls were loose and gorgeous, living the sexy life depicted in their country's hit movie *I Am Curious Yellow.* Our African prince was as dark as the dark interior of his continent and had tribal scars in neat rows on his cheeks. The Norwegian boys took us skiing, shushing the powder off the slopes as they "christied" effortlessly ahead of us. We all partied a lot and gathered together in The Paperback Bookshop, owned by an American ex-patriot named Jim Haynes, a handsome Lothario just a few years our senior. The girl from Brookline was getting an education her parents never dreamed of.

I shared "digs" in a converted coal cellar with a beautiful girl from Ohio named Emily Ann Possehl. We both loved theater and quickly became lifelong friends. Advanced calculus proved daunting; I flunked the final exam but went on to triumph in plays given by the Edinburgh University Dramatic Society. We put on Tennessee Williams's *Orpheus Descending* at the Edinburgh Festival's Fringe in 1960. There was the main festival and then there was "the Fringe," where college groups and after-hours acts played. It was more fun to be part of the Fringe. The Scottish drama critics wrote reviews of me that my father might have penned, and when I later returned home to the States I was more determined than ever to go to New York and begin my career.

That November, a week after my twenty-first birthday, I voted in my first election. I cast my ballot for John F. Kennedy, and it was the most exciting vote I ever made. When JFK became president, those of us who elected him felt we were on the threshold of a new and brilliant era. He spoke of a vision he had for the nation, of opportunity and democracy for all people, of going to the moon, of a "peace corps," of the importance of education, and of the arts. Young people felt a sense of purpose because he made us feel important and as though we had something to give to our nation and to the people of the world who lacked the privileges we had.

Although I grew up during World War II, my memories of Roosevelt are dim. I remember my mother's excitement when the war ended at last and the anticipation of my father's return from England. My first substantial political memory is of the hearings during the House Un-American Activities Committee's investigation of Alger Hiss in the late 1940s. I recall my mother bent over the ironing board, her eyes glued to the scratchy black-and-white TV. The summer heat and the hot iron beaded her forehead with drops of perspiration as she hushed us into silence. The hearings were the national postwar epic, and the pursuit and elimination of Communists was our collective resolution. The giddy days after World War II turned somber as the country sought to eliminate the spies in our midst.

My parents were Republicans, as were all their friends in the medical world, but I always sensed that I was born a Democrat, although I never knew one growing up. In August 1952, while my parents and their friends, highballs in hand, cheered on the presidential primary campaign of the war hero Dwight D. Eisenhower, we children grouped around the Monopoly board in the next room and aped their celebration. I alone found the studious figure of Adlai Stevenson compelling—whether to be different or because war sickened me, I do not know, but the Democrat in me was alive then and there at the age of twelve.

In the three years that Kennedy was our president, I met my first husband, Robert Alexander, in an acting class, and together we pursued our careers in the New York theater. I was on the subway when word ricocheted around the car that the president had been killed. Tears streamed down all our faces, black and white, young and old, our communal dreams smashed in an instant. Still, we persevered through the 1960s, those of us in our twenties bucking up against an old guard, attempting to right wrongs in civil rights and in human rights and to reverse the stranglehold of the military in our society. "Beware the military-industrial complex," said the old soldier Eisenhower on his exit from government. Beware indeed! While we preached peace and love, the Pentagon was stealthily stockpiling weapons of mass destruction, until by 1980 there were fifty thousand or more in the United States and the Soviet Union.

My son Jace was born in 1964. I worked through my eighth month of pregnancy, performing a cabaret act with four talented comedians. One evening a drunk in the front row looked up at my swollen belly disguised beneath my empire dress and pronounced to one and all that I was about to "drop a kid." That was the end of my nightclub career. I continued to pursue work, however, because Bob and I needed the money. I auditioned again for Joseph Papp one afternoon, hoping to be awarded a role in his "Shakespeare in Central Park" program that coming summer. Joe said, "Jane, you look like you're about to have your baby any minute." "No, Joe," I replied, "I just saw the doctor this morning, and he says it'll be another week or so." He tolerated my audition, trying, I suppose, to envision a lovelorn Rosalind beneath the protrusion. I didn't get the job but hoped he would remember me for future roles. I climbed on a bus at 105th Street for the long ride downtown during rush hour, and by the time we reached 42nd Street I was in full labor. Jace arrived three hours later, a healthy six-pound baby boy.

All one's protective instincts emerge when children enter your life. I was more concerned than ever with the proliferation of nuclear weapons and their testing. I read all I could on the subject. Kennedy and Khrushchev had signed a treaty ending atmospheric testing, but the buildup and underground tests continued. Hadn't the devastation of Hiroshima and Nagasaki taught us anything? What were we doing stockpiling so many of these deadly instruments when a few were all that were needed to obliterate the world? Why were we spending so much money on weapons when there were so many people to take care of first?

My mistrust of the Pentagon was at an all-time high in the late 1960s. The Vietnam War was obviously a huge mistake, and although I was cognizant that marching against it could jeopardize our troops, my brother among them, I went ahead and did it anyway. I joined the thousands who placed flowers in the rifle butts of the soldiers circling the Pentagon to keep us out, at the same time that I was sending cookies to Tom in Saigon. The young men of America were dying daily because of the flawed and specious reasoning of a few men in Washington, D.C.

I was performing regularly in regional theaters by 1965 when I met the man who became my life partner, Ed Sherin. He cast me as Saint Joan for the Arena Stage company in Washington, D.C., where he was artistic director, and our working relationship developed into lasting friendship, and then two years later into love. We were both married to other persons, we lived in townhouses close by each other, and his three sons were good friends with my son. Time and work separated us often because my career was burgeoning back in New York and we were becoming involved in the movie world as well. Our marriages floundered, and as we navigated the rocky terrain of divorce, it became clear that our future was together.

Shuttling children back and forth between households is difficult for everyone, but Tony, Geoffrey, and Jon were as much the focus of my maternal affection when they were with us as Jace was when he was not commuting to his father. Ours was a boisterous household, heavy on the testosterone, since the four boys and Ed played football, watched football, body-surfed the Atlantic's waves, and fished the waters together. I cooked a lot and looked adoringly at this extremely handsome quintet. We all outgrew my small New York apartment and moved to the country to accommodate expanding feet. In 1975 Ed and I were married, while the boys exuberantly pelted us with confetti and tied tin cans to the muffler of our car.

A few years later I began to have a recurring nightmare. I awoke in a sweat one evening, my heart pounding. I dreamed that three of the boys and I emerged from a camping trip in the woods one sunny day to find thousands and thousands of people walking north, their belongings hanging from wagons and off their backs. "What's going on?" I asked. A man pointed to the headline of the *New York Times:* "400 Mile Long Cloud of Radiation Blankets the Northeast." Helicopters were dropping leaflets warning us not to eat shellfish or newly picked vegetables. I begged a policeman to let me go past the barrier to find Ed and Tony. He relented, and we began the trek of several miles to get home. In the noonday sun we stopped by a pond to cool ourselves. The boys played in the water and then silently gathered freshwater clams. We were very hungry and ate them, tacitly understanding that we were going to die. This is the point in the dream when I always woke up.

The nightmare visited me a dozen times over the course of three years until finally I read an article written by the pediatrician Dr. Helen Caldicott about the dangers of nuclear weapons and radioactive fallout. I immediately joined her new organization, Women's Action for Nuclear Disarmament (WAND). I wanted to educate others about the issue, but I didn't know how to proceed. Helen told me that I should never fear talking about the things I was passionate about, and that it would be a surprise to me to learn how few people were in fact talking about these issues. She was right. I began to speak publicly about nuclear weapons and radiation, and people were interested and grateful for the information. My nightmare soon ceased. I was confronting my fears and doing something about them.

The connection between the military and the weapons manufacturers was easy to understand—they fed off each other—but I hadn't yet made the connection between politicians and the manufacturers. I was naive enough to believe that if our elected officials knew the truth they would act on it. The truth was that nuclear weapons were more dangerous than anything mankind had ever invented and that radiation poisoning was an insidious and slow death that would mark generations of those affected. There was absolutely no need for so many weapons of mass destruction in the world, and the detritus from their manufacture was deadly. No one had devised a totally safe method of handling or disposing of poisons like plutonium and uranium, and with the worldwide proliferation of nuclear materials, an accident was guaranteed to happen. It did at Chernobyl in 1986.

But Nero fiddled while Rome burned, and our politicians neither ratified a comprehensive test ban treaty nor did anything substantial to reduce the almighty power of the military. I wasn't against a strong defense system, but the amount of money awarded annually to our Defense Department was overkill by any standard. I thought that if just 10 percent of its monstrous budget were dedicated to worldwide peace efforts we would be moving all the nations of the earth toward a more secure future. But the military-industrial complex of which Eisenhower warned had a stranglehold on our society that was not to be broken. Congressmen made sure that a base or a weapons manufacturing plant was located in their own backyards, thereby enriching the corporate manufacturers and their stockholders, who then contributed significantly to the next election campaign.

These were the issues that consumed me during the 1980s. I was fortunate to be part of a fine film on the subject of nuclear holocaust called *Testament.* It dealt with radiation poisoning in a highly personal way, following the daily life of a family after bombs devastate the United States. I played the mother of three children dying from radioactive fallout. It was my nightmare all over again. But it was a movie, and no more real than my dream had been. It was the real thing I was hoping to prevent.

When Mikhail Gorbachev became the leader of the Soviet Union he envisioned a road toward democracy and a world with reduced weapons. The cold war ended. The stockpiling of weapons did not.

My frustration with our political leaders was mitigated by the happiness in my personal life. Ed and I had an excellent marriage despite two careers that often found us in two different cities, if not on two different continents. He might be directing a TV film in Hungary while I was working on Broadway, or vice versa. The separations were short mainly because we traveled to visit one another every few weeks whenever we could. The boys attended college and were beginning to pursue careers. Jace had wanted to be an actor and director from the time he was very little and would make a good living at it from the age of seventeen. Tony tried book editing and then would find his métier editing films instead. Geoff would try many things, from Hollywood agent to skiing instructor to restaurant manager, before he settled on cooking, his first love. And Jon, who had long since determined that the last frontier was the human brain, would dedicate his life at the age of sixteen to the study of neuroscience.

My own career was solid in the three arenas of stage, movies, and television. I was receiving awards for my work and turning down more roles than I had time to play. Although I gravitated toward the theater, I made my living in movies and television. I was invited to portray many great ladies in history, from Saint Joan to Calamity Jane to Georgia O'Keeffe to Eleanor Roosevelt. The research I did for these roles was extensive and always made me the wiser for it. Dad had been right after all: all knowledge *did* serve me.

After playing Eleanor Roosevelt on a TV miniseries in the 1970s I began to be approached about running for office, either locally or nationally. I would explain that I had only pretended to be Eleanor, that in reality I had none of her skills. The truth, however, was that I had overcome my shyness about public speaking by copying Eleanor. One year in the 1920s she had vowed to accept all speaking engagements in order to surmount her fright of speaking in public. I decided to do the same thing in the 1970s. It worked. Although I always felt most comfortable with a script in hand, I no longer needed to hide behind a character to get out in the public eye. With my strong opinions on issues and my hatred of injustice, I almost *was* ready for political office. But I loved acting and the ambience of the theater too much to give it up.

The theater was the perfect home for me. It combined make-believe and all the joy of performing with a rigorous art form. Unlike many of my fellow performers, I did not sit around New York or Hollywood waiting for "the big break" but chose instead to take good parts in good plays or screenplays wherever they might be. I was always drawn to the classics—Shakespeare, Ibsen, and Chekhov, to name a few—and found myself working in the regional theaters where they were most often produced. Doing a play like Eugene O'Neill's marathon *Mourning Becomes Electra* was exhilarating. I played Lavinia, based on the Greek Electra, at the American Shakespeare Festival in Stratford, Connecticut, in 1970. She moves in the first scene from a tightly wound young woman obsessed with murder and revenge to a beautiful seductress in the final act. It was like climbing Mount Everest—four and a half hours of intrigue and emotional hills and valleys. There is never enough time to explore all the nuances of a character; certainly a run of only a few weeks or even a few months is insufficient, but the satisfaction of performing in the play nightly and learning something new with every performance has never diminished for me. I've played more than a hundred different characters, no two alike, in plays and films that were mediocre or masterpieces, and I've never tired of the work, the collaboration with others, or the ambiance. The company of players is the best in the world.

Learning to act is a lifelong pursuit, and it has brought me into contact with all kinds of people and all kinds of art forms. Because, as an actor, you are your own instrument and you inhabit the world of the writer, you make use of literature, design and other visual arts, and sometimes music, in building a character. I would search museums and libraries for the right elements to enhance and reveal the life of my character.

I was an inveterate museum-goer from the age of fourteen, when I'd take the trolley to the Boston Museum of Fine Arts after school and wander the halls of Greek antiquities. By chance one day I discovered graphic erotic scenes on the red and black vases; the surprise and delight of seeing them openly displayed drew me to them as much as the subject matter. But there was so much more to see: a tiny ivory Minoan snake goddess, the rich portraits by Sargent and Copley, and the vivid colors of Van Gogh. I revered painters and counted as my close friends three young men who painted brilliantly. We explored galleries together, and they taught me about the great painters and sculptors.

Another teenage friend took me to concerts and introduced me to classical composers both old and new. I listened to Milhaud and Webern but did my math homework to Mozart concertos. My first husband loved jazz, and so my musical lexicon expanded. I myself played the guitar and read Alan Lomax's *Folksongs of North America* backward and forward. I bought Dylan and Rolling Stones records in equal proportion. Another friend was a poet, and we pored over compendiums of poetry and scratched haikus to each other. My tastes were eclectic and wide-ranging, and as I aged I acquainted myself with everything new that came along. There seemed no end to the possibilities of human imagination, and I was glad I had been exposed to so much.

The only art form I knew really well, however, was theater. There simply was not time in life to know more than one or two art forms profoundly. The theater was a perfect whole, a world unto itself for the time the play lasted. I was content to play my role in it. Then I was asked to play a greater role in the real world.

CHAPTER TWO

The Audition

It was a cold January day when the call came from Senator Claiborne Pell's office asking whether I would be interested in being the chairman of the National Endowment for the Arts. I thought the caller was kidding. "Don't you mean, be on a grants panel?" I laughed.

President William Jefferson Clinton had been inaugurated for his first term a few days before, and although I had voted for him, I had neither campaigned for him nor even sent any contribution. Why was I being considered to run one of his agencies? Particularly an agency in the crossfire, as the NEA was.

The caller, Alexander Crary, a longtime aide to the senator, explained that my name would simply be sent over to the White House as one of many possible candidates. He said that other senators were also submitting names. I was flattered, if bemused. The only thing I'd ever run was my household. Well, that wasn't entirely true. As president of my class I had mastered *Roberts' Rules of Order* and run many a meeting. I'd also produced several films, taking responsibility for casts and crews of a hundred people or more. Still, in the larger scheme of things, these experiences had barely gotten my feet wet.

"How long do I have to think about it?" I asked.

"The weekend," was his wry response.

There are only a few people with whom I consult when faced with major decisions. One is my husband, Ed Sherin, and another is my son, Jace Alexander. They are smart and articulate, they represent different generations, and I trust them implicitly. They have an ability to advise without pushing their own agenda, qualities that make both of them remarkable stage and film directors.

Ed encouraged me to throw my hat in the ring. He knew how deeply I cared about the agency; after all, I was an NEA "baby." We both were. Back in 1967 the NEA had given a $25,000 grant to the playwright Howard Sackler to develop *The Great White Hope* at the premier theater in Washington, D.C., Arena Stage. I was a member of the company, and Ed was artistic director. Howard, Ed, and Arena's founder, Zelda Fichandler, together fashioned an extraordinary play that later moved from Washington to Broadway and was then made into a film. The play won every major award in 1968, including the Tony and the Pulitzer, and virtually sealed my acting career and that of James Earl Jones when we both received Academy Award nominations for our movie roles. I owed a lot to Arena Stage and the NEA.

Jace thought I would be good for the NEA because I would be the first working artist to take the helm of the agency and I understood the problems of artists.

I also consulted my dearest friends who were involved in the arts in one way or another. I had been close to Susan Dowling, Jane Milliken, Susan Sollins, and Tina Howe since college. Although they felt the job would be a perfect marriage of my creative instincts and my political activism, they were also concerned for my well-being. Susan Sollins thought that the politics of the NEA situation might be immutable and ultimately drain me. She made sense, and I thought about the negatives but decided in the end to give it a try. I thought it also might be possible to turn things around for the agency.

When an actor is in a new hit play on Broadway, in a terrific role, everything falls into place. Such was my life in 1993. The play was *The Sisters Rosensweig* by Wendy Wasserstein, and I was Sarah, a banker who has repudiated her Jewish heritage and during the course of the play retrieves it with the help of her two sisters and a new love in her life. My costars were Madeline Kahn, Frances McDormand (later replaced by Christine Estabrook), and Robert Klein, and to perform with them nightly was sheer delight. I was content. At the age of fifty-three good new roles were hard to come by in the theater and in film, and so I was particularly grateful to be a part of *The Sisters Rosensweig*. We were in the midst of transferring the play from its successful off-Broadway run at Lincoln Center to the Barrymore Theater on Broadway when I was thrust into consideration for the NEA.

It was another week or so before I heard from the White House. A woman named Susan Clampitt, who was working in the personnel office and helping to put together the administration's team, called to ask a number of questions. Had I ever done drugs? Was there anything in my past that might embarrass the administration? Things of that nature. I answered truthfully that I came of age in the 1960s and not to have inhaled back then was out of the question. If she chuckled, I didn't hear it at the other end of the phone line. Fortunately, in more ways than one, I had a peculiar allergy to marijuana that resulted in excruciating pain behind my eyeballs, and so I sat out the drug scene of my generation. I told her that I had always been a political activist, marching against the wars in Vietnam and in El Salvador, for civil rights, for the Equal Rights Amendment, and always against the stockpiling and expansion of nuclear weapons. This activism was de rigueur for many of us in the 1960s and 1970s, and although I hadn't abandoned any of my political feelings during the 1980s and 1990s, the steam had gone out of demonstrations. They no longer exerted the pressure on government that they once had, mostly because the media had tired of covering them.

All in all I came across as a pretty clean candidate. Susan told me that I would need to present a financial disclosure statement to the Senate, that the White House and the judicial branch would also require extensive background material, and that I would be hearing from the FBI soon. She told me that I was one of about forty people being considered for the job.

Pulling together my life employment history and financial record was a mammoth task, but I set about it with the help of my able assistant, Rosemarie Rogers, and my accountant of twenty-three years, James Powers. I had to list all my jobs from the time I was sixteen years old and provide the names and addresses of each employer. This was daunting, to say the least, because of the numerous engagements I'd had as an actress; some had taken only an hour or two, such as the recording of a voice-over narration, and none, not even performing in a hit play, had lasted longer than a year. When the list reached more than three hundred, I began to give up. Digging up all the names and addresses of employers and the salaries they paid me proved to be almost impossible. I did the best I could, and that seemed acceptable to the White House.

The FBI, however, was a different story. They were humorless and seemed to know all about me. I wondered what my file contained and how far back it went. At the University of Edinburgh, during my junior year studying calculus and Russian (in between extracurricular drama society productions), a group of us had gone to the Soviet Union. This was in 1960, during the coldest part of the cold war. We hooked up with a tour chartered by the Scottish Union of Students, a socialist organization on campus. Although my American friends and I had no interest in socialism or communism, we did have an interest in our pocketbooks, and the tour made it possible for us to go cheaply. Tagging along with SUS, we attended a huge conference of Communist youth in Moscow. There were about three thousand delegates from all the countries behind the Iron Curtain and from other Communist nations worldwide. It was exciting to be with so many different university students and to hear the multitude of languages. Each country provided some form of entertainment nightly in the cavernous halls. When it came time for the Scottish Union of Students to perform, they came up blank and turned suddenly to my guitar-playing Californian friend, Red Williams, and to his folksinger, me.

Red and I gave it about three seconds' thought and then burst into a medley of Woody Guthrie's Dust Bowl ballads and other songs from the 1930s, like:

I don't want your millions, mister,
I don't want your diamond rings,
All I want is the right to live, mister,
Give me back my job again.

We thought the Depression statement was harmless enough but understood its obvious appeal to this crowd. We underestimated the KGB and Radio Moscow, which shortly thereafter beamed to the world that this was the way the youth of America were headed in the 1960s, that our embrace of communism was only a heartbeat away.

Red, whose nickname had only to do with the color of his hair, returned to the United States before I did and was detained for hours at customs. Back in Edinburgh I learned that we had been something of a cause célèbre and that Missouri Senator Stuart Symington had been on a British talk show defending us. Folly of youth!

Was this incident in my FBI file, I wondered? Did it matter anymore now that the cold war was over? The investigator assigned to me was very thorough. We had a few phone conversations before meeting. She was specific: "What is this gap of three months in your employment record in 1972?" "My God, I'm an actress!" I replied. "I'm lucky it was only three months!" When she finally came to my door for an interview, I thought I was looking at Jodie Foster in a movie. She had a pert little figure in a nicely cut blue suit, above the knees, straight blond shiny hair, and she was young enough to be my daughter. The new FBI, I thought. No stereotypes here.

Her major question was about why I had visited a psychiatrist two times in 1989. "Change of life," I responded. "I beg your pardon?" "It's a tough time for a woman, going through change of life; I wanted to talk to another woman about it. I went only two times because the therapist I consulted was too young to understand what I was going through." She dutifully wrote all of this down. I got the impression that all would have been over if I had visited a psychiatrist with any regularity.

I guess I passed the test. Later I learned that the FBI interviewed between twenty-five and fifty of my friends and neighbors from Los Angeles to Boston, people who had known me from the early 1940s to the present: teachers, relatives, landlords, producers, and so on. Where the agents got their information I will never know, but I subsequently heard from people I'd not heard from in decades, saying that the FBI had contacted them. All this to be the head of an arts agency? In peacetime? I'd learn that government process was how things were done and that it was not to be questioned by interlopers like me.

While this comprehensive background check was going on and I was exhaustively putting together the paperwork requested, we were mounting *The Sisters Rosensweig* in the new theater. Previews were going well, and I was excited to be back in my favorite kind of theater, the great proscenium house of the 1920s, of which Broadway has many. The wide apron in front of the curtain and the gentle rise of the orchestra where the audience sits create a space wonderfully suited to display the best an actor has to offer.

Then my husband and I received the call that would turn our lives upside down. The telephone rang in the late afternoon of a dour March day. The caller identified herself as an assistant district attorney of the County of New York. "Is this Jane Alexander?" she asked. "Yes," I replied, thinking that this was yet another call concerning my consideration for the NEA. "Could you and your husband come to my office at your earliest possible convenience?" she said. I knew by her tone something was very wrong, but she declined to discuss anything on the telephone. Sensing urgency, I said, "How about tomorrow morning at nine?" "That would be fine, we're down near City Hall in lower Manhattan." "Yes, I know where you are, my husband has been there many times," I replied, without elaborating.

Ed had been directing numerous episodes of the TV series *Law and Order* for several years. It is one of the few shows based in New York, and its hour-long story is split into two parts: the cops of New York City, who maintain the law, and the district attorney's office, which keeps order. After shooting in and around City Hall regularly, Ed had gotten to know some of those who worked for District Attorney Robert M. Morganthau.

We arrived promptly at 1 Hogan Place, wound our way through a maze of third-floor offices, cluttered with the debris of bureaucracy and decades of dust, and found our assistant district attorney. Stereotypes again exploded as a lovely brunette answered the door, ushered us into a ten-by-ten space, and sat us on government-issue chairs amid boxes and boxes of papers.

No amenities here. She jumped right in: "I don't know how to tell you this," she began, "but you have nothing."

The story unspooled itself over the course of an hour or more. A former client of our accountant, James Powers, had apparently asked the DA's office for help in retrieving money that Powers owed him. In the course of investigating she had discovered that Powers was systematically embezzling nine of his clients, including us, and had been doing so for over five years. Ed and I were dumbfounded. Jim was a friend! He had been in our lives since the early 1970s. He had come to family events and parties. He had always been the soul of courtesy and immaculate in his accounts. Or so we thought.

We listened with growing dismay and despair as she reeled off a litany of abuse that crossed all our financial transactions. It was true that we had nothing. He had virtually wiped us out: no pension fund, no life insurance, no stocks, no bonds, no savings accounts, no cash on hand. He had refinanced our summer home, and worst of all, he hadn't paid our taxes for the last five years. How could this have happened? It was easy. We trusted him, and he violated that trust. He committed fraud on a major scale; he forged our signatures and once even my voice!

The assistant district attorney suggested that we set up a sting operation in order to arrest him. Because we weren't the only victims, James Powers was considered an enemy of the people and New York would handle his prosecution. That was the good news; at least we and the eight others did not have to hire lawyers to go after him. Not immediately anyway.

I phoned Jim to tell him that we needed to meet because the FBI was sure to call him about our finances in the course of its investigation for the White House. He seemed cool as a cucumber, but he must have been panicking to think that his books might be opened to the FBI. I arranged to meet him at eleven o'clock a few mornings later. Of course I never showed up, but the district attorney's detectives did. They were New York's finest policemen, and their long-standing rivalry with the FBI about who would bust a crime first was legendary. It was a great disappointment to them when Powers exclaimed, as they burst through the door and put the cuffs on him, "Ah, the FBI. I've been expecting you."

My nascent steps toward public service in the Clinton administration ground to a halt. There was no way, it seemed, for me to give up my work as an actress when we were in such financial straits. It would take years and years to get back on our feet again. And then a stroke of good luck occurred.

The creator of *Law and Order,* Dick Wolf, had repeatedly asked Ed whether he would take over the job of executive producer. Ed had declined, preferring to free-lance as a director rather than assume the burden of day-to-day responsibility for the show. But the current executive producer was moving back to California, and Dick, hearing of our catastrophe, called quickly once again and said, "Your loss is my gain." Ed laughed and thanked him for his perseverance, accepting the position at once. It was our saving grace. Ed would be making good steady money, on a hit show, and in four years we would be in the black again, our debts eliminated.

A few weeks before Jim was arrested I had shot some major commercials as the new spokeswoman for the regional Bell companies. They were seeking to expand as full-service providers of information and sales across phone lines, and they needed the help of Congress to do it. They thought some influential television advertising might turn the trick. They paid me a huge amount of money, and I had called Jim to make sure the check was where we could get at it quickly in case I needed to return it. I couldn't very well be a spokeswoman for the "Baby Bells" if I became the NEA's chairman. The day before he was arrested Jim cashed the check and spent the money. It was just one of our assets that was never recovered, and later I had to repay the regional Bells because they weren't going to run the spots I had contracted to shoot.

With Ed about to secure some ongoing financial stability with his new job, we decided that it might be possible for me to work for the government after all. I revised my financial statements for the White House and the Senate and included letters from the district attorney's office confirming the prosecution of Powers.

I think I was in shock. I don't remember crying over the event except once. I do remember Ed's anger. I remember our family and friends jumping in to help with offers of money and with support and commiseration. With every loss there is hope. But I also remember losing a vital part of myself, the part that had trusted so freely and surely. I would question everyone's motives for a long, long time.

A week or so later, in March 1993, *The Sisters Rosensweig* opened on Broadway and was an immediate sellout. My dressing room was very special. It was right on the stage, and all I had to do was open my door, climb up some stairs behind the set, and enter my character Sarah's house; my backstage life was seamless. The dressing room was special as well because of all the great theater stars who had occupied it in the past: Katharine Cornell, Paul Muni, Jessica Tandy, Gertrude Lawrence, Deborah Kerr, Geraldine Page, and Ingrid Bergman, to name a few. Katharine Hepburn, I was told, had put in the high platform on which a mattress rested so that she could take naps whenever she wished. I followed suit and did likewise. I was grateful that my work life was so fulfilling and fun, and I looked forward to every performance. Madeline Kahn and I had some delicious moments together onstage when the audience would be convulsed in laughter. The wave of their delight would sweep over us and hang in time. These are the kind of stage experiences that actors live for. Why, I wondered, was I even contemplating leaving the theater? One reason certainly was that I wanted to give something back to an agency that had made my career possible; another was that I thought I might be able to make a difference in the negative perception that Congress had of the agency; and a third was that by September I would have been involved in the play for a year and would probably want to do something new. In any case it was a bit late to be pulling out.

By the beginning of May the field had been winnowed, and I was one of two candidates for the NEA chair. My friends kept my candidacy confidential, and no one at the theater knew that I might be leaving at the end of my contract in August. Calls from the White House stepped up as I received FBI clearance. "Nannygate" had submarined the appointment of Zoë Baird to be U.S. attorney general, so I was careful to check that my housecleaner did indeed have her green card and that I had paid up her Social Security taxes. This kind of issue was of considerable concern to White House Counsel Bernard Nussbaum, with good reason: the Republicans were finding loopholes like this one to prevent confirmation of several of the president's nominations to important posts. I kept coming up clean, making his job much easier.

Meanwhile New York's case against James Powers was proceeding. The nine of us who were victimized formed a support group and independently hired a lawyer and a detective to try to track down the missing money that the DA's office had not recovered. We learned a lot about our former accountant. He was heavily into horses and horse-racing; we thought perhaps he had gambled away all our funds, but the gaming commission came up blank. He supported his lover and housed him in fine condominiums down south. He had invested in dubious real estate ventures in a number of states with our money.

Jim Powers had provided each of his clients with quarterly reports, which Ed and I diligently read, not knowing they were mostly bogus. We learned later that he had whited out the actual numbers on a bank or investment house statement, typed in his own numbers, and run it through a copy machine. He also had cleverly hidden any loss one of us might have had in a bank account by covering it with funds from another's account. This is called kiting; it is illegal, and he became very deft at it. What surprised us was that Chase Manhattan Bank, which held most of our accounts, let it happen without ever picking up the phone to call any one of us to alert us to our accountant's activities. Jim may have been our accountant of record, but it didn't take a rocket scientist to see that something was awry with the multitude of transactions taking place in any given month or the numerous overdraft fees he was incurring. Power of attorney is not, after all, a license to steal.

Although the most devastating blow was the nonpayment of taxes—Powers would dutifully fill out the forms, we would sign them in his office, and then he would never mail them to the IRS—what personally disturbed me the most was a visit I made to Merrill Lynch on the morning he was arrested. I sat with the broker, feeling numb as she recounted how Jim had cashed in this asset or that stock. "What about the trust funds for my nieces, nephews, and godchildren?" I asked. "Oh my, I thought you knew. They're mostly gone too—down to a few dollars each." I burst into tears. This was too much. The few thousand dollars in each was accumulating to help pay for their college educations. Jim knew that, and this seemed downright cruel. "Why didn't you call me?" I cried to the broker, who had met or talked with me several times in the past decade. She seemed confused. "Oh dear, well, I guess I thought you knew what was going on." It was the same refrain I heard elsewhere. Jim had been very convincing. He even convinced an employee of a mutual fund in Massachusetts in a recorded phone call that *he,* a basso, was Jane Alexander! The poor fellow on the other end sounded confused and extremely embarrassed but decided to err on the side of political correctness, I guess, and released the funds to Jim.

The strain of getting our financial affairs in order took its toll on both Ed and me, but Ed assumed most of the burden, for which I was grateful. Every paycheck we received went immediately to our debtors, the IRS being the most formidable and unforgiving. They agreed to waive the penalties for nonpayment of taxes but insisted on the interest accrued on back taxes, which in some cases amounted to even more than the original tax. They were sympathetic as individuals but undeterred in their mission of restitution. They would have taken our house if we hadn't been able to meet the payments, and I'm sure that has happened to many people who don't have the income we did. We were fortunate too in having excellent and conservative new accountants charting a path to get us back on our feet again. In due time a jury convicted Powers, and a judge sentenced him to twelve years in prison, but we never recovered the money he had stolen.

In early summer I was called down to Washington to meet some people in the White House. I suppose this was my "audition." I moved through security at the gates, where my bag was carefully searched, and I was handed an ugly pink plastic tag to wear with a large letter "A" stamped on it. It hung around my neck from a flimsy chain, reminding me not so much of Hester Prynne as of a criminal mugshot. I never did find out what the "A" signified. I knew it wasn't "Alexander" because every other person inside wore the same badge of visitation. I wondered whether they were as embarrassed by it as I was. The Secret Service agents, who were everywhere, wore discreet little pins identifying *them* (if you happened to miss the not-so-discreet radios in their ears).

It is always a thrill to go to the White House. With nothing overbearing or imposing about its design, it truly is a house, of gracious proportions and graceful lines. It has probably outgrown its office capacity as government has expanded through the decades, but there is something heartening about the fact that the nerve center of our country is still contained in a few rooms connected by a rabbit warren of backstairs and cubicles. The intimidation is all in the mind. It seems uniquely American and reflects the people's ownership of the president's house and the very basis of our democracy.

I was led up those narrow backstairs, wondering how the hefty three-hundred-pound Howard Taft and other porky presidents had done it, and then I was ushered into the outer office of the First Lady. In a few minutes Hillary Rodham Clinton arrived. I was struck by her warmth and liveliness as she greeted me. The two of us went into her modest, rather spartan office, where we chatted for only about ten minutes, and then spent another five or so minutes having what is known as a "photo-op." We talked mostly about Eleanor Roosevelt, whom we both admire immensely.

My turn as Eleanor in a seven-hour TV miniseries back in the mid-1970s was one of the most rewarding roles in my entire career. Because ABC kept postponing the production, Edward Herrmann, who played Franklin, and I had a luxurious two years in which to do research. We probably could have earned Ph.D.s in American history by the time we finished, we were so immersed in their lives. I played Eleanor from the age of seventeen to sixty-three, with the help of a lot of makeup. The opportunity to get to know this remarkable woman through inhabiting the role was a great gift to me. I felt the ugly duckling that Eleanor believed herself to be emerge into a swan in her later years, through perseverance, determination, and compassion. She taught me how to overcome adversity, and it was a lesson I took to heart in my own life from the 1970s on. I suspected that Hillary Rodham Clinton viewed Eleanor similarly, and I knew she wished to emulate her in the White House.

I was puzzled that the First Lady asked no questions about the National Endowment for the Arts. The interview was soon over, and I was back on a plane and back onstage that night. Only recently was I told that she was not supposed to be meeting with me at all that day, that in fact the other candidate for the NEA job was lobbying so intensely that they were about to give it to her. That candidate had a good record of nonprofit arts work in a major state, was an old friend from Arkansas, and had been important to the Clintons during his campaign for president—a lot of plusses, to be sure. But I knew nothing of this at the time. All I was told by those in the White House who were backing me was that I needed to do some lobbying of my own.

Promoting myself was completely alien territory to me. As an actress I'd never been good at it, even when I knew I was absolutely the right choice for a role. I could audition, hiding behind a reading or a screen test, but I could never bring myself to pick up the phone and call a director or producer to say that I was the best choice, or even that I was dying for the part. I'm sure I lost many a fine role, or at the very least was never even in consideration. After all, how can you win a race if you don't even tell anyone you want to run? This is a primer for elected office. Perhaps I thought I could squeeze out of it because the NEA chairman was appointed by the president, rather like a command performance. Well, it wasn't exactly like that, so I parked my shyness in the corner and got on the phone.

I called a prominent writer in Arkansas and asked whether he would write a letter to the president. He did. I called a professor I'd met in Utah and asked whether he would write to Senator Orrin Hatch recommending me for the agency, and he did. All in all I called about a dozen people around the country who I thought would be influential. I was pleased that they all seemed delighted to help. Quite independently, the gallery owner Richard Feigen was compiling a list of supporters from the visual arts world, and my friends in the theater were doing the same for the performing arts. They sent a substantial number of signatures to Washington backing my candidacy to head the NEA.

I also was asked to meet privately with five individuals who were prominent in the arts and in the Democratic Party. They needed to know my views on First Amendment issues before they went to bat for me. Would I stand firm on issues of freedom of expression when and if the going got tough? I assured them I would, little knowing just how tough it was going to get. I liked these five men and women very much and came to rely on their judgment and support throughout my subsequent tenure at the NEA. They were a secret cadre of support for me and the agency.

And because I wanted to be absolutely surefooted in the area of the law relevant to being head of the NEA, I consulted a prominent New York lawyer to school me on the First Amendment and other legalities I might encounter. He taught me that freedom of expression does not mean that all forms of speech and art are protected. Obscenity is no more protected than yelling "Fire!" in a crowded theater.

There was one person whose advice I needed more than anyone

else's, and that was Roger Stevens. One of the great men of the theater in the twentieth century, Roger had brought the NEA into being in the mid-1960s. President Lyndon Johnson then appointed him the agency's first chairman. He founded the Kennedy Center as well and went on to be its unsurpassed chairman from 1971 through 1988. Ed and I had done half a dozen plays with Roger, in Washington, in New York, and on the road. Perhaps the most famous was *First Monday in October* by Jerome Lawrence and Robert E. Lee, in which Henry Fonda played a curmudgeonly old justice of the Supreme Court modeled after William O. Douglas and I played the first female justice appointed to the court, predating Sandra Day O'Connor's 1981 appointment by three years. It was enormous fun to play, and the run in Washington was sold out and extended for many weeks. Eight of the nine real justices of the Supreme Court came to see it, and Chief Justice Warren Burger came twice. He was most gracious, inviting me to the inner sanctum of the Court, his chambers, and making me cinnamon toast and tea. I remember him sweeping enthusiastically into his chambers after a long morning on the bench and saying, "I'm sorry I kept you waiting. Let's have some tea!" Then he hung up his black robe carefully, donned a brown cardigan sweater, and proceeded to shake cinnamon and brown sugar on the toast for us.

The great liberal William O. Douglas was no longer sitting on the bench in 1978, but he so loved Hank's portrayal of him that he gave us a reception in the lofty marble rooms of the Supreme Court. It was a great party and a hot ticket: Douglas was just as legendary as Hank Fonda, and although he was infirm and sitting in a wheelchair, it seemed that all Washington wanted to pay homage to him. Virtually everyone who was invited showed up: all the justices, Vice President Walter Mondale, and members of the House and Senate. It was the first time I met Senator Ted Kennedy, who would be so important to me when I was at the NEA fifteen years later, and Mark Hatfield, the distinguished senator from Oregon. I was also introduced to Thurgood Marshall, the first African American justice and a prominent lawyer in the civil rights movement in the 1960s. Stars were in my eyes. The room was crowded with statesmen (no women to speak of), men I admired, who had come to honor not only William O. Douglas but

Hank and me! This was the first and only party the Supreme Court ever gave for thespians, I am sure. And it was SRO.

Roger Stevens produced not only *First Monday in October* but more than three hundred plays in his long and remarkable life. He had been chairman of the Democratic Party's finance committee in 1956 and was later influential in John F. Kennedy's dedication to the idea of federal funding for the arts and the humanities, a dream the young president never lived to see come true. As the first chairman of the NEA, Roger not only knew its history and the ins and outs of politics but also knew me and whether I would be capable of doing the job. I called him.

"Roger," I said, "they're seriously considering me to head the NEA. What do you think?" There was a long pause at the other end of the line. Oh dear, I thought, he thinks I'd be disastrous in the role.

"Always talk to the president," he said, skipping over the preliminaries and my agenda. It seemed a foregone conclusion to him that I'd get the job, just as I'd gotten parts he envisioned me playing. He chuckled, with some delight I think, at the prospect. This was a man I cared for very deeply, and he never questioned my ability to take on this new role. That meant a lot to me. His words reverberated over and over in my head: "Always talk to the president." They would continue to reverberate for years to come.

When *would* the president talk to me, I wondered. I had seen the First Lady briefly, I had talked with some of her staff, and I had met with personnel and White House lawyers, most notably Bruce Lindsey, one of the president's closest friends from Arkansas. There were definite hints that I was the front-runner. But no one had ever mentioned the president or whether he even knew I was alive.

One summer day in my New York apartment the phone rang, and it was the White House telling me to expect a call soon from the president. I was very excited. This was it. He was going to ask me, and I was going to say yes, six months from the time I'd been first contacted. I waited. I cleaned up the apartment, which I was rarely in since it was summer and Ed and I preferred commuting from our home upstate. I cleaned the cupboards, which were bare. Because of the embezzlement, we would sell the apartment as soon as we could get a decent price for it, so we didn't bother keeping it stocked. I waited. I cleaned the refrigerator, which contained only mustard, plastic envelopes of restaurant ketchup, and some old ice cubes. My stomach growled. I was so hungry. Maybe I could just duck downstairs quickly and grab a sandwich at the deli on the corner.

I made it back in record time, tuna on rye in hand, to see the message light blinking.

"This is Air Force One calling Ms. Jane Alexander. Ms. Alexander, please pick up if you're there, the president wishes to speak with you."

Damn. I missed it. My big moment. I desultorily downed the sandwich, waited for another hour, and then thought I'd better pick up my dry cleaning in order to have time for a nap before the evening performance of *Sisters*. What would you say are the chances of missing two important calls from the president of the United States in two dumb ten-minute periods? I hit the jackpot again. When I got back there it was on my machine for the second time: "Ms. Alexander, the president is trying to reach you. This is Air Force One calling. Please pick up." I could hear the static in the background; they were in the air this time. I was mortified. I called my friends in White House personnel and told them of my errors. An hour later Bruce Lindsey called and told me the president wanted to offer me the position of chairman of the National Endowment for the Arts and that he would soon publicly place my name in nomination. I thanked Bruce and slouched off to the theater. I never got a call from the president again.

There was much ballyhoo when the press carried the announcement of my nomination on August 7, 1993. The *New York Times* put it on the front page, and almost every paper wrote positively. The conservative press made me laugh by writing that I was "beholden to Hollywood." Hah! I may have made forty television and feature films, but my heart has always belonged to the theater, and I was beholden to no one I knew of on the West Coast.

Many lovely letters of congratulations came with the morning mail; most touching to me were the letters from those who remembered my mother and father and knew how proud they would have been had they lived to see this day. Flowers and gifts flowed in from old friends and family. Telegrams arrived from celebrities and politicians, some of whom I knew, others whom I didn't, all wishing me well. There was excitement that a working artist would be heading the National Endowment for the Arts.

It was a very busy week. Madeline Kahn, Robert Klein, and I were finishing our run in *The Sisters Rosensweig*. It had been almost a year since we began rehearsals, and every last performance was now precious to us. We had never had a cross word, and our admiration for one another had only grown. It would be hard to say good-bye. We had talked about what we would be doing in the future, but until the president's announcement I had had to keep mum about my plans. Madeline sent me a funny, cryptic note when she heard the news, and Robert immediately launched into his schtick, which was brilliant political satire. I missed them already.

At home we were preparing for Geoffrey's wedding. Geoff was Ed's middle son, and I had known and loved him since he was three years old. He was now thirty and marrying the beautiful Hope Leezum Namgyal, the daughter of my good friend Hope Cooke, who had been the queen of Sikkim. Little Hope, as we called her, was a princess of that small Himalayan country but had grown up in the United States after her mother fled the Indian takeover in the early 1970s. I had also known Little Hope from the time she was a toddler and felt that this marriage was a good one. Geoff had been searching for the right profession since graduating from Boston University. He had had a natural affinity for cooking since childhood; the Culinary Institute of America, just up the road from us in Hyde Park, New York, turned out to be perfect for him. He graduated from there in June and was eager to take up his new life as a chef. Ed and I had watched the deepening love of Geoff and Hope during the year they were living with us. Hope had graduated from Georgetown University and was such a bright young woman. It seemed the world was their oyster.

The large old hickory tree was festooned with Tibetan prayer flags the morning of the wedding. Geoff's fellow CIA graduates provided the food, and my friends, including "Big" Hope, arranged the floral bouquets. Our four acres of sloping lawn looked enchanting even though the summer drought had left the brook-fed pool half-empty and stagnant. Buddhist monks chanted prayers during the hour-long ceremony, their sweet faces and sonorous tones lending the hot afternoon an exotic air. We toasted the newlyweds and danced into the evening under a white tent.

The next day I rang down the curtain on my year with *The Sisters Rosensweig*. Ed put Hope and Geoff on a plane for Sikkim for their honeymoon, and I collapsed with a fever that I self-diagnosed as too much excitement. Blessed as I am with a strong constitution, I was up and about again in twenty-four hours, ready to immerse myself fully in the business of the NEA.

CHAPTER THREE

The Rehearsal

The "murder board" first assembled one hot August night. They were a team of people gathered by the White House to prepare me for my confirmation hearing before the Senate Committee on Labor and Human Resources. The team comprised three people from the White House personnel office, three lawyers, a D.C. lobbyist, two senators' assistants, a White House Fellow, a publicist, and a remarkable woman named Melanne Verveer who hosted the buffet dinner in her home. Melanne was deputy assistant to the president and deputy chief of staff to the First Lady. She was the captain of my confirmation team and the one responsible for the arts and humanities agencies in the Clinton administration. Her modest, unassuming style masked impressive fortitude and a finely honed intellect.

We sat in a large circle in the living room exchanging pleasantries until the discussion veered toward the continued threat of Republican attacks on the Arts Endowment. How could I deal with it in my upcoming courtesy calls to the senators? The annual appropriation bills were to be debated shortly in Congress, and Senator Jesse Helms and others could be counted on to try to eliminate or curtail the Endowment. A woman named Ricki Seidman, an indefatigable powerhouse in the campaign to elect the president, had no illusions about the Republicans' ability to use the NEA to their advantage. She'd been through the wars on the campaign trail and knew how bloody it might get. She seemed weary and restless and hot. There was no political correctness about her; while the rest of us were clothed in conservative Washington dress, she wore a tank top and shorts, her bountiful flesh cresting the hem at her thighs. If I had expected a certain formality in the denizens of the presidential office, it was blown apart by Ricki. She was "down home" all the way. But that was the first and last time I saw her as a member of my team; she became the president's scheduler and lasted only another year in D.C., a victim of burnout, I presume. But she was memorable that night, and memorable too for the role she played in getting Bill Clinton elected.

The murder board met seven times in the early weeks of September before my hearing on the twenty-second. I was force-fed more facts than I'd consumed since taking the SATs in high school. The NEA brought 125 hours of arts programming to public television in 1990, reaching 310 million people. Thirteen thousand artists-in-residence in the schools reached four million students and teachers through the NEA in 1990–1991. My briefing book was the size of the New York telephone book. I was drilled and grilled each time we met.

But facts were only part of my education. The real reason we were meeting was to rehearse me in the appropriate responses to questions about controversy. The NEA had been under fire since 1989 because of the work of a handful of artists, most notably the photographers Robert Mapplethorpe and Andres Serrano and the performance artist Karen Finley. Special-interest groups like the American Family Association and the Christian Action Network were stirring the coals again, bringing new alleged outrages to the attention of Congress in a renewed effort to eliminate the agency. The latest controversies involved a gay and lesbian film festival; an exhibition called "Abject Art" at New York's Whitney Museum; some photographs by Joel-Peter Witkin; and the distribution of ten-dollar bills to undocumented workers crossing the Mexican border as part of a project of the Museum of Contemporary Art in San Diego.

It was fortunate that I had seen none of the works in question and could respond noncommittally when asked about them. The talking points in my briefing book suggested that I say:

- I am not thoroughly knowledgeable about the actions taken by the former administration, nor am I thoroughly knowledgeable about current controversies.

- In the future, I look forward to working with the Senate on those issues and all other issues regarding the Endowment.

My confirmation team put me on mock trial, playing the roles of some of my worst adversaries: Jesse Helms, Dan Coats of Indiana, Strom Thurmond. It was easy to see why they were called the murder board: they shot you down each and every time. It was a quick lesson in the first principle of tai chi: learn to deflect. When someone asks you a question, the answer you give is *yours,* not theirs. You have no obligation to give them the answer that *they* want to hear. Helms was not a member of the committee, but his point of view was important to understand; the senior lawyer of the group, Jim Fitzpatrick, played him uncompromisingly:

"Miss Alexander, how will you make sure that the taxpayer does not have to pay for obscene art like Robert Mapplethorpe's homosexual photographs, or that blasphemous one by Andres Serrano called *Piss Christ?*"

"Senator, I have not seen the photographs you mention, so I cannot respond directly to your question. I will work to see that the NEA continues to uphold its mission of funding excellent art. As you know, we are prohibited from funding obscenity as defined in a court of law."

This was the kind of noncommittal response that was sure to drive Helms and company crazy, but it was also the truth for me. The obscenity clause was a kind of catch-22. The NEA was supposed to reject grants that it deemed to be obscene, yet what was considered obscene was to be determined only in a court of law. In addition, the 1990 NEA authorization statute stated: "Artistic excellence and artistic merit are the criteria by which applications are judged, taking into consideration general standards of decency and respect for the diverse beliefs and values of the American public."

And therein lies the rub, the very nexus of the problem of art and politics. Whose excellence and whose decency? In a pluralistic nation like ours, how do we respect the full range of diversity in art without treading on someone's beliefs and values? I was to become quite conversant on these questions in the next four years, but in preparing for my confirmation hearing, neophyte that I was, I was just struggling to learn my lines.

My days were jam-packed. Even as I was scaling the learning curve, I was looking for a house and recruiting senior staff, as if my chairmanship were a fait accompli. Our Santa Monica condo was mortgaged to the hilt thanks to Powers, who had refinanced it without our knowledge, but it was on the market, and I thought we might get enough for me to buy a D.C. house. But the final check amounted to only four thousand dollars, so I settled for a one-bedroom rental in a chicly renovated building downtown, a block from Pennsylvania Avenue.

I had been dreaming of a place where I might have weekly salons, invite visiting artists, mingle them with members of Congress, and give haven, after hours, to colleagues in the administration, including our sax-playing president. After-theater parties had been such a staple of my early years in New York, where actors met painters and music invariably sparked song and dance, that I envisioned a similar ease for hardworking Washington. Surely everyone would welcome R&R like that. Now the dream was eroded; a seventeen-by-twenty-foot living room was not conducive to such visions. Oh well, I thought, perhaps intimate dinners of eight, bringing together the best minds of our generation? If I could find the time to bring it all together? Dream on.

The selection of my staff was a more realistic pursuit. The federal government has strict rules about who serves. Federal employees are divided into those who dedicate their lives to public service—civil servants, or bureaucrats—and those who are hired by the administration in power, called executive service, or political appointees. The civil servants are promoted through fifteen grade levels in a complex set of steps that take years to achieve. Executive service pops people into plum positions without any past service. This dichotomy can create palpable tension between the two types of service, or at the very least lethargy on the part of some civil servants as they wait for a hostile administration to give way to a friendlier one. Fortunately this was not the case with those who staffed the NEA. They were all dedicated to the agency, and it was known as an exciting place to be employed.

Some of those on my senior staff I happily inherited. They were public servants with special skills of their own. My speechwriter, Keith Donohue, was a writer of fiction. A. B. Spellman, who had been in many authoritative positions at the Endowment and would be in many more, was a respected writer on the subject of jazz as well as a fine poet. And Larry Baden was skilled in management and administration.

For my senior deputy I chose Ana Steele, who had been serving as the agency's acting chairman and had been with the NEA from the beginning in the mid-1960s as an assistant to Roger Stevens. Ana's long career in government, all of it at the Endowment, was of immense value to me. She was its history. In fact she kept copious notes all the time, head down, pen constantly running across her notepad, reminding me a little of Madame Defarge knitting the names of the guilty in the French Revolution. But there was not a traitorous bone in Ana's body; besides, she was a fan of my acting, having started in the theater herself, and that didn't hurt.

With the help of White House personnel, I had my pick of recruits for the nine political appointments. A quiet steel magnolia named Scott Sanders, from Columbia, South Carolina, became the deputy chairman for public partnership. Scott had run her state's arts council when Richard Riley was governor, making it one of the finest in the nation. Riley had been head of Clinton's transition team and was now secretary of Education. The NEA's subsequent focus on arts education was secure because of these two advocates.

Susan Clampitt joined us from the White House, where her job was being phased out. I hired her as director of programs, a coveted position because of its close association with artists and their grant applications. Susan had run museums and been involved in a multitude of arts-related businesses. Like Scott, she was a strong supporter of Clinton and the Democratic Party.

In the arena of policy and research I wanted someone who already knew how the NEA worked, was conversant with issues of diversity and multiculturalism, and could help me redefine the agency's mission in the coming years. Olive Mosier was bright, with an inquiring mind, and because of her long association with the National Association of Local Arts Agencies (NALAA) she was the ideal person for the job.

Alexander "Sandy" Crary was ready to leave Senator Pell after a long career as his aide in charge of the arts, humanities, and related fields.

He had a remarkable memory for names and faces and a fine reputation for dignity and integrity. I asked him to be my White House liaison, and later my chief of staff.

The other important liaison was the person who would interact with members of Congress and their aides. This was a vital position for the Endowment because of the attacks on the agency. I needed someone who wasn't afraid of battle, who shared my own liberal philosophy, and who thoroughly understood the issues and Congress. When I heard retiring Ohio Senator Howard Metzenbaum read a strong speech to the Senate in support of the NEA, I knew that the speechwriter, his aide Richard Woodruff, was my man.

Another extremely vital position was that of public relations. The NEA had been a whipping boy in the press for years, and the public had a confused image at best and a disgusted image at worst. Ginny Terzano had been at the agency for a while, and I wanted her to stay on. She knew her job well and was feisty, and I knew that together we could turn it around. So did the White House. Ginny was so good that by December they stole her away to work directly in the president's press office.

Personnel offered me numerous candidates in exchange. My interviewing method was perhaps unorthodox, but it accomplished what I needed to know. I would put forward a hypothetical scenario of the most egregious kind of grant possible, one that would give the press a field day—something with sex in it, preferably homosexual, and a little religion thrown in. Then I asked the candidate how he or she would handle it. Most of them bluffed their way through, smiling nervously as they detailed a strategy of containment, but if acting has taught me anything it is to observe body language. I watched helplessly as one poor young woman flushed pink, then turned scarlet; red welts began erupting on her neck and face. She was related to a high-ranking official in the White House, and without getting too personal, I had a hard time explaining why she was not suitable for the job.

Finally, after searching for weeks, a woman named Cherie Simon walked in. She was petite and snazzily dressed, carrying a pale pink wool coat over her arm. She moved right to the sofa and sat down in the middle. She had worked as a producer for *ABC News* and most recently in media for the political fund-raising organization Emily's

List. I spelled out a wild scenario, and her eyes lit up. She smiled ever so slightly and replied, "What a challenge! Sounds like fun." I hired her on the spot. Any woman with a pale pink winter coat, subject to mud and slush, is a risk-taker. In addition, when she sat in the middle of the sofa I knew that she had a strong sense of herself. I proved to be right on both counts.

The lawyer who became general counsel for the Endowment had to be someone skilled in First Amendment issues as well as grounded and secure in the articulation of the NEA's position, not only to the press but also to the White House and the Department of Justice. Several years before I arrived four performance artists had sued the NEA because of the decency clause, which they regarded as unconstitutional, and the case was on appeal. The case of the "NEA Four," as Karen Finley and the others were known, was important and complex and ultimately went all the way to the Supreme Court. My choice for general counsel was Karen Christensen, who had been at National Public Radio dealing with similar issues. Her goal was to be a federal judge, but she came on board the NEA with little convincing once she understood how important her role was. Because of her innate wisdom, and the lawyer-client privilege inherent to our positions, she was my adviser and confidante.

Rounding out my immediate staff were my assistants Stephanie Madden and Noel Boxer and my secretary LaVerne Walker. Stephanie, like me, had dual interests in the theater and politics. She was adept at both, and as one of those closest to me she understood my needs and wants particularly well. Noel Boxer had been an advance man on several Democratic campaigns and came highly recommended from the White House. He became my scheduler, a major position of support for a chairman who had little time to call her own. My secretary, LaVerne Walker, had spent many years working in Senator Ted Kennedy's office. She was lively and beautiful and kept confidences as well as she kept files and folders.

These were my generals, my soldiers, my cast and crew. An organization is only as good as the people staffing it. The confluence of this senior group at the NEA and the events that rocked the agency in the next few years was a most fortunate one.

I had a lot of advice in those first months after my nomination.

Someone had the good sense to tell me to call Sharon Rockefeller, who was president and CEO of WETA, the area's public television station. Sharon knew the Endowment's issues well. Public television was doing its own battle with conservatives who were concerned with the content of programming and who sought to eviscerate the budgets of public media entities. She was also the wife of the junior senator from West Virginia, Jay Rockefeller, and had numerous friends on the Hill. We had breakfast together one morning; she thoughtfully had prepared notes on what she felt was most important for me to do immediately upon confirmation:

- Do not let the right wing or the left wing define you.
- Ask for a grace period from the artistic community.
- Meet with members of the religious right.
- Develop new supporters in Congress—the next generation.
- Let people know that the White House is behind you.
- Meet with corporate CEOs and foundation heads.

The advice was excellent, and I followed it to the best of my ability.

I also met with the leading grant-makers in the arts. A dozen of us sat down at the Mellon Foundation in New York one afternoon and talked about the NEA. The foundations were major partners, matching grants we gave and donating funds for special initiatives. They knew the inner workings of the Endowment far better than I did since most of them were regulars on the panels. They wished to see a reconfigured agency with a clearly defined policy about government grants. They said there was money to be tapped from other government agencies, especially for arts education. They also thought we needed to redefine the cultural wars by taking a strong position and by creating new language for the argument on the value of art to society.

Although all these suggestions were great, my head was swimming. These people had interacted with the NEA for a long time; they recognized the importance of the public and private sectors working together. I hadn't had time to understand sufficiently the role of either.

I left the luncheon a bit dazed from the onslaught of information and lingered momentarily on the New York City sidewalk. A gentle giant of a man, who had been fairly quiet during the discussion, came to my side. He was the retired chairman of Time-Life and had recently devoted his energies to the restoration of the city's Bryant Park. He knew the arts issues because in the 1980s he had been Ronald Reagan's choice to chair the President's Committee on the Arts and Humanities. Although he was used to the echelons of power, there was nothing driven about the man. He did not want to tell me what to do, he just wanted to offer me a hand or an ear if I needed it. Andrew Heiskell became a mentor to me at that moment. He told me to call him if I ever wanted to talk.

Kitty Carlisle Hart had been the chairman of the New York State Council on the Arts for twenty-five years. If anyone was in a position to advise me it was she. I eagerly looked forward to the opinions of another woman in a similar government position. She invited me to her spacious East Side apartment one morning; I browsed through the multitude of photographs adorning the piano, the walls, and the tables in the grand living room she had shared with her late husband, Moss Hart. I heard her breezy voice on the telephone in the other room as I mused on the long and fruitful life she had led, as an actress, as the wife of a famous playwright and director, and now, as a widow, the best-known arts council leader in the country.

She entered the living room with the most enchanting smile on her face, her small frame radiating health and elegance. There is no one I know who dresses so smartly all the time and manages to keep the decades at bay with such ease. It was natural for us to talk about clothes.

I had thought that I'd profile American designers by wearing only their suits and gowns. Memories of Nancy Reagan being lent Bill Blass and Galanos creations flooded my mind. Kitty put a quick stop to that. Never borrow from anyone, she said. Don't leave yourself open to charges of owing favors. I didn't tell her that the embezzlement had left me virtually bankrupt without a clothes allowance, but I listened carefully as she detailed the number of outfits I'd need and suggested that perhaps friends would donate their unused suits and gowns. She sweetly offered to give me some of her own.

"Kitty," I said, "look at me! I'm five feet seven and a half inches tall, and I weigh about 140 pounds in my stocking feet. You're the size I was at puberty. I don't think this is going to work."

She sneaked a good look at my large figure seated on the sofa next to her own diminutive size 4 and allowed that perhaps her offer *was* pie in the sky.

Of course the bulk of our conversation was not about clothes at all but about the job. I asked her myriad questions, which she answered succinctly and most candidly. She told me it would be rough, but to stand firm. Once she had been brought to tears by one assemblyman on the floor of the New York statehouse, but she held her ground. With regard to my staff she said to tell them: "No surprises, no secrets." She also told me not to leave them alone for more than a few days, that a leader needed to be present. Kitty was another mentor from then on, and she introduced me to Schuyler Chapin, who soon became New York City's commissioner of culture. He and I shared many confidences in the ensuing years.

I was staying with old and dear friends in Washington before my furniture arrived in the new apartment. Bardyl Tirana and I had known each other since we were teenagers. President Jimmy Carter had appointed him in 1977 to run the Civil Defense Agency in the Pentagon. Bardyl, after some months of investigation, had convinced Congress that the policy of evacuation in case of a nuclear bomb was ridiculous and not worth a dime's expenditure, and that the agency, and his job, should be abolished. My friend now had a successful law practice in D.C., and he and his wife Anne, a painter, lived in a grand old house dating from before the Civil War. I would tumble home to them at night, and Bardyl would coach me on the wiles of politics and listen as I recounted the events of my day on the Hill.

The business of meeting the senators had begun. Melanne accompanied me on my first few courtesy calls. After the disastrous initial meeting with Strom Thurmond, I got a welcome reprieve in the form of the most liberal man in the Senate, Howard Metzenbaum. The senator from Ohio was a collector of modern art, and his office was chock-full of work by artists like Red Grooms, Jenny Holzer, Frank Stella, and Robert Rauschenberg. What a rare pleasure it was just to sit in it! But

Metzenbaum was retiring in a few months, and his forthright and out-spoken defense of the NEA and freedom of expression would have few inheritors. Yet even this champion of new art had difficulty with the latest contretemps, known as the "border art fiasco."

Ana Steele, in her capacity as acting director of the Endowment, briefed me thoroughly on the "border art" piece, although she was con-strained from soliciting my advice on what to do about it. She had a difficult decision to make. The NEA had given a grant in 1989 to the Museum of Contemporary Art in San Diego for a very large project called "Dos Cuidades/Two Cities: The Border Project." The $250,000 grant was part of an overall budget of about $1 million spread over sev-eral years. The project engaged numerous artists to explore issues involving the shared border of the United States and Mexico. To date it had met with considerable success, bringing together disparate groups of people through everything from exhibitions to educational activities to artists' residencies. It had given employment to dozens and dozens of artists.

One work among many was called "Arte-Reembolso/Art Rebate." The three artists involved dispensed crisp new ten-dollar bills to incom-ing Mexican workers, most of whom had no legal papers. The artists wanted to bring attention to the fact that these workers were not a bur-den to the U.S. economy but in fact contributed to it through the dis-bursement of cash like the ten-dollar bills they were being given. They had signed receipts for each bill and intended to display the receipts at a later date. The project's budget was $5,000, of which the NEA con-tributed approximately $1,250.

When Congress got wind of this project there was a huge outcry. It was hard to know what it was that bothered them most—that the workers were illegal aliens or that the taxpayer was shelling out ten-dol-lar bills through the NEA and this was called "art." It was, to the critics' mind, just another instance of abuse on the part of the agency.

There was not one senator I spoke with who would defend the grant, not even Howard Metzenbaum. I sat there pontificating about the long history of controversy that currency had in the visual arts of our nation. I talked about the painter William Harnett, whose depiction of a bill had been so realistic that his painting was banned a hundred years before. I was going on too long, I realized, as I watched the good senator's eyes glaze over.

Within days the NEA decided that the agency was within its rights to ask for its portion of the money back, citing as the reason that currency was not considered art supplies. And it was not really within the purview of a U.S. government agency to support citizens of another country. The brouhaha over what looked like a freebie to non-Americans completely obscured any discussion by members of Congress of the art itself. As a political art project it was in fact successful, bringing attention to the plight of immigrants. But Congress had no interest in the worthiness of the art itself. In any case, the controversy was all moot before I became chairman.

I never spoke of the grant again, but secretly I wondered: had the artists handed out little engravings of Alexander Hamilton the size of a ten-dollar bill—which cost ten dollars each to produce—rather than his picture on the real thing, would it have made any difference? After all, a ten-dollar bill is also just paper; the gold that makes it worth something is safely locked away in Fort Knox (we trust).

A visit to the junior senator from Kansas, Nancy Kassebaum, reinforced my perception of congressional thinking. She told me point-blank that I could not defend controversial art and to not even bother to try. Kassebaum was the ranking minority leader on the Committee for Labor and Human Resources. She was bright, fair-minded, and straightforward. She always told me exactly what she thought, and she always did exactly what she said she was going to do. I appreciated this enormously.

Senator Ted Kennedy, the chairman of the committee, had an unblemished record of support for the arts and the humanities throughout his long career. His personal life had been marked with moments of darkest despair for decades, but in 1993 he was a new man. His power and strength as a human being radiated to all around him. He reminded me of a lion with his mane of snow-white hair, regal profile, and large girth. It had been two good years for Teddy. He had fallen in love with the beautiful lawyer Victoria Reggie and was deeply loved by her in return. Their marriage was a good one. He was the revered patriarch of his extensive family. As chairman of a powerful committee, he was intent on passing health care legislation at last, and his staff of about forty-five was one of the sharpest on Capitol Hill.

The walls of his office were covered with the artwork of "his kids"—his own, his stepchildren, and all his nephews and nieces. He pointed with pride to the poems they had written, and there was also a fine seascape painting of his own on his wall. The message was that art was part of the lives of all those close to him.

He told me that the NEA had almost been lost completely in 1989 and 1990, the argument for it submerged in the rhetoric of extremists. That was when New York Senator Alphonse D'Amato tore up a copy of Andres Serrano's photograph *Piss Christ* on the Senate floor and Jesse Helms claimed that Serrano wasn't even an artist. They called for the elimination of the agency. A compromise, which saved the day, had been hammered out behind closed doors by Kennedy and Pell, on the Democrats' side, and Orrin Hatch and Nancy Kassebaum for the Republicans. This was when the "decency clause" became a part of the NEA's reauthorizing statute. It seemed harmless enough to these good senators to ask the NEA to take into consideration "general standards of decency and respect for the diverse beliefs and values of the American public," and also, "Obscenity is without artistic merit, is not protected speech, and shall not be funded."

If hell is paved with good intentions, this authorizing language is an illustration of it. My predecessor, John Frohnmayer, had lived with the havoc it wreaked, not fully grasping the pitfalls inherent in a simple concept like "general standards of decency." I had read all about it in Frohnmayer's book *Leaving Town Alive,* written after President Bush unceremoniously asked him in 1992 to resign as chairman after three tumultuous years. Attempting to abide by the language of the statute, Frohnmayer had denied grants to Karen Finley and the others. Then the NEA Four turned around and sued the agency, charging that the decency clause was unconstitutionally vague. Frohnmayer was a lawyer and a good man. He was caught in an impossible bind, trying to please the conservative administration and members of Congress who had appointed him and at the same time serve artists, for whom freedom of expression is the bedrock of creativity and of our First Amendment rights. What happened to John Frohnmayer set the stage for me. At least I had been nominated to be chairman by the more liberal Clinton administration and had less to fear in that regard. And it was gratifying to know that there were bipartisan champions like Kennedy and Hatch who would go to the mat for the agency.

When I met Orrin Hatch, I was stunned that I was actually sitting down with him. My husband and friends and I had been riveted during the hearings for Clarence Thomas's appointment to the Supreme Court. I had been disgusted at the way Hatch, as a ranking minority member on the Judiciary Committee, had treated the witness Anita Hill. But then, as a woman, I was disgusted by the behavior of most of the men questioning her, from Alan Simpson's snide remarks to the almost total silence of Ted Kennedy. Yet here I was, in the lair of the beast, and he wasn't so beastly at all.

His incisive eyes never left mine during almost forty-five minutes of conversation, as if he were memorizing my face for future reference. He was the only member of Congress I met who talked about the sacrifice it had to be for me to give up my acting career to take on the NEA. I didn't look at it that way, but it was nice of him to say so. He spoke of decency but did not ask me what my definition was or what I might or might not fund. He talked of his relationship with Ted Kennedy and of how they worked closely together to get things done; they were not at two opposite ends of the pole, he asserted, as many people thought. And he told me the story of his boyhood in Pittsburgh, where his mother struggled in order to give him piano lessons and where he saved his pennies to take the streetcar, then walked two miles to sit in the peanut gallery to hear the symphony. It was clear that the arts meant a great deal to him personally.

As a Mormon in his state of Utah, he was perhaps inclined to support the arts. The state of Utah has the oldest arts council prototype in the nation, founded in 1899, and an even longer history of arts support. When, in 1847, Brigham Young arrived with his dedicated band of pioneers at the great expanse now called Salt Lake and declared, "This is the place," the very first building they erected was a theater cum social hall. Music, drama, and the visual arts have always been valued by the Mormon faith because of their life-enhancing qualities.

Senator Claiborne Pell of Rhode Island may not have had any religious incentive to promote the arts, but it was in his bones and his heritage just the same. One of the original founders of the Endowments for the Arts and the Humanities, Pell was still the most eloquent member of the committee. I spent a fine half-hour in his office, as I did with Senator Jeff Bingaman of New Mexico, Christopher Dodd of Connecticut, Bill Bradley of New Jersey, Carl Levin of Michigan, Tom Harkin of Iowa, Paul Simon of Illinois, and Paul Wellstone of Minnesota—Democratic supporters all. Senator Bob Kerrey and I spoke of our Nebraska roots and my dad's family still there. I found personal connections with almost everyone in one way or another. My career as an actress had taken me to many of our fifty states, and just a few words about each place, or someone I knew there, went a long way toward breaking the ice.

Dianne Feinstein of California, who had the busiest office I visited, seemed to have a fairly conservative approach to the arts and public funding. She told me that when she was mayor of San Francisco she had to cancel an "inappropriate" statue of the mayor who preceded her, George Moscone, who had been assassinated along with the gay politician Harvey Milk. The statue, like most art in public places, was controversial. She didn't wait for history to determine its value but decided to bend to the wishes of those who deemed it abominable. She got hell for her action, she said, but it was necessary for a leader to decide what was appropriate to do with public funds. This approach was more in line with Republican thinking, and unexpected coming from a leading female Democrat. I paid attention.

On the GOP side I sat down with Dave Durenberger of Minnesota, Judd Gregg of New Hampshire, and the infamous Dan Coats of Indiana. Coats, as a conservative Christian, had real problems with some of the alleged NEA grants. He told me that John Frohnmayer had sat in the very chair I was sitting in three years before, and then "the mess occurred." I said that my life in art had been in pursuit of excellence and that I expected to continue in that pursuit at the Endowment, if confirmed, but I didn't think that content restrictions were a good idea. Where do you stop and where do you begin? He surprised me by saying that he agreed with me—and then added that he would prefer that the agency took care of it internally.

When we parted, I still did not know whether he was going to vote for me, but he had urged me to return to Indianapolis to see how the Indiana Repertory Theater had grown. More than thirty years earlier I had spent two months at the theater. Although I had enjoyed playing Lizzie in *The Rainmaker,* I did not tell the senator of my terror at being there during the Cuban Missile Crisis. Indiana was on red alert for sure. As soon as the Soviet presence in Cuba made one transgression, the ground missiles in Indiana's dark soil were poised to rocket toward the annihilation of those Commie bastards. Warning sirens rang in the night, rehearsing us for the real event, and blurbs on the radio told us where to go. It was supposed to be a lucky thing that I found myself in an environment with so many underground bomb shelters. Funny, I didn't look at it that way. Two weeks later it was all over, Nikita Khrushchev having the good sense to retreat at last.

One day Melanne Verveer arranged for us to have breakfast in the small basement restaurant of the White House, patronized by the president's busy staff and those lucky enough to be invited. She invited along an ace lobbyist on the Hill whom she wanted me to get to know, Liz Robbins. Liz was nobody's idea of central casting, not in Hollywood's wildest dreams. Hollywood might have cast her as a Beverly Hills shopper on Rodeo Drive, never as a lobbyist in the halls of Congress. When at work she wore tight suits that revealed her knockout figure, her skirt a good four inches above her knees. Her reddish blond hair cascaded blowsily down her back, and her slingback or open-toed heels were so high it was a wonder she could maneuver the marble floors of the Capitol Building. But maneuver she did, and quite brilliantly. She knew everyone on a first-name basis, it seemed, and she dispensed kisses as freely as she did her infectious smiles. All the guys stopped and said hello. She introduced me to dozens of congressmen emerging from the House or Senate chambers one afternoon and even snagged the vice president for a quick "Hi, Al! Have you met Jane Alexander?" as a phalanx of Secret Service men parted in her wake.

I was astounded. Who was this creature? And what kind of goods did she have on all these fellows that they paid her such mind? It turned out that Liz Robbins was simply a superb lobbyist. She took on many nonprofit organizations as her clients and often volunteered her time for causes she believed in, like the arts. The packaging she wrapped herself in was just the initial attention-getter—pretty clever in a town where lobbyists are a dime a dozen.

There were two senators who made indelible impressions on me at this time. Alan Simpson, Republican from Wyoming, was a tall skinny cowboy with a broad smile and expansive manner. He led me up a few steps into his cluttered cubbyhole of an office and sat me down on a leather sofa. We quickly found out we had something rare in common: Bill Cody. Al hailed from Cody, Wyoming, where his grandfather had been the lawyer for Buffalo Bill and his Wild West Show. I told him that my own grandfather, Dr. Daniel Quigley, had ministered to Cody, and that my grandmother had been the best friend of his daughter, Irma Cody. Alan Simpson and I had both grown up with many Buffalo Bill stories. This connection made us friends almost instantly. But there was more.

I liked Al and trusted him from the very beginning of our relationship. He gave me the best advice of anyone at all: "Follow your gut, and don't take any crap from anyone." Bold words, but a nice drink of cool water at a hot time. He then shuffled through some papers on his desk, citing negatives the Christian Coalition and other right-wing groups had sent him about me. My leftist activities had included supporting nuclear disarmament. "Wrong," the senator said. "The Soviet Union collapsed because of the policy of 'mutually assured destruction' (or 'MAD,' as it was generally designated) and the buildup of nuclear weapons."

"I think we peace activists made a real difference," I replied. The senator would have none of this, and we went on to discuss other things.

Later that night I recalled the first marches I had joined to "ban the bomb." In the late 1950s Benjamin Spock, the great baby doctor, was mobilizing many of us to protest the deadly element strontium 90, which had crept into the milk that children drank. The testing of nuclear weapons in space had created a fallout of radiation onto the grasses our cows were eating. A few years later, in 1963, President Kennedy and the Soviet Union's Khrushchev signed the ban on atmospheric testing of nuclear weapons. No one could ever tell me that we who marched had made no difference. As Margaret Mead said: "Never doubt that a small group of thoughtful committed citizens can change the world; indeed it is the only thing that ever has." This had been my credo for as long as I could remember, and I think it still was as I tackled the NEA's foes in Washington.

Daniel Patrick Moynihan, the distinguished senior senator from my home state of New York, was a great friend to the arts. He dispensed with preliminaries and went right to a book cataloging the artworks under fire from the Whitney Museum's latest show. He read the descriptions of several pieces and then happily hit on what he was looking for: "Ah yes, here we are—*Skull Fuck*." The consonants swirled on his tongue as he briefly allowed me a glimpse of the accompanying photo. Then he insouciantly tossed the book on the table and exclaimed, "Comes with the territory!" His professorial eye twinkled, and I breathed a sigh of relief. Here was a fellow who understood, really understood, the nature of what we were grappling with. Controversy was inherent in the world of art.

He went on to say that of course the arts needed support because they were not cost-productive, they all had "Baumol's disease." William Baumol had written a book in the 1960s explaining that the performing arts would never be self-supporting because the size of the performance space never varied. Unlike production costs, it didn't increase. In other words, a concert hall is a concert hall is a concert hall. And a Mozart string quartet will always require four musicians, not fewer and not more. You couldn't expect to charge three hundred dollars per ticket to keep pace with inflation. The argument made eminent sense to Moynihan, who was chairman of the Finance Committee, but it never impressed others sufficiently. I didn't see the senator much after that first meeting; regrettably for the NEA his time was consumed with the country's financial matters and with health and welfare issues.

As usual in September, when the budget is decided for the coming year, a lot was happening on the Hill. And also as usual Jesse Helms was after the NEA again. His annual bill to eliminate the agency entirely was handily defeated by a vote of 85–15. The only surprise was what else he might have up his sleeve in the form of amendments. In September 1993 Helms called for the elimination of grants to individual artists and an increase in the amount the NEA gave to the states.

I met briefly with California's junior senator, Barbara Boxer, just before she went to the floor in the agency's defense. She had impressed me in the past with her stance on runaway defense spending, but I wasn't prepared for what she did this day. She stepped up to the microphone and said, "Give Jane Alexander a chance." Ted Kennedy and Claiborne Pell also chimed in, while Nancy Kassebaum was at work behind the scenes telling her GOP colleagues, fence-sitters like Dirk Kempthorne and Larry Craig from Idaho, "Jane Alexander will make it all right."

I sat in the vice president's anteroom off the Senate floor and watched it all on cable TV. Al Gore was not there, but his aides were scurrying around and intermittently explaining to me what was happening. It all looked good. Jim Jeffords, a fine independent thinker from the state of Vermont—where they grow those kind of folks—rose to the occasion too, despite his membership in the Republican Party. He told his colleagues that the photos of babies' corpses by Joel Peter-Witkin that Helms and others were circulating in the cloakroom and on closed-circuit television were *not* in fact produced by the photographer at the time he received an NEA grant. He asked that the two amendments be tabled. There was a roll-call vote, the amendments were tabled, and that was the end of it for 1993. It now looked likely that I would be confirmed as the Endowment's chairman, even before my hearing in a few days, because of the confidence placed in me during the roll-call vote. The pressure was on, but I was glad to be going into fiscal year 1994 with a sound budget of $174 million, the same as the year before.

Leaving the Senate floor area, I bumped into Al Simpson, who told me that the boys in the back room were chuckling under their breath over the photographs—the usual response to crude art, I guess, when it isn't outrage. As we were talking, Jesse Helms suddenly appeared. Al said, "Come on, you should meet him," and hustled me toward my nemesis.

Helms, one should never forget, is from the South; he has the manners of a courtly southern gentleman. He looks like the grandfather that he is, but with eyes as sharp as black buttons on a teddy bear. Simpson introduced us, and there was a slight pause before Helms lifted his hands above his head and slowly stroked imaginary horns.

"You can come to my office and feel my horns anytime" were his first words to me. All I could do was laugh. Here was the devil as a dirty old man! Well, if not dirty, at least naughty, very naughty. He then said that he was inclined to support my nomination—because his daughter's name was Jane Alexander. Was that her married name, I asked? No, he replied, it was his wife's middle name—Jane Alexander Helms Knox was her full name now. This was all a bit eerie. We got back to basics when he asked me to take his objections seriously. I assured him that I did, that I had been in front of audiences all my life and that I listened very carefully. I took them seriously, but I couldn't imagine that Helms would ever believe that I could think as he did. He left us, and Al Simpson naively suggested that all Jesse needed was a little attention paid to him. I doubted that very much.

Ed and I took a quick trip to Los Angeles the weekend before my hearing. There were others in our family who had lives too. My eldest stepson, Tony Sherin, and his wife, Amelia Jones, were expecting their first baby any day. Tony had a good career as a film editor in Hollywood, and Amelia taught art history at the University of California in Riverside. We were able to spend a few hours with them and, as new grandparents-to-be, excitedly discuss the impending birth.

My son Jace had switched from an acting career to directing and was attending the American Film Institute. We visited him at his new apartment in the Hollywood Hills. Now I had a good picture in my mind of where our boys lived. My agent, Joan Hyler, gave a lovely dinner party for me—a farewell to film and theater for a few years. She generously gave me many of her suits and evening gowns for my new D.C. life. On Sunday night we attended the Emmy awards ceremony and ball because Ed was nominated for the first time for his direction of *Law and Order.* He didn't win, but the evening was exciting anyway.

On Monday we packed up our Santa Monica condo and arranged

for a mover to take all our furniture to my apartment in Washington. We then rushed exhaustedly to the airport to make my final murder board meeting before the big Senate day on Wednesday morning. I had never been so busy in my life; this, I found out, was just preparation for the months to come.

I was ready, and eager, and willing.

CHAPTER FOUR

Curtain Up

Opening nights have always been exhilarating for me. Like a racehorse at the starting gate, I can't wait for the bell. At the same time I've always known I am just at the beginning of a long process. I may know my lines and the bare bones of character and emotion, but it is in the repetition, the playing of the role over and over and over again, that I begin to plumb the depths. Discovery is a never-ending part of the game, and one I welcome. The risk of what I might find is exciting and not to be feared. This is what kept me coming back to the theater year after year. I've done more than a hundred plays, and each character has brought me something new, and the reminder that the extent of human emotion and experience can never be exhausted.

Actors approach a role in essentially two different ways. Some actors seek first to know the look of a character and the details of his or her life. Does she wear hats, bite her nails, stoop when she walks, or lisp slightly? Once they have a sense of the outer look and behavior, they can begin to build a character and understand what is going on inside.

Other actors start by trying to understand the underlying emotions and motivations first, before they dress their character or know how she moves. Both methods reach the same result eventually, given enough time.

I subscribe to the latter way of creating a role, and it can often take a very long time to understand what is going on in a character's psyche. As much as I've pondered and deliberated the whys and the wherefores, there are some things that come to you only through osmosis, and through the doing of them again and again. It is not unlike sports in that way. Who can say how your brain tells a multitude of muscles what to do and when, finally putting it all together to ace a shot?

I approached my confirmation hearing in much the same way I do the opening night of a show—with excitement and an understanding that I would perform as best I could. The day dawned bright and blue. At 9:00 A.M. I hopped in a cab to the White House, where I met Melanne, and together we proceeded to the Senate's Dirksen Building on the Hill. The corridors outside the hearing room were crowded with people and press in line to get in. After making our way to Kennedy's office to wait while the senators arrived, we chatted quietly with members of my confirmation team, who, like sports coaches, were there for last-minute pep talks. Senators Jeffords, Pell, Simon, Metzenbaum, and Kennedy lined up for their entrance, I behind them. Moynihan could not introduce me as planned because he had another meeting; he sent a note saying that he felt "awful." It meant that the other senator from my home state, Al D'Amato, would present me. There was some irony in this: D'Amato had led the attack on the Endowment a few years before, but if his willingness to present me meant he had had a change of heart, that was all to the good. My other presenter was an old friend from the state of Oklahoma, Senator David Boren, another Republican but a great arts supporter.

We entered the chamber, cameras flashing on either side. The senators mounted to their leather seats behind the curved mahogany table, a good six feet above the witness table below. I spotted Ed, Jace, and my stepson Jon seated directly behind my designated chair and went to greet them. The crowded room held many of my friends and family who had come to support me on this big day.

Senator Boren took the seat to my right, and Senator D'Amato to my left, as we faced the committee. I don't know when, historically, those in power elevated themselves above everyone else, but psychologically it does the trick, reducing the supplicant to a state of intimidation. For a fleeting second I felt like Alice in Wonderland. Over a raft of cameras and cameramen sprawled at odd angles on the floor before me, I looked up in childlike anticipation. The gavel came down, and the room hushed as Chairman Kennedy told David Boren to begin. He spoke of the work I had done with young people at the Oklahoma

Summer Arts Institute, where we had first met in the 1980s. It was a special place that Ed and I had been to a number of times to teach acting and directing. We had fallen in love with the state and its people. Boren spoke thoughtfully of my qualifications for the position and my love of the arts.

Al D'Amato then told the committee of his confidence in me and in my ability to restore public confidence in the NEA. He said, "Art in any society serves as a focal point for thought and discussion." (Where was Andres Serrano in that "discussion," I wondered, when "Big Al," as New Yorkers called him, had publicly harangued the artist just a few years earlier?) He graciously commended my family for supporting me in the move away from home, which he knew was not easy, and wound up saying he looked forward to my "endeavors as . . . a star on the nation's stage."

Some of the committee spoke to my nomination, and then I was asked to make my statement. This is what I said:

"Thank you, Mr. Chairman, Senator Kassebaum, and members of the committee. I am pleased to come before you today as President Clinton's choice to head an extraordinary agency, the National Endowment for the Arts, which has meant so much to me and to so many others. . . .

"In 1945 a man I barely knew, my father, returned from the war. He had been gone most of my young life. In an effort to get to know me, this handsome stranger took me one afternoon to the ballet. It was surely the seminal experience of my life. The ballet was *Copelia;* it was danced by lighter-than-air magicians from Copenhagen, Denmark, American ballet companies being few and far between at that time. Although I was barely six, that performance transformed my life—my waking thoughts and my dreams. How could human beings defy gravity with such grace? Hovering in the air like hummingbirds? How was the corps de ballet able to execute their steps in such perfect unison? How did such beauty come to exist? You didn't see it in the real world, not costumes like that, or lights, or scenery, or the seemingly limitless extension of the human body itself.

"I was introduced to art, and from that moment on it never left me. Although I dedicated myself to becoming a ballerina, it was not to be.

The sheer discipline of the endeavor, the actual pain endured in being *en pointe* was more than I was cut out for. After getting some good laughs as Long John Silver in a fifth-grade production of *Treasure Island,* I switched my allegiance to theater. At fourteen I went with my class to an Old Vic production of *Romeo and Juliet.* I was transfixed by the romance of Shakespeare's tale and wondered if I would ever grow up to play Juliet—did only the British have a lock on theater like this?

"I began my search for a life in the theater, one that would allow me to act the great classic plays of the world. At the time there was virtually only the commercial theater represented by Broadway in New York City and its tryouts and tours, which visited cities across the United States from time to time. Beyond that there was community theater, where amateurs banded together and, for the love of it, put on plays wherever and however. My dream was to be like the great American actress Katharine Cornell and do a play a year on Broadway and then tour that production around the country for a year. But by the time I grew up that kind of theater had dwindled to almost nothing.

"Then in the early 1960s President Kennedy's vision for the arts as a part of everyone's life began to be translated into reality. Congress declared in 1965 that:

> An advanced civilization must not limit its efforts to science and technology alone but must give full value and support to the other great branches of scholarly and cultural activity in order to achieve a better understanding of the past, a better analysis of the present, and a better view of the future. Democracy demands wisdom and vision in its citizens. It must therefore foster and support a form of education, and access to the arts and the humanities, designed to make people of all backgrounds and wherever located masters of their technology and not its unthinking servants.

"This was the "declaration of independence" for the arts and humanities. Senator Pell was its orchestrator, for which we are all deeply grateful. It legitimized the endeavors of tens of thousands in the creative community and recognized the worth of creative thought made manifest through painting and other visual arts, sculpture, architecture, dance, literature, design, music, opera, theater, film, and folk arts. It confirmed that the arts belong to all people and that art is of the people, for the people, and by the people.

"Almost immediately things began to happen, all across the country. With seed money from the Endowment, people took heart and went to work to raise matching funds for small presses, for dance companies, for an opera, for artists to come into their schools, for museums to celebrate and safeguard our heritage.

"I experienced firsthand this renaissance in the arts. From Boston's Charles Playhouse I went to Washington's great Arena Stage. And with the Endowment's help at the height of the civil rights movement, we did a play called *The Great White Hope* with an interracial company of sixty-three. It was the first from a not-for-profit theater to transfer to Broadway. The play won a Pulitzer Prize for its author, Howard Sackler. James Earl Jones and I moved from the theater to a film version and received Academy Award nominations for our performances.

"The impact of the Endowment was not limited to *The Great White Hope.* Significantly, every single theater Pulitzer Prize since has been awarded to a play that originated in the not-for-profit theater and was funded by the Arts Endowment. I think you will agree that's quite a record!

"My first love of theater has continued to this day. This past year I've been performing in *The Sisters Rosensweig,* which began at Lincoln Center, an Endowment-supported arts complex, and transferred to Broadway. Its author, Wendy Wasserstein, a Pulitzer Prize winner, was once awarded an Endowment fellowship in 1982.

"I have performed in Indiana, in Georgia, in South Carolina, in California—in more than twenty states across this vast and wonderful land of great diversity and beauty. As Senator Boren has told you, I have taught often in Oklahoma's remarkable Arts Institute—young people who have never been out of the state but whose commitment and desire to be an artist causes them in fact to be the best I have ever encountered.

"I'm grateful to have been welcomed and to have felt at home in so many places. The life I've led in the theater, in the world of art, has given so much to me personally—particularly from Endowment-supported works—that I wish to give something back.

"Perhaps I can make a real contribution at this difficult time. The Endowment has struggled these past few years to keep itself alive and valued in the public eye. In these twenty-eight years it has awarded one hundred thousand grants. It has been an unparalleled success, perhaps the most successful of any of the independent federal agencies. Directly and indirectly, it has affected most artists and arts organizations alive today and created an arts economy of about 6 percent of the gross national product and over 2.5 percent of our workforce. The Endowment's budget is modest in comparison with other government agencies, but with its $175 million budget last year, it created a twentyfold return in jobs, services, and contracts. In partnership with the private sector it leveraged that $175 million to almost $1.4 billion.

"With all these accomplishments by the Endowment, how has this success story managed lately to be depicted as a villain? A handful of controversial grants have taken the focus from the thousands upon thousands of grants that have enhanced the lives of millions. I respect the right of people to be heard—the voices of those who are disturbed by art and the voices of the creative community. This, after all, is the greatness of our democratic system. But the arts should not be used as a political football by those on the far right *or* the far left. The arts are for everyone. The Endowment is too important to be misused by some who disseminate misinformation for their own ends or attack the Endowment as a campaign platform.

"I believe strongly that the sound and fury of the past few years over that handful of controversial grants must end. When judging the National Arts Endowment, we must look at the complete picture. Let's give the arts a chance to help us heal and understand one another.

"Should the Senate confirm me, I cannot promise that under my chairmanship the arts will be free of controversy. The very essence of art, after all, is to hold the mirror up to nature; the arts reflect the diversity and variety of human experience. We are, as Hamlet says, 'The abstracts and brief chronicles of the time,' and as such, the artist often taps into the very issues of society that are most sensitive. I can, however, assure Congress that I will follow the statutory guidelines on funding to the very best of my ability to ensure that grants are given for the highest degree of artistic merit and excellence. I will be accountable and look forward to working with members of Congress. My goal for the arts is that the best reaches the most.

"As the president's nominee for chairman of the Arts Endowment, if confirmed, I intend to let the American people know the truth about the Endowment and the value of the arts in each and every one of their lives. I am committed to making the Endowment a driving force for education. Arts education helps inspire and motivate students, gets them to focus on creative approaches to problem-solving, and frees the imagination.

"I also look forward to an enhanced partnership with the private sector, which matches dollar for dollar Endowment grants to organizations. I want to work with state arts councils and local agencies to develop new and innovative ways to reach communities everywhere. I hope to travel all across this country to listen to the people about their needs with regard to the arts, from the most rural area to the inner city.

"I have a vision for the arts in this country. That vision is that every man, woman, and child find the song in his or her heart. I see the arts as part of the solution to our problems and not, in any way, part of the problem. The arts are life-enhancing and bring joy. Through the arts, we release the very best that is in our imaginations, and it is through our imagination that we draw the map for our future. Through the arts we learn the discipline of a skill and the accomplishment that comes with collaboration. The arts are a community issue. They bring together; they do not rend asunder.

"Mr. Chairman, I am honored to be considered for this position. It is the culmination of my life in the arts, which has given me much joy. I hope to be able to help provide the people of this country the opportunity to find through the arts some of the richness and joy that I have experienced."

I had written this statement over the course of the month, with little input from anyone. It was what I wanted to say and a position from which I did not deviate. The committee members were pleased. Senator

Pell said it was one of the best he had ever heard, and Senator Hatch seemed visibly moved.

Senator Jeffords was so enthusiastic he said he wished the Senate could all vote immediately, while Metzenbaum called the morning a "deification." There were very few questions after my remarks, and it was all over by 11:00 A.M.

This was a high point for the arts world and me. The hearing was rerun several times on C-Span, and the press the next day was very positive. By all accounts I was a hit.

My family and friends and I celebrated with a luncheon in the Senate Dining Room, and then, curiously, I ran into Jesse Helms again as we were leaving. He acted like my new best friend and took us all into the Senate gallery for a look, and then to tea back in the Dining Room. My friend Susan Dowling was almost apoplectic; she literally could not speak as we sat there at a round table for ten. Her face would redden and then blanch unexpectedly when Helms talked. Susan had been a modern dancer and then a choreographer and was now director of the avant-garde show called *New Television,* which aired late at night on many public television stations. The show often included cutting-edge work by dancers like Bill T. Jones or a group called Pomo Afro Homo, and yes, many of them were gay men. Some of these groups had been cited by Helms in his routine excoriations. And here was Susan, seated next to the enemy.

My niece Katherine, on the other hand, and the courtly Jesse got along famously. He highly recommended the vanilla frozen yogurt, and Katherine championed the choice. They were giggling together—the elderly senator was an obvious charmer with children. My sister-in-law Janice hailed from his state of North Carolina, and it turned out that her parents and Jesse's daughter were good friends and neighbors in the town of Spring Lake. All these coincidences were a little too close for comfort for me, but if fate was thrusting us together, I was willing to see where it might lead.

I had my antenna up, however. My confirmation team had warned me that I should never be alone with Helms, that he would attempt to extract promises and use them against me later. So it was with some alarm that I felt the senator pulling me aside as we all rose from the table, saying he wanted to speak with me a minute. I'll never forget Susan Clampitt inching toward Helms's back as he cornered me against the wall, trying to overhear and bear witness should it be needed. It wasn't.

His request was mild: Would I please see Anne-Imelda Radice, the former acting chair of the NEA after Frohnmayer was let go? Of course I would, I replied. Radice had a withering reputation among artists, not unlike a modern-day Bloody Mary. But I was curious to meet her and to listen to her perspective. Helms then said that he would support me, but that if the controversial grants continued, he would be right back on the Senate floor. I told him that I understood, and that was that. No promises on my part, but an understanding from him of what I already knew to expect. Katherine then gave the old codger a big hug good-bye. Oh to be ten again! "As innocent as a new-laid egg," as the Gilbert and Sullivan song goes.

We all went our separate ways, most of us flying back to New York and our homes. Until I was voted in by the entire Senate and then sworn into office, there was nothing for me to do in D.C. It was a welcome hiatus. I called Tony and Amy and discovered that my big day was even bigger than our family had imagined. Evan had been born that same evening.

The phone rang all the next day—news of the baby raced around our family, and news of the hearing's success was trumpeted in the papers. In the parlance of Broadway, the reviews were raves. Ted Kennedy called, jubilant, and said, "When I saw you in the halls with Jesse Helms, I figured things were going okay!"

At around 7:00 P.M. the First Lady called to offer congratulations. I in turn thanked her for all she was doing on the health care issue and told her how fine the president's speech on the subject was. She said, "Yes, I was so proud of him." I was too shy, given the weight of health care, to ask her when I might be seeing or hearing from the president himself. In fact it was beginning to dawn on me that the arts and humanities had been relegated to the domain of the First Lady and that perhaps I would never hear from the office of the president.

My few meetings with Bruce Lindsey had been restricted to person-nel matters, not policy, and the last time I had seen him I had asked, almost in parting, what the administration expected of me. "Stay out of the headlines," Bruce replied. I took that to mean no negative press, as it would reflect badly on the president. Good press, obviously, would reflect positively. The only other directive I ever received from the White House was to keep a diary in case of litigation. This was ironic in light of the fact that a few years later everyone in Washington was jettisoning his diary after Senator Packwood's scrawls helped oust him from the Senate on allegations of sexual harassment.

A few days later Al Simpson called to tell me that as minority whip in the Senate it was his job to count heads on the Republican side of the aisle and that there was one opposed to my confirmation. He said he would work on him. Three hours later Melanne called to tell me I had been unanimously confirmed. Al Simpson had gotten Trent Lott to change his mind, the first of many things Al would do for me.

I made the move to Washington within the week. My new assistant, Noel Boxer, and my new driver, Larry Manley, who had been with the agency for nine years, met me at the airport. As we rounded a bend on Rock Creek Parkway just below the Kennedy Center, we inauspiciously crashed into the car in front of us. Nothing was hurt except Larry's ego, which was severely bruised; he'd never had an accident before. Noel and I hailed a cab and went on our way, leaving poor Larry to pick up the pieces.

I visited my office for the first time. It was a wonderful space in the Old Post Office Building at 1100 Pennsylvania Avenue. Nancy Hanks, the visionary chairman of the Endowment from 1968 to 1976, had secured the building for the arts and the humanities agencies, and it was named for her. My office was in a corner on the fifth floor, with light streaming in from huge windows on the south and west sides. This was a major plus for me because the ubiquitous government-issue fluorescent lights would have done me in. I have a peculiar reaction to fluorescence: after about an hour I feel desperately drowsy. I'd had visions of the chairman snoozing away during staff meetings or while entertaining foreign diplomats.

The walls, painted a soft gunmetal blue-gray, were fourteen feet high with nineteenth-century moldings at the top. The room was almost a perfect square with a turret in the corner for plants and an armchair. I was very happy. Surely this was the best office in D.C., other than the oval one up the street.

The party began. It was a whirlwind week of running from one function to another. The artists who had been awarded the National Medal of Arts were being honored, and there were receptions and luncheons and dinners to celebrate them and their accomplishments. My indoctrination as a speaker came suddenly when Senators Kennedy and Simpson asked me to say a few words at a reception they were jointly giving in the steaming jungle atmosphere of the Botanical Gardens. Underneath the huge phallic pod of a kapok tree I managed to squeak out my gratitude and excitement about the occasion, and the medalists.

That night at dinner, given by the National Cultural Alliance, I was seated next to Congressman Ralph Regula of Ohio, and Ed was next to his wife, Mary. Ralph was then ranking minority representative on the House appropriations subcommittee covering the arts. It is fitting that the first House representative I would talk with was the man who would become most important for the NEA a year hence. He was easy to talk to; we spoke of his Ohio farm in Canton and his love of the land. He liked being on the Interior subcommittee because it dealt with the land and Native Americans as well as with the arts and humanities.

The chairman of the subcommittee was the legendary Sidney Yates, who hailed from Chicago. Every artist in the country knew of his dedication to the arts and humanities agencies. He had chaired the subcommittee since 1975 and every year invited prominent artists to testify for the NEA. I had testified twice, in 1983 and 1991.

But Ralph was the man I was seated next to this night. His wife Mary confided in Ed that they had not been invited to any of the National Medal of Arts events at the White House, and their feelings were hurt. She thought it was partisan. This was the first whiff I got of partisanship, if that was what it was. The Regulas were, after all, used to a Republican president, and he was a loyal party man. Bill Clinton was the first Democrat to be elected in twelve years, and this was the first arts event he was officially overseeing; perhaps the invitations were in great demand. Nevertheless, I put in a call to the White House the next morning to have the congressman and his wife placed on the guest list.

The medalists of 1993 had been nominated by the NEA's National

Council on the Arts and then approved by the president. This out-standing group of honorees included the baritone Robert Merrill, the playwright Arthur Miller, the artist Robert Rauschenberg, the movie director Billy Wilder, the stage director Lloyd Richards, the dancer and choreographer Paul Taylor, the singer Ray Charles, and the writer William Styron. Not a lot of women. We stood together chatting in the newly spangled Blue Room of the White House waiting for the president.

Bill Clinton finally walked in the room, and everything stopped. It was my first glimpse of him in the flesh. He was tall, taller than I had imagined, maybe six feet four, with a surprisingly lithe body. His complexion was ruddy, and his eyes were sky blue. Even if he weren't the president it would be hard not to look at him. He radiated warmth and pleasure at being with people. I held out my hand: "Hello, Mr. President, I'm Jane Alexander," I said.

"I know," he replied with a smile. "Thanks for doing this for us."

He moved through the circle with grace and ease, shaking hands, remarking on some special thing about each person. He sat on the settee with the blind Ray Charles, and they laughed together as if they had known each other as boys, Clinton remembering how much the song "Georgia" had meant to him during his own childhood in the South.

At the ceremony on the South Lawn, the president continued to infuse his remarks with a personal touch, departing from his prepared text. He spoke of the impact that Styron's *The Confessions of Nat Turner* had on his thoughts about race when he read it. He recalled a concert that Ray Charles gave on June 24, 1967, that so excited him he couldn't get to sleep until five o'clock in the morning and had to jog three miles in the middle of the night. This was my first exposure to the president's prodigious memory for detail, an ability I found increasingly astounding.

Twice in his remarks the president referred to me and to Sheldon Hackney, my colleague at the National Endowment for the Humanities; he welcomed us both and said that this was the kickoff for the nation's celebration of Arts and Humanities Month. There were hundreds and hundreds of arts advocates and artists in the audience. It was hard not to feel that a new day had dawned in the culture wars.

That night the White House held a gala dinner for the medalists, their families, and a few invited guests. We mingled in the East Room under the watchful eyes of George and Martha Washington, who hung in nineteenth-century gilt on the walls, as we waited for the current occupants to come downstairs. Bob Rauschenberg switched his Jim Beam for Jack Daniels when they ran out of the former and proceeded to get pleasantly buzzed. Ed and I wandered the smaller rooms admiring the paintings. Walter Annenberg chuckled as he told us how Jackie Kennedy had wheedled out of him the great portrait of Ben Franklin, musing with his thumb under his chin, that now dominated the Green Room.

We all lined up to greet the Clintons and have our pictures snapped with them. "How'd I do today?" the president asked me. "Wonderfully," I replied, the stardust blurring my vision.

I sat next to the writer Oscar Hijuelos, who asked, "How did I get here?" I didn't know, but I could guess he came from a list celebrating diversity. Of course he *was* an award-winning author, but I knew that the administration was trying to be as inclusive as possible by reaching out to people of color, disability, and rural parts of America. Once, at a White House meeting about NEA personnel, when I proposed an African American candidate who was disabled and came from the Pacific Northwest, the eager response was, "Oh good, three for one!"

Oscar told me that the NEA had changed his life. He said that when he received the money for his fellowship in literature he immediately quit his job, moved to Italy, and wrote *The Mambo Kings Play Songs of Love,* which became a best-seller and later a movie. It was a tale I would hear again and again from artists, and one I never tired of.

When the Marine Band's violinists strolled through the candlelit dining room playing "Stardust Memories," Leontyne Price stood suddenly and began singing in full operatic voice, and when she finished Robert Merrill at the next table did the same. The mood in the room was giddy, and this spontaneous act left us all entranced and agape. It was a first and a last time, as I never saw it happen again at an arts dinner.

Every president since Johnson, with the exception of George Bush, had invited me to the White House for a gala event. During the 1960s, when I was acting at Arena Stage by night and protesting the war in Vietnam during the day, I was invited to the festivities after a state dinner. I changed into an evening gown after my stage performance and arrived at the White House to see Andy Warhol and Fred Astaire milling in the crowd, watching President Johnson cut a rug. I had the gall to ask Fred Astaire if he would like to dance. He sweetly declined. But before I knew it I was dancing with the president. It was no secret that Lyndon Johnson liked to dance and that he was pretty good at it, but for those of us in the antiwar movement being in his arms was tantamount to defecting to the enemy. I thought of the great chance I had to tell him what I thought of him and the war, but rhythm got the better part of me and I shut up and let him fox-trot me across the floor. He was tall, with southern charm and a way with the ladies; Bill Clinton reminded me of him, although no one could match Johnson in the dance department.

Ed and I have always liked to dance, and if the band is good we can go on for hours. The president and First Lady took the floor for the first dance, gazing into each other's eyes, while the Marine Band played a conservative beat. Soon the rest of us poured onto the floor, with Senator Simpson and his striking wife Ann dominating the space equally as much as Ed and me. We waltzed and waltzed and waltzed, something the Marine Band plays well, and headed for home sometime after midnight.

I rose early the next day to do a remote hookup for the *Today Show* with Katie Couric. At this point in time the press was all rosy; Katie asked me some questions regarding content restrictions, but with only a few minutes on air I could easily field them.

The party continued. The Endowment held a huge luncheon for the National Arts Medalists in the Great Hall of the Library of Congress. The hall had just been restored, to the tune of $80 million, and had not even opened to the public yet. Its giant marble staircases on either side wound up to balconies where tables were set for three hundred people. The ceiling, forty feet overhead, was encrusted in mosaics, romantic images, and literary bon mots and glowed ornately like something out of the sun king's palace. I was wearing white, and someone remarked that I looked like an angel come to the rescue.

If I was an angel, then Garrison Keillor, the emcee for the afternoon, was God. As his deep basso voice reverberated from a microphone high up on a balcony platform, it all seemed deeply profundis or just plain ridiculous. To top it all off, I was sworn in by Sandra Day O'Connor wearing her flowing black robe after a morning at the Supreme Court across the street.

Nevertheless, I took the vows seriously.

I, Jane Alexander, do solemnly swear that I will support and defend the Constitution of the United States against all enemies, foreign and domestic; that I will bear true faith and allegiance to the same; that I take this obligation freely, without any mental reservation or purpose of evasion; and that I will well and faithfully discharge the duties of the office on which I am about to enter. So help me, God.

Justice O'Connor told the crowd that I had predated her as the first woman justice of the Supreme Court, and I then said something about life imitating art. Then we all had lunch, each clink of a fork on a plate resounding in the cavernous space. I chanced to look up and caught a glimpse of the nineteenth-century muses rendered sweetly above the arches. They were four ladies in flowing pastel garb, and each was given a literary theme: *Romance, Fancy, Tradition,* and *Erotica.* How fitting, I thought! Wonder if the fellows across the street know that nineteenth-century minds espoused study of this? I doubted it. In any case, you had to be looking up to notice these gentlewomen.

At least the people gathered this day had a high opinion of art, and certainly of the artists we were honoring. I spoke briefly about each honoree and what they meant to me personally, following the president's lead of the day before and chucking my prepared speech. The day came to an end; the week came to an end; the months of anticipation came to an end. The hard work was about to begin.

CHAPTER FIVE

The Production

The National Endowment for the Arts was founded with strong bipartisan support. That does not mean it emerged full-blown and without a struggle; from the very beginning of our nation there had been contention about government support of the arts. George Washington mentioned the arts in the first draft of his inaugural address:

> I trust you will not fail to use your best endeavors to improve the education and manners of the people; to accelerate the progress of arts and sciences; to patronize works of genius; to confer rewards for inventions of utility; and to cherish institutions favourable to humanity. Such are among the best of all human employments.

For whatever reason, now lost in the cloud of history, those remarks did not survive until the final speech. Too bad. We could have used "best endeavors to improve the education and manners of the people," at the very least.

Washington's colleague John Adams wrote in 1780: "I must study politics and war, that my sons may have liberty to study mathematics and philosophy, geography, natural history and naval architecture, navigation, commerce, and agriculture, in order to give their children a right to study painting, poetry, music, architecture." The world's nations have not yet given up war, but with the infiltration of the computer and attendant technologies into all strata of society it may ultimately be possible. Politics will always be around.

John Adams spent two years with the Continental Congress as that body shaped the U.S. Constitution. Its members sought to protect the varied interests of all concerned with the least possible restriction or encumbrance. The remarkable document may not have included direct support of the arts and humanities, but the founding fathers did cite the protection of copyright in the Constitution. They wrote that Congress had the power to "promote the progress of science and useful arts, by securing for limited times to authors and inventors the exclusive right to their respective writings and discoveries." This was a major advance for creators of all kinds. Regrettably, the abuse of the phrase "for limited times" has robbed the public today of many works that should reside in the public domain, not in the coffers of large entertainment corporations. But copyright protection is one of the single most important pieces of legislation ever granted to artists and scientists.

Thomas Jefferson believed that the three major faculties of the mind were memory, reason, and imagination, and that they were actively applied through the study of history, philosophy, and the fine arts. Architecture was the umbrella under which all the other visual and practically applied arts nestled. His own creative endeavors flourished in the arenas of design, music, and literature. There is no doubt in my mind that if Thomas Jefferson were in Congress today, we would not have to battle for the NEA.

The nineteenth century saw a burgeoning of all the arts and the development of significant schools of American painting and literature. Although there were traveling players and musicians throughout America, most of the performing arts were imports from across the Atlantic. There was a traditional commercial philosophy toward the production of art, and no government support to speak of. The only real exceptions were the legislative commissions to architects, designers, painters, and sculptors for the construction and decoration of capitols and other government buildings. And the U.S. Marine Band, established in 1790, has the distinction of being the oldest continuing music ensemble supported by federal funds. In 1993 the budget for all military bands was about $183 million, more than the budget for the National Endowment for the Arts. I never begrudged the military this amount of money for its bands, as some people did; their music is good, the Arts Endowment doesn't fund bands, and the military bands have been in existence far longer than the Endowment.

In the late years of the 1800s and in the early 1900s huge private fortunes were created on the back of the industrial revolution. Patronage of the arts increased, and a widespread philanthropic movement began in 1917 when individuals and corporations were able to deduct their contributions to educational organizations, which included the arts. When as many fortunes as had been gained were lost in the Depression of the 1930s, President Franklin D. Roosevelt stepped in and created the Works Progress Administration (WPA), putting millions to work—playwrights, painters, and photographers among them. Dorothea Lange photographed indelible portraits of the Depression under the Farm Services Administration; the directors John Houseman, Orson Welles, and Elia Kazan worked for the Federal Theater Project. The playwrights Arthur Miller and Clifford Odets also began their careers with government funds. And the painters Edward Hopper, Jackson Pollock, and Jacob Lawrence were just three of thousands who decorated government buildings with murals or received federal funding in other ways. Forty thousand artists were put to work at this time.

This first substantial effort at government arts support did not last, however. Roosevelt's enemies in Congress saw the arts as a political tool for the New Deal. By the time the country had committed to World War II most of the artists were either on their own again or part of the war effort.

With the postwar boom in the economy private patronage of the arts expanded again during the 1950s. Concurrently, with the push for higher education for all citizens, the arts were seen as an important element of enlightenment and of daily school curricula. Liberals in Congress were promoting the idea that good government encompassed responsibility for our growing arts institutions. John F. Kennedy and his wife Jacqueline personified the glamour and refinement of the "high arts" and hoped for a time when all people would participate in and appreciate this aspect of a civil life. Just a few short weeks before his assassination in November 1963 the young president said: "I look forward to an America which will steadily raise the standards of artistic accomplishment and which will steadily enlarge cultural opportunities for all our citizens."

By 1965 the arts had their chief governmental enthusiast in President

Lyndon Johnson. As part of his vision of the Great Society arts education was bolstered by Title 3 programs, which dispensed about $350 million to schools for the study of the arts between 1965 and 1970. Regrettably, Congress eliminated this funding after those five years, and we have been trying to catch up ever since.

In 1965 Senator Claiborne Pell and Representative Frank Thompson, Democrat from New Jersey, with the help of Representative John Brademas of Indiana and Senator Jacob Javits of New York, steered bills through their respective committees, and then into law, establishing the National Foundation on the Arts and Humanities. Dissenters on the floors of the House and the Senate were of two minds: first, that government had no business funding art at all, and second, that government funding would ultimately lead to restrictions on the content of the artwork. Both points of view remain salient today.

Still, President Johnson urged passage of the bill, saying: "This Congress will consider many programs which will leave an enduring mark on American life. But it may well be that passage of this legislation, modest as it is, will help secure for this Congress a sure and honored place in the story of the advance of our civilization."

A month later the first National Council on the Arts, the artists appointed to vote on the first grants, met at the White House with Roger Stevens as chairman. President Johnson swore them in, making this fine statement:

> Our civilization will largely survive in the works of our creation. There is a quality in art which speaks across the gulf, dividing man from man and nation from nation, and century from century. That quality confirms the faith that our common hopes may be more enduring than our conflicting hostilities. Even now men of affairs are struggling to catch up with the insights of great art. The stakes may well be the survival of civilization.

No president, before or since, has spoken so loftily about art. Even to contemplate that the survival of civilization depends on our relationship to art is a profound thought, and one that is given no credence today in the world of politics. We can only speculate on how much more President Johnson might have given us if the war in Vietnam had not brought him down. He continued to speak in the same vein with the final inauguration of the twin agencies, the National Endowments for the Arts and for the Humanities, six months later: "It is in our works of art that we reveal ourselves, and to others, the inner vision which guides us as a nation. And where there is no vision, the people perish." The idea that human beings cannot live without vision is impossible to prove, but a guiding force for artists is surely the idea that imagination is liberating. It is our imagination that envisions change, that sees new possibilities for society. Both art and science rely on imagination and creativity to build new constructs. Perhaps that is why the founding fathers linked science and art together in the constitutional copyright clause.

The enthusiasm for the Endowment was at an all-time high in the mid-1960s. The awards reflected a desire to shore up institutions while nurturing individual artists. The first grant of $100,000 was given to the foundering American Ballet Theater and probably saved it from extinction. Ten grants were made to choreographers, amounting to $100,000, and fifty grants went to composers, also $100,000 in total. The nod was given to education with grants to teachers for art sabbaticals and to art school graduates to broaden their experience. There was an ambitious plan to aid artists in their housing, and $500,000 was granted to create new laboratory theater companies. The total appropriation for fiscal year 1966 was $2.5 million.

I remember the excitement at Arena Stage when combined grants from the NEA, the Ford Foundation, and the Rockefeller Foundation allowed our company of thirty actors to have ongoing classes in movement and speech, just as the great European companies had. In addition, we were performing plays in repertory, as did the National Theater in London, the Berliner Ensemble, and the Moscow Art Theater. True repertory, where plays are rotated nightly or every few days, was rare in the United States. It was a superior schedule for actors, giving us the opportunity to play drama one night and comedy the next, and not wearing any one actor down with a particularly heavy role eight times a week. But the burden was borne in the costs needed to maintain a technical crew to strike and remount the different sets for each performance and then to run the shows as well. The repertory experiment never lasted long in American theaters because of the price. But in 1966, at Arena Stage, we were giddy with enthusiasm, and we began to believe that, given time, we too might be a world-class theater.

In 1967 the NEA's budget shot up to almost $8 million. But then, in 1968, a scant two and a half years after the Endowment was founded, it was already in some trouble. The Vietnam War had split the country asunder, and many artists, myself included, let Johnson and the hawks in Congress know how wrong we thought they were. This did not endear artists to the president, or to the legislators; some writers who were scathing in their criticism were particularly out of favor. I believe the president was hurt by those he felt should have rewarded him for creating the NEA. He did not go to bat for the agency in its congressional reauthorization, as he had done at its inauguration.

The NEA needed to be reauthorized for another three years and was also asking for a significant budget increase. Arts organizations nationwide had been stimulated by the government grants, and there wasn't enough money to award the thousands of applicants petitioning the Endowment. But Congress did an about-face. They groused about some of the grants, as they groused generally about the "flower children" and "hippies" of the late 1960s, and then they barely reauthorized the agency at all, putting it on trial by giving it just one year. As if warning the arts world not to get too out of line, they also eliminated grants to individual artists. Roger Stevens's success in getting a budget increase of $600,000 was due only to his own personal persuasiveness.

To look at the final vote tally is to look down the pipeline of history. The majority of Republicans and southern Democrats voted against reauthorization, while the northern Democrats voted for the bill. The handwriting was on the wall almost from the NEA's beginnings, but no one was reading it very seriously or choosing to analyze what it might be saying. We were all so caught up in the Vietnam War that the culture wars barely registered at the time. We should have understood more of the dynamic between militarism and art. Throughout history artists have been a dissenting force and frequently on the unpopular side of an issue or a war—or at the very least, calling attention to it. Governments have been embarrassed by artists, feared them, and sought to silence them again and again. Hitler first incarcerated artists and homosexuals early in the 1930s, before he targeted the Jews. China still imprisons artists today. The Czech writer Václev Havel remains the world's most famous artist to have survived prison and become his government's leader. The closest the United States ever came to jailing its own artists in the same way was during the House Un-American Activities Committee (HUAC) hearings of the late 1940s and early 1950s when Senator Joseph McCarthy of Wisconsin spearheaded investigations that resulted in the "blacklisting" of many in the film and theater communities for alleged or actual association with the Communist Party. It's debatable whether our democracy could ever be guilty of the abuses perpetrated in fascist or totalitarian countries, but there will always be tension between those in power and those who dissent, and artists are always on the front lines of that dynamic.

When Lyndon Johnson told the world he was not running for president again in 1968, we were stunned. For peaceniks the announcement was cause for jubilation. In retrospect we should have realized that wars do not end so easily. Richard Nixon believed the war was winnable for another agonizing few years, the death toll of our soldiers mounting with each passing week. But Nixon as president was unpredictable. He did ultimately end U.S. involvement in Vietnam in 1972. Shortly thereafter he paid a visit to our nemesis, Red China, paving the way for today's trade agreements. And "Tricky Dick" from Whittier, California, looked the eastern establishment he so detested full in the face and increased the Arts Endowment budget a thousandfold. Leonard Garment, a lawyer and musician, who advised Nixon during his presidency, told me that the budget increase was made to appease the liberals and anti-war activists, and not because the president adored the arts. In any case, the move was a welcome one for the NEA.

Nancy Hanks was Richard Nixon's choice to head the Endowment in 1969. She had distinguished herself working for the Rockefellers, producing an important document, "The Performing Arts: Problems and Prospects." Nancy Hanks was something of a genius with the agency. She was tenacious and scrappy, by all accounts, and had a winning southern charm to boot. By the time she finished her second term, retiring in October 1977, the NEA's budget stood at almost $124 million.

The agency that Nancy Hanks created is essentially the agency I inherited. There were programs in music, dance, theater, opera, presenting, museums, visual arts, folk arts, arts education, design, media, literature, and expansion arts (for community-based projects). She convinced Congress to reinstate grants to individual artists, and applications poured in from all over the United States. Panelists who were experts in a given art field came together to winnow down the submissions and forward the worthiest to the National Council on the Arts. The Council was a twenty-six-member body appointed by the president and confirmed by the Senate. They were prominent artists and arts patrons who gathered several times a year to vote on the panels' recommendations for grants. As chairman I then signed off on all the grantees voted by the Council; I could reject those they approved, but I could not give a grant to any applicant the Council had rejected. The system worked, and, although like any system, it was capable of being abused, it was still sound in principle.

My first month at the NEA was a nonstop blitz of doing media interviews, going to receptions, getting acquainted with staff, and being welcomed to Washington. My new apartment went unpacked until my goddaughter, Cordelia Persen, was kind enough to come over one afternoon and put everything away just as I might have done it. At least at night I slept well, I was so exhausted.

In a cavernous room on the ground floor of the Old Post Office Building I shook hands with the 275 people whose boss I now was. As a group I told them that I was here because the NEA had made my career possible, that I wanted to turn around the negative image of the agency and let the world know of all the positive things they had been doing for the country. Most important, I told them, was that, with Bill Clinton as president, we had an administration that was totally supportive of the agency.

My predecessor, John Frohnmayer, had been handpicked by President Bush and then, when the going got tough, was summarily dismissed by that same president. Of course I could not be assured that this was not going to happen to me, but the flush of events surrounding the National Medal of Arts led me to believe that my president was going to stick with us. In any case it was something the staff needed to

hear. They had been tossed about in the past few years by the controversies, by Frohnmayer's exit, and by the subsequent hard line taken by
Acting Director Anne-Imelda Radice. Although their friend and fellow
staffer Ana Steele had been most recently in charge, they all knew that
the next chairman was the key to their futures. I did not intend to make
things any worse. I also told them I would be a hands-on chairman and
that my door was always open.

I began preparations to tour all fifty states almost immediately. It was
hard for me to believe that ordinary citizens opposed the NEA, as many
critics in Congress suggested. Who would oppose a theater or museum
or arts festival in their own backyard? Most people polled about arts
education are strongly in favor of it for their children. I suspected that
vocal religious right groups had co-opted the entire argument about
government funding for the arts, based on a few grants out of thousands that they made sure were well publicized. But I needed to hear
from people in their own towns on the subject. I also wanted to see for
myself what the NEA was funding in America and inform the public
and their legislators of the grants in their districts. My scheduler, Noel,
set to work planning an ambitious itinerary that would put me on the
road a few days each week but have me in the office a few days as well,
as Kitty Hart had suggested.

I also began organizing the first federal conference on the arts. Surprisingly, there had never been such a conference. There were many
issues to discuss: the value of the arts to society, new ways of financing
the arts, the new technologies, and arts education, to name a few. The
artists of the country were disgruntled, and rightly so. They were being
treated as if they were all arrogant SOBs out to create work that would
agitate most Americans and insult their values. Conceptual artists were
being ridiculed for their minimalist work; gay artists were being excori-
ated for having a political agenda; the commercial art market had collapsed; and documentary filmmakers had few avenues of distribution.
These were just a few of the problems. Arts administrators were constantly seeking new sources of funding just to keep pace with rising
costs. As government funds declined, their jobs became extremely difficult. Artistic directors were spending as much as 50 percent of their
time on fund-raising rather than on the work at hand. In addition it

was hard to nurture the audiences of the future when our nation's schools had cut the budgets for arts education. We needed a forum to discuss these things, and quickly, before the relationship between artists and the public soured even more and while the media were still interested in what I was doing with the agency.

Because I was the new kid on the block, the media were eagerly reporting my exploits. In that first month I was the subject of interviews in the *Washington Post,* the *Los Angeles Times,* the *New York Times,* the *Washington Times, USA Today,* the Associated Press, Reuters News Service, Gannett, Knight-Ridder, *Newsday, Arts News,* and *GQ,* which photographed me in a flattering but unchairmanlike pose. I was also the subject of a number of editorials, not all of them positive. If Frank Rich had been my nemesis when he was writing theater criticism for the *New York Times,* he seemed to be continuing in that vein now that he was assigned a weekly column in the editorial section. He wrote that my performance before the Senate committee was

> in a characteristically safe style that suggested Helen Hayes playing a Congressional wife of the 1950s. . . . Politicians want to be all things to all people. Real artists don't. Jane Alexander, who even won the endorsement of Charlton Heston during the confirmation process, has already proved herself a master politician. If her leadership of the endowment is to be more than ceremonial, she is going to have to play the role of independent artist with more conviction than she ever has before.

Frank was right that politicians seek the middle of the road while artists take the fast lane, but I felt that I needed to know the political territory better before I could move with any decisiveness. I was hardly a "master politician"—it takes years to learn the game, and there are only a handful of men, no women yet, who qualify. Ted Kennedy is the undisputed champion. Frank and I would find ourselves quite enmeshed in the politics of the NEA during my chairmanship. If I had been hurt or angered in years past by his theatrical criticism, I came to truly respect his opinion on the editorial page. Times change.

Andrew Heiskell also wrote an op-ed piece for the *New York Times* suggesting what I should do at the helm of the agency. He outlined three guiding principles:

- There should be clear standards of artistic merit.
- The First Amendment is the first principle.
- Art can heal instead of dividing.

These precepts made a lot of sense to me, and I incorporated them into my daily thinking.

It was on an early morning C-Span talk show that I encountered my first negative call-ins. In fact nine out of the ten callers had negative comments about the NEA. "Why don't artists get a job?" was one. Shades of my mother when I was in my early twenties trying to make it as an actress! My mother had grown up in South Boston never knowing any artists. She couldn't understand that demonstrating Polaroid cameras in Macy's and waitressing were just jobs to pay the rent and put food in my mouth while I sought a career in the theater. She didn't know that the business of learning the craft—the voice lessons, the scene study, the singing lessons—were a commitment to a lifelong process; that the business of artists was one of reflection, observation, constant learning; and that sometimes doing "nothing" was the most important thing I could be doing. "Why don't you get a job?" was my mother's silent reproach when I failed yet another audition.

I knew how to answer these questions on C-Span, but I was irritated when they put Congressman Spencer Bachus from Alabama on after me. He called for the agency to be abolished and then, almost in the same breath, lamented the loss of the Alabama Symphony due to lack of funds. If this was the level of thinking at least I wanted to be able to countermand it, but C-Span didn't give me a chance. I vowed that wouldn't happen again.

A few days later I was on CNBC's *Equal Time* with Republican Mary Matalin, who was married to the outspoken Democrat James Carville, one of the president's major defenders. Mary's Democratic foil on the show was Jane Wallace. Their style was bouncy and breezy compared to the seriousness of the male interviewers I'd encountered. I let my hair down. I confided to ten million viewers that I was amazed at how much information one had to process in Washington and then be prepared to talk about it or to make a decision. How could anyone know anything, really? I mused. Mary's response rang true: Washington is a very "fast" town; here "everyone is flying by the seat of their pants."

On television, in addition to the morning news programs, the indefatigable Charlie Rose interviewed me for his late-night PBS show. Charlie had made the trip that day from New York to the Arlington, Virginia, offices of WETA in order to have several of us in D.C. on camera. He was very late getting to the studio, and so I found myself in the captive company of Ben Bradlee, executive editor of the *Washington Post* from 1968 to 1991, and Senators John Kerry and Phil Gramm.

I had met Ben in the mid–1970s at the premiere of *All the President's Men*. Jason Robards had done a wonderful turn as Bradlee in the movie, and I had played the "slush fund" bookkeeper who blew the whistle on John Mitchell, Nixon's attorney general from 1968 to 1972 before he was convicted of perjury and obstruction of justice. Dustin Hoffman and Robert Redford played Bernstein and Woodward, the tireless reporters for the *Washington Post* who cracked open Watergate.

It was a great film to be a part of, coming as it did on the heels of Nixon's 1974 resignation. Those of us of a liberal persuasion could feel self-righteous about our beliefs at last. Yes, we *were* right about the Vietnam War, and yes, Nixon *was* a dirty dog. But the film was more than just a historical triumph; filmically it was outstanding because the brilliant Alan Pakula directed it. Jason Robards went on to win the Academy Award for his portrayal of Bradlee, and even I was nominated in the supporting category for my four minutes on screen.

Ben and I chatted about these things while Kerry paced about waiting for Charlie Rose. Then Phil Gramm pulled me aside and told me he would back me at the NEA; he had heard I was a good person and hoped I understood the mistakes that had been made at the Endowment. I demurred, knowing little at the time of Phil Gramm other than that he was from Texas. He hadn't yet announced his intention to run for president. Finally Charlie burst apologetically through the door and in his rush seemed not to know what he and the men were to speak about. Haiti and Somalia, someone reminded him. Charlie was definitely airborne—"flying by the seat of his pants."

I thought of all the improvisational theater I had done early on in my career. Chicago had produced a brilliant troupe called Second City. Its leader, Paul Sills, was the son of an outstanding teacher of improvisation named Viola Spolin. Some of the group came to New York in the early 1960s, including Alan Arkin and Barbara Harris. Mike Nichols and Elaine May had also begun their careers improvising. I became part of a quartet of actors—Olympia Dukakis, Alan Alda, Dana Elcar, and me—that Paul Sills engaged to explore more improvisational techniques in a workshop. At twenty-two I was the youngest of the group, but probably the most grateful for the experience.

The main tenet of improvisation is to accept what the other fellow gives you. In other words, if an actor appears onstage, looks at you funny, and says, "What's wrong with you?" you accept that something might be wrong with you even if you are trying to hide it. Improvisational technique is wonderful grounding for a future in almost any kind of theater or film, and also for life. It keeps you on your toes and alert to the behavior of those around you. You may not like what the other actor is doing to you, and you may feel unprepared to interact, but you *have* to respond. As in Washington, you are "flying by the seat of your pants."

I wondered whether those who interviewed me at this time knew I was winging it. How could I possibly know the answers to all the questions I was asked? My life had been spent in the world of entertainment, and here I was suddenly in an entirely new environment with entirely different rules of the game. I had crammed a lot of information into my head the past few months, and I had followed my gut instinct, as Al Simpson suggested I do, but it was not the same thing as knowing the lay of the land because you live there. The learning curve was steep. Improvisation may have been great for the theater, but I doubted whether it was any good for carrying out the responsibilities of government. Yet so many in Washington seemed to be doing it. It was virtually impossible for a newly elected member of Congress to know very much, or even to learn very much in a two-year term. I was not alone.

My first order of business was to get to know the workings of the agency as well as I could. I had read Michael Straight's biography of Nancy Hanks and Livingston Biddle's book about the NEA. Biddle was the third chairman of the Endowment, appointed by Jimmy Carter in 1977. He had published a few novels and had been the pen behind much of the visionary legislation creating the Endowment, helping Senator Pell shepherd it through Congress in 1965. His book was workmanlike and very helpful as a history of the agency.

Frank Hodsoll, the fourth chairman, had not written a book, but he did take me to lunch. His observations were useful, and he chuckled when he pointed out that much of the offending art had been granted awards under his Republican chairmanship in the 1980s. Frank and I were old friends going back to college days, when a bunch of Yalies would come to Bronxville and date us Sarah Lawrence gals. We had belonged to the same group in the early 1960s but had gone our different ways politically as the decade ended. The problems about controversial art that threatened the agency when I arrived had not been of great concern during Hodsoll's tenure. The Mapplethorpe and Serrano controversies erupted a scant few weeks after Hodsoll's departure. Although he may have been responsible for signing off on the grants that the American Family Association decided to make a cause célèbre in the late 1980s, Frank had also helped keep the Reagan administration and its budget director, David Stockman, from gutting the agency altogether. Frank later became a high-level official in the Office of Management and Budget under President George Bush. He was good at finances, and he slowly pulled the NEA back up over the course of his seven-and-a-half-year chairmanship, until the NEA's budget for fiscal year 1990 was the highest it had ever been at $171 million.

I called up Anne-Imelda Radice, who had been acting chairman of the Endowment after Frohnmayer left. She was brought in by conservatives in the Bush administration to keep a tight rein on the kind of art being funded. Jesse Helms had asked that I see her, and so we sat down to lunch together one day. She was frank and not at all hostile. In fact, with her connections to conservative leaders in our society, she became very valuable to me as a "mole." She would call occasionally to give me a "heads-up" on action by Republican legislators or the religious right against the Endowment. I was grateful for her help.

John Frohnmayer's book *Leaving Town Alive: Confessions of an Art Warrior* was the most helpful of all considering the political climate that blanketed the agency. I knew from the outset that I did not want to fall into the trap John had fallen into, particularly that of rendering judgment on a piece of art and then broadcasting that judgment through letters or public means. Whatever a chairman said was bound to be used by the right or the left for their own purposes in such a volatile climate. Frohnmayer's pronouncements had unintentionally inflamed the situation and ultimately led to the NEA Four's lawsuit against the agency. Because the chairman is the final arbiter in the process of approving grants, and the expectation is that he or she will speak about the art publicly, it was maddening to some people when I did not voice an opinion. But to me it was like trying to respond yes or no to the question "Do you still beat your wife?" You're damned either way. I withheld my personal opinions about works of art. Given the tenderness of the current state of affairs, it seemed best to remain neutral. If the art was deemed excellent by a panel of peers and then passed on by the National Council on the Arts, it was asking for trouble to then offer up my opinion, whatever it was. My role, I determined, was to make sure that the process was fair and conducted without a political agenda. In any case the agency worked on a system of peer review, not dictator fiat.

The heart of the agency is the panel system. In 1993 more than one thousand citizens came to the Endowment to sit on panels in the various arts fields. They reviewed almost 17,000 applications, forwarding about 4,000 to the council for recommendation. The average panel was made up of twelve to fifteen people who met for two to five days. It is an honor to be asked to panel and few refuse, although the compensation is low and the time taken away from one's own work is considerable.

My first visit was to a literature panel chaired by the writer and publisher George Plimpton. Sitting around a large rectangle of tables were a dozen other writers and one layperson who knew literature well but did not make her living by it. The process is confidential, and its demands can be daunting. Each panelist had read all or part of approximately 350 manuscripts over a period of months before arriving for the weeklong adjudication at the Endowment. It was an enlightening and ultimately moving experience to witness the technical discussions of a writer's work by his or her peers. They knew the value of an NEA grant, many having had one of their own at some time, and they weighed the pros and cons of the works before them with utmost gravity. After all, out of those 350 submissions only a dozen or so would be recommended to the National Council for a grant. Dropping in on these advisory panels became my favorite activity when I had a few free minutes.

In addition to visiting panels in all the arts fields I also held meetings with each program director (PD). Besides the chairman, the men and women who ran the programs were the most important people at the Endowment. They knew their fields backward and forward and had the closest link with the artists and arts organizations that applied for grants. They would spend hours on the phone with applicants, shepherding them through the complicated procedure and commiserating with them when they failed to receive the coveted grant. Many of the directors were artists themselves, or had been. I had enormous admiration for the program directors but was somewhat alarmed to discover that they ruled their individual areas like fiefdoms, with very little understanding of what was going on in other fields. Traditionally each program received a yearly appropriation of its own, and so there was quite naturally a lot of internal lobbying for more funds and in some cases external lobbying of congressional staff members and even congressmen who had a pet love like music or dance. Although this mode of operation had been going on since the Endowment's beginnings, I did not view it as healthy, especially at a time when we were so vulnerable to attack. Divided we fall.

I was also concerned about the standards of artistic merit, which seemed to vary in the different fields depending on how the criteria of excellence and artistic merit were interpreted. Some PDs were loose about the standard of excellence, watching the panelists pass on applications that were not always the best. Perhaps they felt that an applicant deserved a grant, having applied and failed many years in a row, or perhaps an applicant had always received a grant and it was de rigueur for them to continue to be funded despite a decline in quality. The PDs did not overtly control who was recommended and who was not, but their leadership exerted a subtle influence nevertheless. They knew their fields better than anyone, having visited sites and pored over applications. They also put the panels together and often relied on panelists they knew rather than taking a chance on a newcomer. Although charges of cronyism had been leveled at the Endowment in the past, I sought to expand the pool of panelists so we could escape accusation in the future. As chairman I relied heavily on the PDs to choose first-rate panelists, to maintain the highest standards, and to make sure the entire process was followed correctly and fairly. If they failed the agency and me everything would topple. As my brother, who is a captain with Trans World Airlines, says: "All error is human error." Fortunately the margin of error in most of the NEA programs was small, and I could point with pride to the system of adjudication.

The next step in the tier of responsibility was the National Council on the Arts, a highly prestigious body of people. In the first years of the agency some of the most famous artists of our time served: Marian Anderson, Leonard Bernstein, Agnes De Mille, Richard Diebenkorn, Ralph Ellison, Charlton Heston, Harper Lee, Gregory Peck, Sidney Poitier, Richard Rodgers, David Smith, Oliver Smith, John Steinbeck, Isaac Stern, and George Stevens Sr., among others.

The Council members are nominated by the president and confirmed by the Senate, as is the chairman, the only difference being that they are in for a six-year term and the chairman for four. Some of the Council members in 1993 had in fact been serving as long as eight years while they awaited the nomination and confirmation of their replacements. There were prominent people on the Council for my first meeting. The painter William Bailey, the poet Donald Hall, the architect Hugh Hardy, the dancer and choreographer Arthur Mitchell, and the opera singer Roberta Peters were at the top of their fields. Others making up the complement of twenty-six members were well-known arts patrons, advocates, or administrators from different areas of the United States, many of them appointed by the Bush administration. Altogether they were a fine and thoughtful group of people.

The Council came together four times a year to vote on the slate of applications recommended by the panels. In November 1993 we were looking at about thirty-five hundred applications in the fields of Presenting and Commissioning, Literature, Design and International programs. Panelists had winnowed out the applications considerably, but

Council members still received an enormous package in the mail a few weeks prior to coming to Washington. The description of applicants sent forward for recommendation and also for rejection was the size of two huge phone books. The Council did not have the luxury of two to five days of deliberation, as did the panelists, but the Council usually had a good idea, having read the panelists' comments, of which grants should be awarded.

The Council came to town on a Thursday to attend review sessions given by the staff on the applications. That night we all had dinner together at a restaurant, and I threw out a question for discussion. If the criterion for awarding grants was "artistic merit and excellence," was that criterion ever mitigated by political content? For example, would the NEA award a grant to a painter whose subject matter was a Nazi beating a Jew? A lively discussion followed. In this age of political correctness libraries and schools are removing books like *Uncle Tom's Cabin* and *Huck Finn* from their shelves as offensive to African Americans. Where do we draw the line? When does art cease to be art and become propaganda, or perversity? The consensus that evening seemed to be that the criterion of "excellence" by a jury of one's peers is the fairest way to adjudicate art, and that the NEA panels were doing a pretty good job in their advisory capacity. The panelists, it was noted, also represented diverse beliefs, coming as they did from different racial and ethnic backgrounds and from different parts of the United States. Still, I was left with an unanswered question. What were the limits of acceptability?

My opening remarks the next morning at the public meeting of the Council were focused on arts as a community issue and on arts in education. These were surely soft-core areas that everyone could get behind, or so I thought. It turned out later that, with dwindling resources, many arts organizations didn't want to see the pie carved up into any more pieces. Individual artist grants were also at a premium, and there were many worthy applicants for every awardee. In the literature program alone only 3 percent of the individual fellowship applicants were funded.

My nascent plan was to increase the focus on community arts and arts education, in the belief that Congress would then be inclined to give us more funding overall. With the decline of arts education in our nation's schools since the 1970s we were also in danger of losing our future audiences. I looked past the assembled Council to the back of the huge room where the staff and the public sat. Perhaps two hundred people had gathered to hear what I had to say at this first meeting. There were also journalists, most notably conservatives, scribbling away and hoping for a slipup on my part that would fuel the next round of salacious controversy. I had been before audiences so often in my life that the size of this one did not faze me, but the thought crossed my mind suddenly that this was real life, not make-believe. My stress on arts education, as positive and innocuous as it seemed, shifted the focus and could possibly rob other programs of the limited funds available. I could read anxiety on the PDs' faces from a distance of a hundred feet, and I took note.

The Council proceeded to vote on the applications recommended by the panels. In the "Presenting and Commissioning" program, which awarded grants to theaters and performance spaces, there was some discussion of a Santa Monica, California, organization called Highways Inc.

Highways was the collective of the performance artist Tim Miller, one of the NEA Four who had brought suit against the Endowment along with John Fleck, Holly Hughes, and Karen Finley. In 1990 they had accused John Frohnmayer of rejecting their grants on the basis of content after they had been recommended by the panel. The NEA Four had recently come to an out-of-court settlement with the NEA in which they had been awarded $252,000. Their legal case had then expanded to include a challenge to the constitutionality of the "general standards of decency" language in the agency's 1990 reauthorization, and that second suit was now under appeal in the federal courts.

The mere mention of Miller's name in some right-wing circles was enough to stir things up again. Nevertheless, Miller, whose solo theater piece, called *My Queer Body,* had been performed to great acclaim in a number of venues nationwide, had been awarded yet another NEA grant since the rejection by Frohnmayer. He was highly ranked by the panel, and I was prepared to take the heat should the Council vote positively for his organization, Highways. The Council did vote in favor of the Highways application, with barely any discussion, noting the high accord the Presenting and Commissioning panel had given the Santa Monica group. The right-wing reporters smirked with satisfaction. They had their story, and soon the conservative staffers on the Hill would be telling their bosses that it was business as usual down at the NEA under Jane Alexander.

Coincidentally that same night I decided to go and see Karen Finley perform. She had been ridiculed for so long by Jesse Helms and the media as the woman who smeared chocolate all over her body that, as a fellow female performer, I wanted to see her work. Her limited engagement at George Washington University attracted a crowd of mostly young people. Her work was raw, not in the sense of being exploitative but in being unformed. She needed the aid of a good director, but she definitely had something to say, and her talents as a visual artist were considerable.

Later I went backstage to say hello. I shook her hand and said I admired her performance. She seemed nonplussed and quickly excused herself to feed her new baby. After four years of doing battle with the NEA her suspicion was understandable, but her husband thanked me and said, "It means a lot." I was meeting her on her turf, and it was ground that I understood well. As actors we are so vulnerable; we open ourselves up to the audience, and it always hurts when they reject us. The battering that Karen, a serious artist, had taken the past few years was more than most artists could have sustained. It had surely taken its toll on her.

That first meeting of the National Council on the Arts under my aegis had gone well. I didn't have a moment's hesitation about approving the grant to Miller: the process had been carefully followed, and his work had been highly ranked. In addition I had the majority of the prestigious Council members behind me should we encounter turbulence ahead. I turned my thoughts to the business of running the agency, preparing for my road trips, and getting to know the strata of Washington's political and social life.

CHAPTER SIX

The Scene

Washington is divided into those who stay and those who come and go. The diehards, the ones who make their home there for years or decades —or even centuries in the case of some families—reign supreme. But since the city's reputation is built on politics, the current federally elected interlopers and their attendant media blitz are sources of much curiosity and speculation. There is always a subtle race to be on the inside with these transients, despite the tension between the two camps.

Many of the old homes in the District are gracious and architecturally pleasing. If you live in Georgetown or neighboring Cleveland Park you can almost forget that Washington was contrived as our nation's capital on the shifting soil of a swamp. You can *almost* forget. The banks of the muddy Potomac swell with the rains and leave mosquito-infested pools in their wake. The summers are insufferable and seem to arrive earlier each year, almost obliterating the name of spring except for a crowning glory of cherry blossoms one week in April.

The nature of the city and its geographical location are obscured by the number of Yankees who occupy the territory. But it is indeed a southern city. It hasn't the charm of Savannah or St. Petersburg or Chattanooga, but it is southern at its core. It moves with the pace of the old South, and many of its venerable transplants migrated from the South—the holly and magnolia trees as well as the resident human population.

The avenues that L'Enfant laid out like the spokes of a wheel are lined with oversized edifices of stone, belying human frailty. Still, a sense of history stirs beneath the swell of daily life. Just as visitors to

Athens step more softly at the base of the Acropolis, one can take pride in this city of monuments. There is no other American place where citizens feel ownership so strongly. We can all recite the story of the Revolution, and the symbolism is ours to embrace, whether our forebears were European, African, Hispanic, or Native American. This city is also ours; it was created out of an idea of freedom for all people, and collectively we built these huge tributes of marble and stone. We paid for them with our hard-earned money, and through them we pay homage to those who went before us. Washington is like a gigantic mausoleum in which we honor the dead and their accomplishments in museums, in libraries, in monuments, and in tombs.

But the city is a living entity too, and the contrasts are startling. A veneer of sobriety masks the raucous business of state taking place in the Capitol Building, where the present rages on with relentless disregard for the lessons of history. What congressman ever has time to cross the street and indulge an afternoon in the archives of the Library of Congress or browse among the treasures of the Smithsonian? The Capitol Building itself is replete with historical paintings and sculptures, but only a few people, like Senator Robert Byrd, the self-taught senatorial archivist, seem able to expound on their nuances.

If the city appears to be in control, one has only to turn a corner and walk a few blocks to the north or the south or the east to hit chaos. Poverty lives cheek by jowl with the smug comfort of our nation's leaders. *Sic semper tyrannis.* The graffiti-less walls of granite give way to the profane scrawls and slogans of a restless citizenry. Congress will not let the District grow up to be the independent city it needs to be; it holds the purse strings and selectively cleanses the face that is shown to the world. I can think of no other city where the hypocrisy is so apparent.

Across from the White House, Lafayette Park shelters the homeless, the layabouts, and the mentally deranged. Although it is no Hyde Park in London, it is also a venue for genuine political protesters who nestle with the others on the ground, and for that we must be grateful. Democracy is tolerant. Many a time in the 1960s and 1970s and 1980s, and even the 1990s, the parks of Washington were meeting grounds for dissenters, for marches, for information on alternative ways of thinking and being. We gathered for civil rights, for poor people, for the earth, for the ERA, for El Salvador, for an end to the Vietnam War, for an end to nuclear weapons, and for an end to AIDS. Some things changed; most didn't.

I have had three distinct lives in Washington: in the 1960s as a young actress at Arena Stage; in the 1970s as a star at the Kennedy Center; and in the 1990s as chairman of the NEA.

In the 1960s my husband Bob Alexander and I made our home in the southwest quadrant of the city, where the poor had been displaced, the buildings had been leveled, and the architect Harry Weese had erected a unique, black and glass structure called Arena Stage. It rose alone in a field of rubble that extended to the next residential structure on G Street, an apartment building called Capitol Park, where we lived. The displaced souls, who were crowded into old housing just east of us, crossed the border frequently, terrorizing those of us who walked the fields at night after the curtain. Their anger was explosive sometimes. There were riots and curfews, and the people set their neighborhoods on fire, the acrid smoke curling over our tidy new homes and apartments. We didn't own a car, and our social life consisted of poker games until dawn, kids' birthday parties, and opening nights. I combed the museums doing research for my roles and took my son kite-flying at the Washington Monument. I was invited once to the Johnson White House because Lady Bird attended our matinees. I was vaguely aware that there was more going on in this powerful city than this corner of cultural life, but my reaction to the political leaders was knee-jerk: they supported a stupid war, they were racist, and they did nothing for the poor, despite proclamations of "the Great Society."

In the 1970s I entered Washington as a known actress of stage and screen. I had won a Tony Award for *The Great White Hope* and been nominated for the Oscar, and I had been celebrated for my performance on television as Eleanor Roosevelt. Ed and I married in 1975. He directed me in most of our Kennedy Center productions, and we stayed at the posh Watergate Hotel. The idealism of the 1960s had given way to the self-promotion of the 1970s. The flower children saw their dreams of communes and peace broken by internecine tension and bad drug trips. Black leaders were dead, in Africa, or incarcerated by the powers that feared them. Feminists were confused about their image: in the name of freedom we were bouncing around bra-less and donning miniskirts that barely covered our bums, to the utter delight and titillation of the male sex. For all the strides that were made in the workplace, the Equal Rights Amendment remained moribund.

As a leading lady of the latest play I was invited to some of the A-list society parties given by the Cafritz family or Evangeline Bruce, who I thought was the most beautiful woman I had ever seen. But it was the events hosted by our gregarious secretary of State, Henry Kissinger, that I remember. He liked performers and invited me a number of times to luncheons and dinners at the State Department. One luncheon was given in honor of Princess Anne. The protocol to observe with royalty, as with our own president, is to not leave the event until after they do. Kissinger, as usual, had invited interesting guests, and the princess and her husband, Mark Phillips, lingered over coffee, chatting with everyone. I was in rehearsal for Saroyan's *The Time of Your Life,* and I was late. Three o'clock came and went, and I sweated, keeping the large company and the leading man, Henry Fonda, waiting. Finally I whispered in the ear of one of the secretary's aides that I felt terrible but that I *had* to slip out. He whispered in Kissinger's ear, who whispered in Anne's ear, whereupon the princess loudly exclaimed to her husband and all within hearing: "Let's make tracks, Mark."

Another protocol gaffe, but not mine this time, occurred when Douglas Fairbanks Jr. and I were invited by President Ford to a state dinner and reception for King Hussein of Jordan. We were starring in Noel Coward's delightful play *Present Laughter,* and so we arrived well after everyone else, after our curtain came down. Doug's distinguished record of service in World War II was earned chiefly by a stint as a secret messenger between Churchill and Roosevelt. His tuxedo jacket was weighted with bright badges of honor, colorful ribbons and pins that he was rarely able to wear except on appropriate occasions such as this state dinner. We scurried up the backstairs, turned the corner, and suddenly saw the president and Mrs. Ford and the king and queen striding four abreast alone toward the East Room and us. Doug panicked and pulled us back down the stairwell. "The king is not wearing his medals. He's not wearing one medal!" Doug whispered. Hussein, also a distinguished war veteran, displayed not one record of service on his resplendent, gold-embroidered jacket. Doug was aghast and quickly ripped the medals from his chest, depositing them in a bulging pocket as we proceeded to the reception, muttering all the while, "What has happened to protocol? It's out the window. It doesn't exist anymore!"

Indeed, protocol does seem to have vanished. Today we still stand when the president enters a room, but people come and go at will, speak before spoken to, and do all those other gauche things that are now part of everyday life. Back in the 1960s, and earlier, you didn't decline an invitation to the White House if you were lucky enough to receive one. Today it is commonplace to call the social secretary with a regret. And I even heard one major Clinton supporter who consistently received invitations sigh and say: "Been there, done that. . . . It's kind of boring after a while."

As chairman of the National Endowment for the Arts, one of the hundred or so agencies of the U.S. government, I was deluged with invitations of all sorts. But the big city social scene of the 1990s was quite different from the scene of the decades preceding it, and Washington was no exception. The big black-tie social events outside of the White House were invariably fund-raisers. You didn't just get invited to a party anymore; you were expected to *pay* for the party in the name of some good cause that all invitees espoused. I suppose this started out as a good idea way back when. Certainly we all remember the initials BYO, for Bring Your Own Liquor, from when we were young and penniless, but now the BYO idea had matured and simply taken on another guise: "Let's give another one hundred dollars, or five hundred dollars, or one thousand dollars, to feed poor starving children, or find a cure for cancer, or elect the Democrats." It's a good way to give a party and to give to a cause, but it's gotten out of hand. You don't get something for nothing these days. And if you have nothing to give you sit out the dance.

I was lucky. As chairman of the NEA I was always invited gratis, which was a good thing considering my financial situation. I decided early on that, although I was a registered Democrat, I had no intention of waving the flag for the Democratic Party or for Democratic candidates when the NEA was in such a morass with the Republicans and I needed to mend fences if we were to survive. The White House understood and respected my opinion, and I was grateful that they rarely pressed me on the issue. So for me political fund-raisers were out. Fund-raisers for arts organizations were often out too because of the delicate nature of the NEA grant process, which required that I sign off on applications. But I did bend the rules a number of times. It was hard not to attend an arts event other than an opening that was not in some way connected with fund-raising.

In the beginning of my tenure there were a few purely social events at which no funds were raised and I was introduced to many of the city's movers and shakers. I was able to gauge the temperature of support for the NEA by attending these events. Senator David Boren and his wife, Molly, gave a buffet dinner party one evening shortly before my confirmation. I found myself huddled around a low coffee table with David Gergen, the commentator and presidential adviser, looming on a small stool to my right, the *Washington Post* and *Newsweek* columnist Meg Greenfield a diminutive presence on my left, and Jack Valenti, president of the influential Motion Picture Association of America, across from me on a sofa with three high-powered lawyers. It's hard to escape the company of lawyers in D.C., where there are rumored to be forty-five thousand of them. The government of the United States is litigious.

David Gergen asked, "How do you define art?" In reply I sounded like the most boring theoretician our educational system ever produced: "Art is the expression of one's perception of life made manifest through the intellect, emotion, physicality, and what we call the soul." Gergen replied that, using that definition, the discussion we were having would qualify as art. "Well," I haltingly responded, "I guess I'm speaking from the point of view of an artist. Perhaps I need to define it another way." The hole I was digging for myself was getting deeper. "Any kid dancing down the street then is an artist?" said Gergen, while the others imperceptibly smirked. "Yes," I said, "but there are levels of art. Art is symbolic, deals with metaphor, and is created in context." I was about to fall in. Gergen didn't reply in words, but he didn't have to. His restlessness was apparent—he'd written me off. Meg Greenfield, who later befriended me, said nothing; her head bobbed like one of those Chinese dolls on a point of wood, and her smile was as inscrutable. The lawyers jumped in with their two cents, and then Valenti said with some finality that his definition of art was simple: "Great art endures; that's the test." "What about dance then?" I said, "the most ephemeral of all the arts?" Not all great dancers have a legacy like Nijinsky's, I thought, whose few rare photographs cannot begin to define his art. "Well, that's my definition," Jack Valenti replied, rising with the rest of them as if on cue. "Great art endures." They headed for the dining room, leaving me scrunched on the silly stool, deflated. In the corner a few feet away sat a fine-looking bow-tied man with an amused smile, taking it all in. As the room emptied he rose and whispered softly in my ear, "Welcome to Washington. Let me take you to lunch next week." Tom Lovejoy was a world-famous biologist and counselor to the secretary for biodiversity and the environment at the Smithsonian. He did indeed take me to lunch. He also taught me the ropes and became a good friend.

In Washington you are only as valuable as the people you know who support you and your cause, and so the modus operandi is to keep increasing your list of acquaintances. Ultimately everyone wants something from Congress or the president, so the focus is on gaining their attention and goodwill. And because jobs come and go with each election, you cross another person at your peril. You never know who might be on top in the future and whose help you might need. Coming as I did from the world of entertainment, where people are readily outspoken, it was quite a change to have to become guarded in my talk. But I soon caught on; when no one responded to my puerile attempts at barbed humor about someone or something, I quickly shut up. Although people hold a great many opinions about others in D.C., they rarely voice them, adding to the city's reputation of being dull.

The functions were social, political, honorary, and arts-oriented, or a combination of all four. Whether at an informal dinner for the ambassador from India, a reception in Senator David Pryor's office displaying the work of Arkansas artists, a function of the Hollywood Women's Political Caucus, in town to lobby for their liberal agenda, or a celebratory two-hundredth birthday party for the Capitol Building, a great deal of business was conducted at these functions. And the star attractions were invariably members of Congress or the administration. If you snagged the president, your group was sure to be in the *Post*'s gossip section the next day.

Ed and I had lived in Los Angeles off and on during the 1970s and 1980s. Washington and L.A. have much in common, not the least of which is the importance of power. Power in politics is what is important in D.C., where your title automatically assures you of a power base. Money cannot buy position, although without campaign finance reform it is looking more and more as if it can. In Los Angeles, however, power often is constituted *as* money. If you can command a certain salary, or percentage points of a film's gross, you are greatly respected. Both cities share a consuming passion for a single arena. In Los Angeles it is the world of entertainment in the form of commercial films, television, and pop music; in Washington it is the world of politics. In either city it is virtually impossible to hold a conversation on any other subject for more than ten minutes. I know, I've tried. New York is far more eclectic in its power structure and its conversations, as are Chicago, Atlanta, and Seattle.

In both L.A. and D.C. I was pitching something to the powers that be. When I was a producer, I was pitching stories to the studio and network executives, and when I was the chairman of the Endowment, I was pitching the value of the agency and the arts to members of Congress. I often felt like a serf. When you want something badly enough you grovel. In Hollywood I wanted to sell my stories, and in Washington I wanted to sell the arts. I longed for enthusiasm but was met usually with stony looks and restless demeanors.

It was easier in both places when I made the pitch to a woman. Women in power are livelier, perhaps because they relate to another woman with more ease, or perhaps because they have not occupied a seat of power for so long. I don't know. I am not prejudiced regarding gender and admire stellar qualities in both sexes, but the patriarchal nature of our society makes it easier for men to do business with other men. The roles are traditional and comfortable. And power rewards power, increasing the comfort zone for all concerned. I had no real power base of my own, either as an independent producer of film or as the chairman of the NEA. The power of my position at the Endowment had been eroded through the years of battling before I ever arrived. Congress held the reins, and they knew it. I was going into meetings with a significant handicap, just as I had in Hollywood, where I had no real clout as a movie actress despite four Academy Award nominations. I sensed that many of the meetings were granted as a courtesy only, and that I wouldn't advance the agenda one iota.

Congress does a little better than Hollywood in terms of diversity, but only a little. An average of 10 percent of high elected offices are held by women; the figure for minorities is about the same. Hollywood's record is rotten. Only a handful of top executives are women or people of color. There is such a sea of old white men in the halls of Congress that I took to calling them "OWMs" behind the scenes. There were plenty of younger men too, but they were usually white and on their way to being old without relinquishing any power if they could help it. Of course I was immensely fond of many OWMs in Congress—Ted Kennedy and Dale Bumpers and Mark Hatfield, to name three. Without taking anything away from that affection, I would have given them up for a balance of women—a number of them old white women like me naturally. I like the idea of the acronym "OWW"; at the very least it demands a response, like "ouch." Women need to be heard and seen more in the legislative bodies of our country. We represent more than 50 percent of the population. The Boston Tea Party precipitated a revolution because there was taxation without representation. We need better representation of women and minorities in Congress.

There were several memorable evenings in my first few months on the job. Al Gore and his wife Tipper gave their first dinner party in the newly renovated vice president's home on the old Naval Observatory grounds on Massachusetts Avenue. The home, which comfortably housed the large Gore family and their dog, was filled with fine American paintings and photographs. Tipper is an all-American girl if there ever was one. That night she was lively, pretty, outgoing, and funny, while the vice president bore a sweetly concentrated look as if he needed to hear again what you were saying.

About forty of us were seated at round tables in the dining room. I was next to the vice president at a table that included the secretary of the Treasury, Lloyd Bentsen, and the secretary of Agriculture, Mike

Espy. Ed was seated next to Senator Barbara Mikulski of Maryland, a pint-sized bundle of dynamism who seemed born to the business of politics. Her voice bellowed in case you overlooked her in a room of tall men, where she was often found.

I turned to my left to speak with Lloyd Bentsen, who inquired about our budget and what the NEA did with its money. He was interested in arts education, but when I told him that the average length of an artist's residency in a school was six weeks or less he was shocked. "How can you do anything in that amount of time?" he asked. How indeed? But artists are resourceful. As much as I would like to see full-time programs of residencies in our school systems nationwide, I learned just how resourceful they are when I later took to the road and observed their creativity firsthand.

I chatted with Bruce Babbitt, the secretary of the Interior, who was surprised to hear that the Endowments were under the aegis of his department's appropriations. Why? he wondered. Because the Smithsonian Institution had long been under Interior, and although it is arguable that the NEA, NEH, and the Smithsonian should have been under the wing of an education committee, no one had moved them since their inception, and so there they remained, with mining, fishing rights, and grazing lands. That was okay, I said: the care of the land and the care of the soul are both intimate needs of the citizenry.

Al Gore said that he thought the arts were "early warning signs" for a culture and that there had been so much going on in science that the arts couldn't process it all and had, in effect, stopped producing. This idea was new to me, and I pondered it a great deal afterward. Certainly the twentieth century overridingly belonged to science, from the invention of the airplane, television, the atom bomb, the computer, silicon injections, and Velcro to the discovery of antibiotics, the pill, DNA, and cloning. More scientific discoveries were made in the last forty years of the century than in all prior history. Science had exploded previously held notions in ways that the arts or humanities hadn't even approached. Was this why the art scene of the closing decade seemed so tame, so stalled in its ability to interpret society's advances or its mores? The arts had produced giants in the twentieth century to be sure, including the dancers Isadora Duncan and Martha Graham, the playwrights Eugene O'Neill and Arthur Miller, the painters Edward Hopper and Jackson Pollock, and the composers John Cage and Duke Ellington. As for the greats of the last thirty years, from about the time of the NEA's inception, the jury was still out. In that sense Jack Valenti was right: "Great art endures"—or *some* great art endures, depending on your publicist and your art form. While dance and most theater presentations peak in the present, other art forms—classical music, for instance—can take decades to know success. Composers peak, on average, fifty years *after* their death.

Still, for all their contributions to the twentieth century, the arts paled in comparison to the sciences. The vice president said that he and his good friend Senator Mikulski wanted to have a series of dinners to discuss such topics. They had held similar dinner-discussions about women after the Clarence Thomas hearings and found them to be highly successful. Count me in, I said.

I began to hold my own small forums around the luncheon table in my office at the Endowment. There was no agenda, however, other than to bring together eight or ten people who might otherwise not meet and to continue to introduce myself to the community. These successful little gatherings were catered by the busiest woman in D.C., Susan Gage, and arranged with impeccable taste by our own Rosemary Cribben who assisted the Endowment with special events. Rosemary believed in elegance and had an instinct for bringing together the right elements, including people. There was always a beautiful bouquet of flowers on the crisp tablecloth and a fine wine served by Gage's suave right-hand man, Guy.

The luncheons were not paid for out of government funds but out of special contributions to the Endowment for such purposes. Rosemary in fact had been brought on board to help us attract additional private giving for all kinds of purposes, from the White House dinner for the National Medal of Arts to fund-raising for ART 21, our big federal conference on the arts. There was nothing Rosemary liked more than to get on the telephone and ask a corporate executive for fifty thousand dollars. Some people have a knack, and she certainly did.

The guests for my first roundtable luncheon included Senators Boren and Thad Cochran, a Republican supporter of the NEA from

Mississippi, House Representatives Ralph Regula of Ohio and Maxine Waters of California, Carol Wilner of AT&T, Robert Aubrey Davis, who conducted talk shows on NPR and WETA, and the painter Sam Gilliam. Maxine blew in with an entourage of TV camera personnel surrounding her for a CBS *60 Minutes* interview. They left her shortly, and it became a breezy luncheon of small talk and fun. Although my guests were invited to come at noon, the senators arrived late after a vote, and Ralph and Maxine left early to cast their House votes on another issue. This was disruptive but common behavior with members of Congress, and one soon got used to it.

It was good to catch up with Maxine again. In 1985 she and I had been part of Women for a Meaningful Summit, an ad hoc group of thirty-five that included Bella Abzug, the former congresswoman from New York, Anne Martindell, the former ambassador to New Zealand, and others. We flew together to Geneva to put pressure on Reagan and Gorbachev to advance the cause of nuclear disarmament. It was a three-day summit meeting between the world's two most powerful leaders, and Reagan had ordered a press blackout. Neither of the leaders, and neither of their wives, had responded to our invitation to meet, so we engaged others in discussion—the Polish embassy, the Netherlands, and so on, none of which advanced our cause one iota. The world's media were going crazy because there were no leaks and they didn't know what to report.

Suddenly, to our immense surprise, we received word one morning that Gorbachev would meet with us on his forty-five-minute lunch break away from Reagan. Sure enough, he came striding in, and we thirty-five surrounded him, pushing our peace agenda and staring at the prominent birthmark on his forehead. The born-again Christians back in the United States were convinced that Gorbachev was of the devil because of this birthmark. Revelation 13 mentions "the Beast" and the telling mark on his head; Gorbachev fit the bill for those who believed. But for those of us in the anti-nuke movement, the Soviet leader was a visionary who saw a path for democracy in communism, one that included the dismantling of weapons of destruction. He spoke with us for his entire lunch break, sharing many of our concerns.

The Reverend Jesse Jackson of the Rainbow Coalition had formed an alliance with our group in Geneva, and he took much of the focus away from us. Nevertheless, for the waiting press we were sitting on gold, and the next twelve hours were a flurry of media beamed worldwide for our thirty-five women. Maxine and I were chosen to represent the group for some TV interviews. I found her thoughtful and committed to a strong point of view; she served her Los Angeles district well because she was a fighter for what she believed in. We now found ourselves once again fighting for a cause together—in this case the arts.

My second luncheon included Katharine Graham, scion of the *Washington Post,* Senators Kassebaum and Metzenbaum, the art collectors Jane and Bob Meyerhoff, Congresswoman Marjorie Margolies-Mezvinsky of Pennsylvania, and the jazz aficionado Thelonius Monk Jr., son of the late great jazz pianist and composer. Thelonius Jr. had done wonderful things with the estate of his father, bringing jazz and jazz greats into public schools. He had fine ideas, but something got into him at the luncheon and he talked almost nonstop, monopolizing all the conversation at the table. It began to be funny; I would try desperately to wrest the subject matter away from him, turning to Marjorie or the others to pick up on it, only to have him beat them to it and reel off another litany of his own. Finally Kay Graham, leading Washington hostess that she was, took complete control. In her most ladylike way she informed Monk that he had talked quite enough and it was someone else's turn. I was sorry that the hour and a half we were together hadn't been more successful, but that one act of Kay's gave me more insight into her indomitable character than I might otherwise have gained, and I was most grateful to her.

Subsequent luncheons proved more rewarding. Dr. Bernice Johnson Reagon was the powerhouse who had founded the a cappella group Sweet Honey in the Rock. She had researched the voyage of African American song from its roots in Africa and elsewhere to present-day rap in the ghetto, and she had an NPR gospel show, which NEA supported, called *Wade in the Water.* She was also a curator in Folkways at the Smithsonian and taught at American University. Although other guests, including Ambassador de Ojeda from Spain and Ed Jones, the manager of the nation's only African American TV channel, were equally interesting, it was the meeting of Senator Orrin Hatch and Dr. Reagon that was memorable.

Reagon described how the arts had been vital to her childhood in the one-room schoolhouse she attended in Georgia—how song and music had infused her life because of her teachers. The senator listened quietly and then said he was glad he was lunching with us because the vote for arts education in the school curriculum was on the floor as we spoke. He was going to vote against it as part of the president's Goals 2000, since he didn't believe an educational curriculum should be mandated at the federal level, but it was just as well that he wasn't there to cast his vote now after hearing Reagon.

It was our turn to remain silent when Hatch and the Spanish ambassador concurred that free trade with China should be opened up despite civil rights violations. Although Ed Jones, Reagon, and I said nothing, you could have cut the tension with a knife. Bernice Johnson Reagon had been at the forefront of the civil rights movement in our country. When Hatch went on to argue that the Soviet Union had collapsed economically because we forced the buildup of nuclear weapons, she quietly said, "But the country was bankrupt internally." The violations against Soviet citizens had been ongoing for almost a century, committed first by the czars, then Lenin, and then in particular Stalin, who had murdered perhaps millions in the name of communism. "The end justifies the means" was their prevailing rhetoric. Reagon knew better; she knew that democracy was founded on tolerance and nonviolence, just as Martin Luther King Jr. had preached, and that a nation ruled by violence would ultimately collapse no matter what economic system it followed. The buildup of nuclear weapons was simply the last straw that broke the bankrupt Soviet system.

Hatch turned the discussion away from civil rights and on to music. He said he was a true fan of gospel music and went out of his way to hear it. Reagon promised to send him some tapes, and as the luncheon came to an end, the senator promised to help Ed Jones keep alive his channel 32, which was badly in need of funds.

I continued these luncheons throughout 1994, bringing together

Democrats and Republicans, politicians and artists, ambassadors and businesspeople. In an Old World sense I felt that get-togethers like these accomplished more than the reams of political paper we were all confronted with daily. Washington was such a serious town, and everyone worked so damned hard. It was pleasant to have this civilized respite in a crowded day. Sadly, when the 104th Congress was elected and the reign of austerity began, it was politically expedient to end this oasis of pleasure. Suddenly serving a glass of fine wine at lunch could be construed as downright immoral.

One evening Sharon and Jay Rockefeller gave a beautiful formal dinner in my honor at their spacious home. The senator toasted me in great style, and then, as if to prove that the arts are for everyone, he related a story of an event in a downtown New York church many years before. He had gone to listen to an all-night concert of Bach and emerged in the wee hours of the morning high on the music and the pianist. Suddenly confronting him in the dark were three huge black guys. Since Jay is about six-foot-five, they must have been especially huge to seem menacing to him. As they advanced toward him, Jay tried to sidestep them when one of the fellows said, "How did you like the concert? Wasn't it great?"

It was a good story on himself, about prejudice, preconceptions, and the reach of art, but what most attracted me to it was the coincidence of a dream I had had the night before. I rose after Jay's toast, thanked him, and then told the guests that the meaning of my silly dream was now abundantly clear. I had dreamed that NPR had a new classical music show, dubiously called *Bach and Forth*. It was now clear to me that as NEA chairman I was to take Bach to the people—to go forth with Bach, with art, into all arenas. Jane of Art! Charge!

The social scene in Washington is most dependent on invitations to the White House. Bill Clinton, the first Democratic president in twelve years, turned the tables on the in crowd. His administration was determined to thank all those who had been a friend to him, and there simply weren't enough places at the table to accommodate everyone. The Clintons were extremely busy shaking hands in receiving lines whenever I saw them. I'm sure every Democrat in the entire state of Arkansas had found his or her way to the East Room by the time the president's first term was over. But the old guard of D.C. was often left out, and these sins of omission took their toll in subtle ways.

Old guard members were the repositories of history, and Bill Clinton was short on advisers who had been a part of former administrations. The old guard was made up of those who had been born in Washington, or who had come and stayed, or whose tenure had ensured a long involvement in the city. Katherine Shouse, in her nineties and founder of Wolf Trap, Virginia's famous performing arts center, was a member of the old guard, as were men who had served former administrations, such as Elliot Richardson, Leonard Garment, and Roger Stevens. Ben Bradlee was old guard, as was Mike Mansfield. Some of the old guard were not pacesetters anymore, but to exclude them was like excluding your great-grandmother from a family reunion. Others were still extremely active and considered a part of the community by dint of prestige and longevity in their field, like Sandra Day O'Connor or Lloyd Cutler. The old guard were the bastions of Washington cultural life. They could be seen with regularity at the theater or concerts, and they contributed financially to these institutions. Their collective memory and expertise were not sufficiently utilized in the current political realm, where the wheel was being reinvented daily.

Whenever there was an event involving the arts, I was top of the invitation list. The Kennedy Center Honors come on the heels of the National Medal of Arts every year. But unlike the latter, the honors program is televised with great fanfare, and the five chosen recipients are celebrated for an entire weekend. The honors predate the medals by eight years, having begun in 1978. The honors are given to famous people in the performing arts, while the medals also include the visual and literary arts and arts patronage.

As a member of the Artists' Committee I had attended the Kennedy Center honors for many years and been present when succeeding presidents hosted. Ed and I always looked forward to the event in December because George Stevens Jr. and others did such a remarkable job of producing the finest awards show in America.

In 1993 the honorees were Johnny Carson, Arthur Mitchell, Marion Williams, Stephen Sondheim, and Sir Georg Solti. Both Mitchell and

Sondheim were former members of the National Council on the Arts. In addition to being great talents in their respective fields of dance and musical theater the two men were dedicated to mentoring young people.

I was to introduce the gospel singer Marion Williams. Only once before had I introduced anyone at the Honors, and that was Henry Fonda back in 1979. I did not know Miss Williams personally as I had Fonda, but I admired her singing.

The State Department hosts a dinner the night before the Kennedy Center event where the honorees are toasted and receive the actual medal in a more informal atmosphere. My dinner partners were Howard Stringer, the ebullient president of CBS, and Majority Leader Senator George Mitchell of Maine. Howard and I discussed the fact that the networks were also facing content issues; the critics were attacking violence and sexual content on TV. Demands were being made that content be restricted and programs labeled in much the same way that feature films were rated R, G, and so on. The networks were resistant primarily because of the fear of advertising fallout, and secondarily because many felt that labeling violated First Amendment rights of free speech and free press.

Because *Law and Order* was one of NBC's highly rated one-hour dramas, Ed was embroiled in the issue quite directly. The show prided itself on the fact that it had no overt violence. Nevertheless, the series' creator, Dick Wolf, felt strongly that any content restrictions were in violation of the First Amendment, and he publicly stated so. One of the show's leading actors, Michael Moriarty, was equally vocal and had made a trip to Washington, D.C., with others in the television industry to meet with Attorney General Janet Reno. The Justice Department was contemplating restrictions, but many in the administration, from the president and vice president on down, hoped that the networks, with due warning, would regulate themselves. Perhaps no one was more concerned about violence among young people than Janet Reno. As state attorney for Dade County, Florida, she had witnessed violence firsthand and the havoc it wreaked. She had strong opinions about gratuitous violence on television.

Moriarty clashed with Reno almost immediately. He returned to

New York outraged by her position and took his case to the newspapers, calling for her resignation. No one else joined him in his crusade, preferring to deal with the issue step by step through hearings on the Hill and behind the scenes. Regrettably his outrage escalated, ultimately leading to his departure from *Law and Order* and his move to Canada. But right then it was enough for Ed to deal with Michael daily and keep him concentrated sufficiently to do the show.

I told Howard Stringer that the major difference between the networks' content battles and those of the NEA was that CBS, NBC, and ABC were commercial entities with important friends in high places who could place strategic calls to the highest-level officials in Washington. The NEA supported thousands of nonprofit organizations across the country, with disparate boards and disparate community impact. We were not organized to be influential in the same way.

George Mitchell and I talked about the changes that had occurred in politics during his time, and in the Senate in particular. He said that there was no loyalty to the Senate as an institution anymore, and that Bob Packwood's decision to stay on in light of the sexual harassment charges against him was indicative of this. A few weeks later Packwood did resign when the revelations became more and more serious. But Mitchell's point was well taken: we were witnessing a profound change in the way politicians conducted themselves. No longer was the institution, the House, the Senate, or the presidency, the hallowed ground it had been before. Now the men and women who had been elected were there to fight for their own agenda and for themselves. Their loyalty had shifted from something larger than themselves to the protection of their immediate position and its future. They cited their constituents more than they did the good of the body politic.

Mitchell asked for my impressions of Jesse Helms and then characterized him as a nice grandfatherly type but also as an "evil man." This was surprising to me—not that Helms might be an evil man but that George Mitchell might think that way. I personally had never characterized anyone as evil, because when I had played a desperate, devious or murderous character I had to become her and make some logical sense of her motives, no matter how twisted. Perhaps there are people in the world who characterize themselves as evil, but I just don't know any. I imagined that Mitchell must have had some horrendous clashes with Helms, but he didn't elaborate.

Ricki Seidman called from the White House on short notice and said that since cameras would be focused on the president and the First Lady at the Kennedy Center, would Ed and I like to sit with them in the presidential box? I thanked her profusely: this would send a strong visual message about the president's support of the NEA. We were whisked from the White House in the president's motorcade, the sirens blaring, the police escort blasting through red lights in a thrilling rush to the Opera House. The president grabbed my hand as we walked the plush carpet to the box and said he was so glad I was doing this job. Like a bashful schoolgirl, I was giddy with the excitement of it all.

Sitting behind Bill Clinton is a lesson in patience. The man is very big, and I couldn't see much of the show. Ed had a better view behind Hillary. I amused myself watching the intractability of the Secret Service man squeezed to my left, who never smiled and whose eyes endlessly scanned the crowd below like a robotic camera. And I watched the shadow play in the dark of an affectionate president and his lovely wife. They whispered, he nuzzled her neck and kissed her fingertips. This was a show for no one but themselves, and it made me happy to witness it. The state of the union was just fine in those waning days of 1993; the world was a lot brighter than it would become a year later.

When introducing Marion Williams, I referred briefly to the "easy" job I had come to D.C. to take on and received an appreciative guffaw from the audience. The tributes to the honorees were, as always, magnificent. And the president laughed loud and hard at a tape of Johnny Carson satirizing his long-windedness at the 1988 convention. The Clintons returned to the White House afterward while the rest of us proceeded to dinner in the vast Kennedy Center lobby.

Ed and I arrived at our assigned table before any of the other guests and toured around to view the place cards. Julio Iglesias was to be on my left, and across the centerpiece was Leon Panetta. I figured the director of the Office of Management and Budget was more important for me to sit next to than a Spanish singer, no matter how alluring, so I quickly switched cards.

Leon Panetta and I hit it off immediately. He was a classical pianist and had an innate love of the arts, as well as an Italian gusto that made him instantly likable and sympathetic. As a member of Congress from 1977 to 1993 he remembered that his colleagues on the other side of the aisle used to bash the National Science Foundation, not the arts.

As the head of the administration's budget affairs, Panetta was the man to talk to about our appropriations. Every November, shortly after Congress approved the coming fiscal year's budget, we began drawing up a budget for the following year. The first step in the long process was to discuss what we wanted with OMB, since our agency's needs had to fit in with the president's overall plan. We had to be realistic but at the same time make our case for an increase based on the nation's needs. The NEA always asked for a substantial increase because it had vast numbers of worthy applicants in the arts and insufficient funds to award them. In addition our current budget of $174.5 million had not kept pace with inflation over the years and should have been closer to $350 million had we received concomitant increases yearly since inception. I didn't have to spell all this out to Leon. He knew our problems. Nevertheless, with a president determined to trim his overall budget, he advised me that the NEA was going to have to remain at the same request level for the coming year.

The social scene in Washington has always been an important way of doing business, as it is in the private sector. What surprised me was that there wasn't more of it, until I realized how hard everyone worked. Except for the occasional presidential golf game, I didn't hear of other outings on the links or carousing in back rooms. A restaurant called the Capitol Grill was supposed to be the place where Republicans hung out, but the times I was there I rarely spotted the known or infamous. After a long day's work people usually dragged themselves home with sheaves of paperwork for an unceremonious evening and hoped to catch enough sleep before the dawn of another long day. Yes, there were lunches, and drinks, and dinners with friends, but the overwhelming impression I got was of a city on overdrive, trying to catch up, and then crashing at the end of the week.

Air travel had made it possible for most members of Congress to fly home on the weekends; just thirty or forty years ago being elected to

Congress entailed a commitment to live in Washington for two years, or at least for the periods when Congress was in session. An investment in the life of the city and in making friends was normal and produced bonds that do not develop now. Today the wear and tear of travel, the erratic separations from family and friends, the increased workload, and the pressure to meet with constituents when at home all conspire to make Jack a dull boy.

I was as guilty as anyone. I worked harder than I ever had in my life but not as hard as most. The president was known to run his staff ragged. He had made the colossal mistake, in the name of fiscal responsibility, of cutting White House personnel by 30 percent when he took office, and now everyone was paying for it. In addition he himself needed little more than six hours of sleep a night, and staff meetings were often held at the ungodly hour of seven-thirty in the morning. All of us who worked for the administration felt the unspoken obligation to keep up with the boss.

But I kept the hours of Congress for the most part. As one who had spent her life in the theater, I wasn't much good to anyone before ten o'clock in the morning despite the fact that I rose between six and seven. Still, I managed to walk the three blocks to the Old Post Office Building and be at my desk between nine-thirty and ten. I'd work until six-thirty and be out three nights a week, usually Tuesdays, Wednesdays, and Thursdays, when most events were held to ensure the attendance of members of Congress. I'd catch the Delta Airline shuttle home Friday nights and return to D.C. on Sunday night or Monday morning. I knew firsthand the conflicting emotions of working in one town and pledging allegiance to home in another.

The "fourth estate" was the fourth major element of the Washington scene, after the president, Congress, and the old guard. Kay Graham straddled dual worlds as a member of the old guard and the publisher of the *Washington Post*. Although Kay's strength as an arbiter of the political and social climate was matchless, it was the daily papers, the evening news, and the Sunday talk shows that sent the staffers spinning. Bad press meant a bad day for those impaled. I could sympathize with this, having been victimized many times in theater reviews, but bad press rarely induced me to change my performance of a role. Bad press in the political world, by contrast, could initiate a whole new look at policy.

The relationships of Washington media stars with those they covered were downright incestuous. Cokie Roberts, Sam Donaldson, Tim Russert, Bernard Shaw, and Jim Lehrer were on everyone's A-list and frequented D.C. social events as much as anyone, as did the *Post* columnists. A few times yearly they expiated their guilt at massive roasts knocking themselves and leading politicians about the ears for their behavior. The White House Correspondents dinner, the Washington Press Club event, and the Gridiron Club roast were hot tickets. Everyone laughed a lot at locker-room humor or frat-house high jinks and then went back to work the next day to prick each other publicly. I suppose these roasts were healthy, but it all seemed sophomoric, and I wished the jokes were better.

The world of Washington is insular and self-perpetuating, like a dog running in circles with its own tail in its mouth. Bad press begets new policy begets bad reaction begets bad press. The press is the barometer for "How're we doing?" When the answer was less than positive, the White House or congressional staff would pull together a focus group to gauge public reaction to whatever event, issue, or policy was at stake. The White House became increasingly dependent on poll results and then would direct its efforts accordingly.

A focus group was pulled together for the NEA, paid for by a private organization. Although I didn't initiate it, I was interested in what this tiny sampling of the public had to say about our agency. I was stunned to learn that fully 90 percent of those questioned had never heard of the NEA. So I disregarded subsequent answers and in my travels set about increasing awareness of what this fine agency does.

There was hardly a day when I did not give an interview in my office, on the phone, or on the road. The press was good to me and the Endowment, with the exception of the conservative press, whose position was known from the outset. I think the press is always rooting for the underdog, and the agency had been down long enough to warrant some sympathy. Media attention was not new to me. I'd been in the celebrity category for a number of years and was comfortable with reporters. I was rarely misquoted and by and large found the interviews I did for the NEA thoughtful and productive.

When a scandal broke, however, as happened later on in my tenure, the race to be the first with the story often resulted in sloppy work. Reporters tended to quote each other, compounding misinformation and leaving us with a mess to clean up. With news outlets owned by fewer and fewer moguls, reporters didn't bother to do independent research but drew their information from the same sources.

Our communications director, Cherie Simon, organized op-eds and letters to the editor as rebuttals or as statements of facts. These worked to a limited extent; they certainly worked better than a little box stating a correction, but nothing could replace the original breaking story. Rumors become truth, and lies become ingrained in the memory of readers, despite retractions and revisions. How many stories can readers absorb or managing editors print on a subject? They have newspapers to sell and TV ratings to court, and they move on to the newest events with great rapidity and little regard for the injured left in their wake. I just wish reporters did their homework better.

The scene in Washington and the varied social events expanded my horizons, enlivened my evenings, and introduced me to a world of supporters, but the important players in the game lived on the Hill during the day. They were not getting invited to the same parties I was. And if they were they did not want to spend time with me. I set about visiting them on their turf.

CHAPTER SEVEN

The Players

"All the world's a stage, and all the men and women merely players: They have their exits and their entrances."

Newt Gingrich was waiting in the wings making a lot of noise, but he hadn't yet made his entrance. It would take the Republican congressional victory of November 1994 before he took the stage in full regalia. Nevertheless, like an actor who has main billing, his presence was anxiously anticipated. Eugene Ionesco wrote a marvelous play called *Rhinoceros* back in the 1960s. The rhinoceros keeps growing until by the end of the play it has taken over the entire room and the lives of the poor people housing the creature. This was a little bit like Newt Gingrich in Congress in 1993 and the early part of 1994. Although the House and Senate were still controlled by the Democrats, his presence loomed large. It was reputed that Gingrich, who loved animals, had a special fondness for rhinos.

The campaign for the presidency had been bitter and expensive, and the war between Bill Clinton and his enemies was long-standing and ongoing. If Clinton invited controversy because of his personal behavior and character, the GOP was determined to bring him down—to have him "hoisted with his own petard," to quote Shakespeare again. As a result, all of us in the administration were also targets. Some whose nominations were shaky at the outset never made it into office: Zoë Baird, Lani Guinier, and Kimba Wood. For those of us who got the job, it was a constant lesson in surveillance. We weren't going to do anything to embarrass the president or make it easy for the other side to snipe. Still, lives were ruined or overturned during the course of the first term. Henry Cisneros was forced out of Housing and Urban Development, and Mike Espy out of Agriculture. The saddest of all was Vince Foster, a close friend of the Clintons who was working for them in the White House when he took his own life. The note he left said it all: "Here ruining people is considered sport." It reminded me of Gloucester's cry in *King Lear:* "As flies to wanton boys, are we to the gods; they kill us for their sport." Washington sport was not godlike, but it *was* bloody.

The National Endowment for the Arts had been a target of the Moral Majority and then the Christian Coalition well before Clinton took office, but the combination of this president and a controversial agency was enough to incite Republican congressional leaders to seek the destruction of both. It was important for me to tread lightly and attempt to appease our detractors.

All government agencies and departments are dependent on the largesse of Congress. The arcane path of any appropriations bill begins with the presentation of the president's budget to the legislators. Subcommittees of the House and Senate then meet to hear testimony on the worth of agencies under their aegis, and then they submit a budget to the full committee. Sometime during the summer, before everyone takes off for the August recess, the appropriations bills are debated on the House and Senate floors. After the recess, in September, the House and Senate reconcile their budgets so that they are in accord and then finally confer with the White House for complete reconciliation with the administration's budget. The entire process can take a year, or even longer if the president and Congress do not see eye to eye. When the fiscal year expires at the end of September and there is still wrangling over the budget, Congress will pass what is known as a continuing resolution (CR) in order to pay the bills and keep the government open. If that doesn't happen, the government shuts down, quite literally. Everyone goes home until the stalemate ends.

The National Endowment for the Arts testified annually before the House and Senate subcommittees of the Committees on Appropriations for the Department of the Interior. There were many committee members I needed to visit in both parties in order to introduce myself as the new NEA chairman and, more important, to press my case for the agency. As long as the Democrats were in control, there was little chance of the GOP killing off our agency, but they could try to whittle it down, as some, like Representative Cliff Stearns of Florida, kept proposing annually.

Democrat Sidney Yates had chaired the House subcommittee for Interior appropriations for almost twenty years. His government career was long and distinguished, and his Chicago constituents had returned him to office again and again since 1948. He was a noncombative and inclusive chairman whom everyone liked and respected. Ralph Regula and other Republicans on the subcommittee had been longtime supporters of the NEA, despite the controversies. They and the Republican leaders in the House might agitate about the Endowment, but they knew they would not get very far as long as their party was in the minority.

Sid Yates was a gallant man. One might have thought, since he was in his eighties, that Sid was slowing down, but that was never the case. His mind was as sharp as ever, and he remained just as committed to the causes and people he believed in. He believed in the National Endowments for the Arts and for the Humanities, and there was no one who championed them more on the House floor. He also deeply respected artists. He may not have liked the erotic photographs of Robert Mapplethorpe, but he never doubted the artist's right to make them or to have them exhibited. Sid adored music and musicians. He and his wife, Addie, would often attend concerts, and at home they liked to listen to symphonic recordings. But Sid's interest in the arts and humanities was far-ranging. He could quote Gilbert and Sullivan and also discuss paintings, films, and folk art.

Sid Yates and I spoke of my wish to increase the focus on arts education and to form more partnerships with other federal agencies, both of which he thought were good ideas. He wanted to increase the Endowment's budget by $10 million for fiscal year 1995. It had risen steadily during the Bush administration until Frohnmayer's dismissal in 1992, when it was the highest it had ever been at almost $176 million. Because of the administration's budget cuts to reduce the deficit and additional cuts by Congress, NEA's budget was approximately $170 million for fiscal year 1994. As chairman of the subcommittee, Sid Yates wielded a lot of power with his colleagues and could usually get the bill he wanted to the full committee on Interior appropriations.

It was problematic that the Endowments were lodged in Interior because the department had many huge issues to address. The staff there were constantly trying to defend and increase the appropriations for other areas of the department—everything from the Bureau of Land Management to Energy Conservation to Indian Health Services. That the arts were "caretakers of the soul" didn't mean much when there was so much land to take care of. This situation resulted in some odd horse-trading. The year before I arrived opposing members of Congress had struck a deal that allowed ranchers to pay a reduced fee for grazing their animals on government land in exchange for funding of the NEA. This, quipped one congressman, was "corn for porn." The following year a similar deal was consummated as "grass for ass." They wrangled one year over whether to give some of the NEA's funding to health care for Indians, which I suppose they might have coined as "sex for Rx."

Sid Yates was a pragmatist. He had been around so long he knew the pitfalls and where we could win points. He was a stickler for the rules and would often pick up the phone to ask the House parliamentarian about a rule to see whether we might use it to our advantage. The rules dictated how representatives conducted business on the House floor, and the parliamentarian arbitrated like the umpire of a football game.

As Sid and I discussed strategy over tuna fish sandwiches at his round office table his indefatigable assistant, Mary Bain, also in her eighties, popped in occasionally with information or messages. I thought of how much they had been through together on the Hill and the many hearings for which they had prepared through the years.

I had first testified before his committee in 1983, and then again in the most turbulent year of all, 1990, when sadness and outrage had prevailed among the artists present at the hearings. Those testifying with me then were masters in their fields: the cellist Yo-Yo Ma, the sculptor Martin Puryear, the pianist Leon Bates, the theater producer Joe Papp, the choreographer Bella Lewitzky, the tenor White Eagle, Arena Stage's Zelda Fichandler, and the visual artists Robert Rauschenberg and Roy Lichtenstein.

In 1990 we were all concerned about the inclusion of an "obscenity clause" in the Endowment's legislation stating that funds could not be used to "promote, disseminate, or produce materials which . . . may be considered obscene, including depictions of sadomasochism, homo-eroticism, the sexual exploitation of children, or individuals engaged in sex acts and which, when taken as a whole, do not have serious literary, artistic, political, or scientific value." Artists and arts organizations that received grants were required to sign a letter accepting this provision as part of the "terms and conditions" of the award. This was known as the "loyalty oath," and at that time Joe Papp and Bella Lewitzky had refused to accept NEA grants because of it. Bella, a mature woman with decades of experience in the dance world behind her, had an interesting discussion with Chairman Yates about censorship:

> Yates: Now that we have the word *pornography* written into this endowment, do you worry about pornography as being an inhibition against any grant?
>
> Lewitzky: Yes, I think it is untenable. . . . It's very easy for somebody to misread something which might look pornographic, but is not in fact. It might be a social statement directed against pornography, and the act of presenting it from their particular vision. . . . I fear censorship, Mr. Yates, altogether, because I know what its ramifications can be.
>
> Yates: Do you ever create any dances that address the subject of love, for example?
>
> Lewitzky: All the time. All the time.
>
> Yates: How do you avoid the possible criticisms of pornography then?
>
> Lewitzky: I would hate to have to start worrying about it, and thank you, that is exactly the point. Because all choreographers now must weigh something they never intended to weigh. . . . I don't want the imposition of censorship to make me mediocre.

Apropos of the mention of "smut," Sid Yates, with his usual flair, quoted Ogden Nash: "You have probably heard of the Smoot-Hawley tariff way back when. This barred all kinds of products from coming into our country. One of the products that was barred was obscene material. Ogden Nash . . . wrote a poem in which he said: "Smite, smut, smoot, rough and tough, smut when smitten is first-page stuff."

Bella Lewitzky sued the government and won in a California court in 1991 on the grounds that the obscenity clause was unconstitutionally vague and that a national entity such as the NEA was incapable of applying local community standards, which of course might vary from town to town. The judge also cited the possibility of a chilling effect on artists, who might self-censor because it would not be clear to them what "obscene" meant.

Joe Papp, whose Public Theater in New York had been awarded NEA grants for years, one of which resulted in a workshop of *A Chorus Line,* also spoke at the 1990 hearing. He said that Congress was hypocritical when they stood and applauded Václav Havel as a hero and the head of state of Czechoslovakia. Because of his writings, Havel had been suppressed and jailed by his government, which violated his right to speak freely. Now this same Congress wanted to muzzle the American artists whom it funded. Papp continued: "If Václav Havel is wonderful, then you cannot put a restriction on art and the government must support the artists. The government must be outspoken for the artists. Congresspeople and the Senate must speak out for the rights of the artist, not circumscribe the artist as they have done."

When it was Robert Rauschenberg's time to speak he went even further:

> History reflects that Hitler attempted to annihilate the Bauhaus before the Jews. Mao and Stalin sent all the scholars and poets and painters to the farms and assigned the farmers to the banks and to official bureaucratic powers. The results we know. The McCarthy period of censorship hysteria in the USA is quite serious but was massively supported.
>
> If we allow this frenzy to control the international model of freedom of the arts, we confuse the world's people and let them down.

(It is interesting to note that in the *Congressional Record* reporting these hearings of the 101st Congress, "Bauhaus" is not included. The sentence reads: "History reflects that Hitler attempted to annihilate the

Bowhows." I have changed "Bowhows" to "Bauhaus," confident that Rauschenberg meant the German school of aesthetics and design, and not dog know-how. This illustrates little more than that no one bothers to read the *Record,* or that if they do they are more ignorant than they should be.)

When it was my turn to testify in 1990, I told the committee that I got down on my knees daily and thanked the good Lord for Sid Yates and all the members of the committee who worked so hard for those of us in the arts. I said that it was astonishing to me that after twenty-five years of enormous success for the NEA, we were having to defend it. "The family of art produces a lot of things," I went on. "It produces ugly babies as well as beautiful ones, but we have to embrace all of that family, and we cannot throw any baby out with the dirty water."

This was a rather ungainly way to speak of censorship after the eloquent testimony of my colleagues, and to talk about "dirty water" sounded pejorative in and of itself. Nevertheless, I made my point, and I was united with my colleagues in voicing our alarm. I knew that Chairman Yates felt the same way in 1990, and that as we sat together over lunch in late 1993 his feelings remained unchanged. We needed to recapture the high ground. The First Amendment, the very cornerstone of our democracy, was written for all Americans: "Congress shall make no law respecting an establishment of religion, or prohibiting the free exercise thereof; or abridging the freedom of speech, or of the press; or the right of the people peaceably to assemble, and to petition the Government for a redress of grievances." If we citizens allowed it to be chipped away, bit by bit, we would sacrifice the essence of what made us a great nation. "Don't fool with the First" the slogan goes. Bella Lewitzky had won in the court—indeed, most courts upheld First Amendment rights whenever a case got to trial—but there was a pervasive feeling on the Hill that Congress should or could continue to make laws subverting or even overturning the right of free expression. I began to feel like a missionary for the First Amendment in my rounds as chairman of the NEA, although I rarely referred to it directly for fear of arousing the same unreasonable ire that had erupted during my visit to Strom Thurmond.

I had concentrated mainly on meeting senators before my confirmation hearing, but it was the House that was vital in the agency's new round of appropriations. I made frequent trips to Capitol Hill, always accompanied by the NEA's congressional liason, Dick Woodruff. With 435 members of the House and 100 in the Senate, I relied on Dick to make appointments with those who might be most helpful. We began with members of the subcommittee on appropriations and then expanded our visits to others who were influential with their colleagues, seeking to neutralize the Republicans and shore up the Democrats.

There was one very influential Democrat I needed to win over. Charlie Stenholm, from west Texas, held sway over about twenty-five colleagues, many of them moderate westerners, who were known as "blue dog" Democrats. The "blue dogs" were unpredictable as a bloc and more conservative than others in their party. They had voted to eliminate the NEA, so I set out to court Charlie. I knew west Texas went on forever and that the arts, like the failing oil wells, were dispersed far and wide between patches of tumbling tumbleweed. I wanted to understand why Stenholm and the others had chosen to abandon the rest of the Democrats on this issue.

We had a frank discussion. I began by telling him how much I grew to love Texas when I made a film there in the 1980s. I was one of the producers and stars of a low-budget feature called *Square Dance,* which introduced fourteen-year-old Winona Ryder to the world. I had spent the better part of a steaming summer in the state, kicking up my heels dancing in country-western bars as research for my role. Just as Texas legend has it, the men were taciturn and charming and the women were loud and spirited. I didn't see any reason why they wouldn't welcome the arts in the farthest corners of the state just as they welcomed strangers in their midst.

Charlie was clear: the gay and lesbian community had made the NEA a battleground, he said. I pointed out that the battleground included controversial heterosexual art as well, and that the NEA did not make the battleground. I suspected that there were plenty of homosexuals in Texas, just as there were in the other forty-nine states, and that they were part of the taxpaying public too. The Tony Alamo boots shuffled under the low table just itching to swing up on top to complete the laid-back cowboy look. His constituents wouldn't stand for it,

Charlie said. They received so much Christian Right mail that nailed the NEA and homosexuals as sinners that we didn't stand a chance. He didn't go on, but the gist of it was that I wouldn't have his vote or those of the other "blue dogs" if I didn't cut out the grants to gays. Stenholm was powerful but not mean. I had the feeling that he was acting on purely political motives, that he himself was not prejudiced. I met with him again a few years later in hopes of convincing him to change his mind, but that never happened. In my naïveté I still believed it was possible for a congressman to lead rather than follow his constituents, and to uphold the constitutional rights of *all* the citizens of his district rather than only those of the very vocal special-interest groups. As time went by it became clear that the money required to get elected led all legislators by the nose. But in the first year of my tenure I still hoped that I could convince the opposition to see the value of the Endowment, in and of itself, without money as part of the equation.

For all those who voted against the NEA, there were still more who were in favor. We could count on all the Democrats except the "blue dogs" and as many as thirty Republicans. Considering that New York was the cultural capital of the world, it was not surprising that most of the representatives from both parties of the New York metropolitan area were committed to funding for the arts. Jerrold Nadler from the city's West Side was a staunch defender, as were Carolyn Maloney from the East Side, Charlie Rangel from Harlem, and José Serrano from the Bronx. Nita Lowey from Westchester County was immensely helpful, and Republican Amo Houghton from upstate New York was one of the agency's leading defenders.

Other Republicans I could always count on were Marge Roukema of New Jersey, Rick Lazio and Michael Forbes from Long Island, and Representative Mike Castle of Delaware, who, as governor, had been instrumental in the creation of a model statewide plan for cultural support. Wisconsin also had a good record of statewide support for the arts, and Republican Steve Gunderson, from the LaCrosse area, worked with me on different strategies to ensure the NEA's success. Gunderson's opponents had "outed" him in 1992, making an issue of his homosexuality, but that didn't seem to bother his constituents; they put him back in office anyway. Still, the whole demeaning business must have taken its toll on him. He was determined to make this his final term in the House, but before going he wanted to be of assistance to those issues he supported.

My favorite woman in the House was Democrat Louise Slaughter, a Kentucky mining gal who had married a fine fellow with a good job in upstate New York. She had represented the Rochester area since 1986, never losing her Loretta Lynn twang or her homespun humor. Louise always told it like it was and never deviated from her positive outlook. I was immensely fond of her, as much for her good nature as for the fact that she could always make me laugh. Louise was head of the Congressional Arts Caucus, and I could count on her to "whip" all its members behind the NEA.

I was enjoying going to the Hill and meeting so many new people. It was easy for me to talk about the Endowment; in fact I was passionate about it. It was difficult to elicit any passion in return, however, except from a few of the legislators already mentioned. This diffidence made me feel uneasy about the chances of Congress making a real and lasting commitment to the agency. I had to explain too much—why the arts needed to be supported, why the nonprofit arts couldn't make it on their own, why kids needed arts education in the schools. I was feeling the same way I had felt when I pitched film scenarios in Hollywood and was told that my stories were too "soft." I had the uneasy feeling that congressmen viewed the arts that way also, and that the arts were a low priority.

There is nothing at all "soft" about the arts or about how artists create, but it is difficult, at best, to assess how artists do what they do. So much of the work is internal; it is brainwork whether the discipline is dance or drama, literature or painting. When the result is truly fine it seems effortless, leading those who don't know better to proclaim that the artist's work is entirely intuitive. In fact great art is the result of years of discipline, repetition, research, experience, technical skill, perseverance, *and* natural talent. The life of an artist is not "soft" but quite rigorous. This is little understood, however.

Congress has an easier time understanding the "hard" priorities of weapons or transportation systems like highways and bridges. Weapons can be actually seen and heard, and their capability can be demonstrated. They either work or they don't. Much of the time the research and development doesn't pay off and Congress is stuck with a billion-dollar fiasco, but it doesn't seem to deter them. Over the past four decades the search for an antimissile defense system alone has cost the taxpayers of America over $100 billion. Members of Congress plow ahead anyway and fund more experiments in antimissile defense and other weapons systems, piling up the pork in their own backyards and not exploring "softer" means of national defense, like the dissemination of culture and goodwill.

It was clear to me that our country, indeed the world, would be a better place if we had strong national and international arts programs. But my life had been spent in art, not in business or politics. How could I expect others to be as passionate as I was when they had not had a life in art? The arts meant everything to me. They were more than just my livelihood. Books, paintings, theater, music, and movies informed me totally about the world. There was grandeur and wonder in the natural world, but there was magic and possibility in the world of the arts, which told me about my fellow human beings and myself. Science might amaze me, but the arts could astonish me. If we were bound by ethics, the arts would tell me how we were bound. If our changing world needed interpretation, the arts would provide it. And sometimes we were transported through great music, literature, or painting into a realm we rarely entered and couldn't begin to define. Who can say how William Shakespeare was able to write about the intricacies of human behavior and emotion so poetically? Or how Cezanne, with blocks of color, gave us Provence? Or how the cave painters of Lascaux, fifty thousand years ago, transmitted their worship of bison with a charcoal line? Or how a late Beethoven string quartet moves us to tears? No, for me the arts were the pinnacle of human achievement, not a by-product. Science could get us to the moon or stars, but the arts told the story of the journey. It is said that Winston Churchill, during World War II, was asked to cut the arts budget of England. "God no," he replied. "What the hell have we been fighting for?"

It was Churchill's kind of passionate and immediate response that I was looking for in our U.S. congressmen—and failing to find. Support of the arts was still considered mandatory by most other industrialized nations in Europe and Asia, which subsidized their artists ninety percent with government funds in most countries. The United States is unique in the world in funding the arts with only ten percent of public money and ninety percent private money. If it was an effort to interest people in domestic funding for the arts in the United States, it was nearly impossible to garner support for publicly supported international programs.

When the United States Information Agency was subsumed by the State Department in 1999, the last formal international arts exchange programs, apart from those at the NEA, disappeared. The Endowment's small international program helped some American artists go to festivals abroad, and it had some fledgling exchanges with Mexico and Canada, but our budget of less than $1 million could not stretch very far. The State Department rarely sends artists abroad; it facilitates international exchange but implements limited funds. I was taken to task more than once by the ambassadors or cultural ministers of other nations who rightly claimed that they imported dance companies, music ensembles, and even some theater from the United States to *their* countries but we did not invite their artists in return. The choreographer Trisha Brown, the composers Philip Glass and Earle Brown, and many others have had significant careers in Europe, Japan, and elsewhere because of the government largesse of those countries, but the United States is not at all generous in return invitations. I am ashamed that the United States of America has no abiding interest in cultural exchange. Too many members of Congress don't even have a passport. They choose to believe that the United States is superior to all other countries and that we have nothing to learn from any of them. They also choose to believe that the marketplace sifts out what is important and ensures that it reaches us. But the commercial art markets of pop music, film, and videos, as valuable as they may be as a commodity, or even as art, do not begin to scratch the surface of what is being created in world cultures.

Iowa's Senator Tom Harkin told me that two pig farmers were sitting outside his office one day waiting to see him. They leafed through the pamphlets on the table and found one on the NEA. When they saw the senator they expressed concern that each taxpaying citizen was contributing only sixty-eight cents in 1993 to the National Endowment for

the Arts. How can we be the best with such a low figure, they wondered? How indeed? We engage in a race for space and an arms race,
but not in a race to promote the best arts companies in the world and
to learn from other nations.

The excitement of my early visits to the Hill began to be tempered as
I sensed just how low a priority the arts and humanities were to most
members of Congress. In addition, I felt that my gender made it difficult for some men on the Hill—that they would have been more comfortable talking politics with another man. There were a good number
of women working on the Hill, as aides, secretaries, and interns, but
since female members of Congress numbered only about 10 percent,
the atmosphere was still that of a male bastion. Bill Clinton had placed
more women in executive positions than any previous president, and
this went a long way toward introducing the public to women in positions of power, but I still sensed unease on the part of some congressmen.

Although my official title was the Honorable Jane Alexander, Chairman of the National Endowment for the Arts, I was virtually never
called "Chairman" (and thank God never "Honorable"). After the initial hellos I was immediately called "Jane" by most people. I observed
that occasionally when my counterpart at the National Endowment for
the Humanities, Sheldon Hackney, and I were at the same event he
would be referred to as "Chairman Hackney" while I was called "Jane"
or "Ms. Alexander." Maybe "Jane" is easier to say than "Sheldon," but
conscious or unconscious, there was a sexist overtone to it.

I chose "Chairman" myself, preferring it to "Chairperson," which
sounded like a lackey designated to pull out someone's chair, or "Chair-
woman," which had overtones of "charwoman." Besides, it amused me
to think of *-man* as a suffix to *wo-*. Some people wondered at that time
why I still referred to myself as an "actress," not an "actor," since we as a
society no longer said "poetess" to designate a female poet, and so on. I
was an "actress" and not an "actor" because the roles that I played were
gender-specific and I *was* that gender. It was unlikely that Robert De
Niro would ever be asked to play the roles I played, and vice versa.

Titles are interesting. If a man or woman walks into a room wearing
a military uniform, he or she is assuredly called by title: "General,"

"Colonel," or "Admiral." Without the uniform, references blur. Many of the men in Congress simply didn't know how to relate to something new on the scene—whether it was a woman in the workplace or new art on a wall.

The last thing I wanted to do was to threaten them, jeopardizing the agency's future, so I dressed conservatively in suits with a skirt hemmed at the knee. I wore low heels and hose of an unimaginative color. This was a departure for me. Although I love simple, classic clothes, my tendency has always been toward aging hippie and ethnic flair. As an actress you can dress pretty well as you damn please and people will love you. In fact the hope and expectation is that you *will* be outrageous, so that there is something to talk about. I was never flamboyant, but I had a way with clothes that was all my own.

Not anymore. In Washington I was boring myself with my daily dress. I'd yawn going through my closet in the morning. But at least I could brighten up with a spot of color. The poor guys in D.C. had to put on the ubiquitous gray or blue suit, white or blue shirt, and red or blue tie. From a distance they looked like dots on a pegboard. The women in Congress livened up the floor of the House with their dashes of color. And some, like Representative Cynthia McKinney from Georgia, were delightful to look at. Mckinney wore gold and white sneakers sometimes, her hair plaited in neat cornrows.

As time went by, however, I came to envy the men the comfort of their dress. Skirts and high heels are truly moronic for working women these days. In a venue that is not supposed to be about sex it is antediluvian to be exposing legs and downright uncomfortable to be wearing stockings and heels. I saw a T-shirt on the street once that said: "I know pain, I wear pantyhose." I could relate.

In any case my dress was self-inflicted. Even the White House gals gently suggested that I dress less conservatively. The First Lady was moving more and more into the mode of pantsuits, and I could do the same. I wanted to, but I had to follow my gut, which told me not to draw attention to myself in any way, to play the role of a soothing, reassuring matron so that it might be possible to have a levelheaded discussion about the arts.

Of course, there were a few men in Congress for whom "levelheaded" was an oxymoron. Robert Dornan, from southern California, just seemed downright crazy. He would be overcome with rage, and I'd expect foam to pour out of his mouth. He was known as "Mad Dog" Dornan, and the NEA was often an object of his wrath. Yet when I met him at a luncheon to introduce me to members of the Congressional Arts Caucus, he not only showed up but was eager to share with me his past exploits as an actor. Perhaps it is a profession he should return to; his bombast certainly didn't serve politics well, and it was a relief when Loretta Sanchez defeated him in 1996.

As a result of all the tension over the NEA, it had not been reauthorized since 1990, so in addition to visiting those in Congress who would help with our annual appropriations it was important to address this other legislative aspect as well. Reauthorization is necessary if an agency or department of government is to be eligible for funding, and it confirms that Congress has faith in an agency; moreover, the language of reauthorization legislation sets down the rules under which appropriations are granted. If there is contention about those rules and it isn't decided by the deadline for appropriating funds, then the requirement is often waived. The NEA was not the only department of government operating without reauthorization: parts of the Bureau of Land Management had not been reauthorized for years, and even the Department of Justice was conducting business without reauthorization. Pat Williams, the lone congressman from Montana, was a member of the Committee on Economic and Educational Opportunities and, as subcommittee chairman, was steering the agency through the reauthorization process once again. He was a smart westerner with a fervent belief in First Amendment rights and a love of the arts and humanities that extended beyond the wide-open plains of his large state. Pat thought that this year we might have a chance at reauthorization since I was newly on board and controversy over the NEA seemed to be quieting down compared to 1990 and 1991. Senators Kennedy and Kassebaum, who were in charge of our reauthorization in the Senate, agreed. We began to strategize how to best present the Endowment to the respective committees in the months to come.

Fortunately I was not the only one visiting Congress on behalf of the NEA. Advocates for the American Arts Alliance (AAA), which represented theaters, symphony orchestras, dance companies, museums, and opera companies, was an omnipresent force for the NEA and for any other issues that might have a negative impact on these nonprofit groups. The American Council on the Arts (ACA), an independent national advocacy organization, was also very active, as was the National Association of Local Arts Agencies (NALAA), the National Assembly of State Arts Agencies (NASAA), and the National Association of Artists' Organizations (NAAO). They represented their own constituents and also sought federal funds for the arts because doing so was in their constituents' interests. When Congress trod on First Amendment rights for artists, these groups were joined by People for the American Way, the Campaign for Freedom of Expression, and others.

All and all, the collective force was considerable for the arts on the Hill and could result in impressive media coverage when needed. The only drawback was that the arts advocacy groups did not represent any collective force that translated financially into campaign contributions. There was no "Arts Pac," no political action committee composed of artists and arts advocates who had given massive amounts of money to elect congressmen. Artists were notoriously unorganized across America, except for those two hundred thousand or so—only 10 percent of the estimated number of artists nationwide—who belonged to unions. Pressure was brought to bear through numbers: numbers of people who would vote for a given candidate, and the number of dollars contributed to that candidate. The religious right, for example, knew how to deliver the votes, while corporate America was expert at delivering money. The arts and humanities could deliver neither.

We brought the arts advocacy groups together in my office every few months so that we represented a unified field and there were no secrets between us. I was forthright with them about what we were doing, and they soon became equally outspoken. There had been tension in the past about how the Endowments funds were to be divided. When some members of Congress sought to increase the amount that the NEA gave directly to the fifty states, naturally NASAA encouraged it. My goal was to minimize the tension by having us all work together, not do "end-runs" to Congress behind anyone's back and to the detriment of any other group. NASAA agreed that it would not press Congress for a greater allocation of NEA funds to the states—that 40 percent or so was sufficient ultimately—and that if we all worked together, we might do better in the long run. I was proud of our accomplishments and grateful in the ensuing years, when the NEA's budget was cut so radically, that we friends stayed together.

The other important players for the NEA were those in the administration: the White House staff and the cabinet members. Early on I decided that we could maximize the NEA's small budget by creating partnerships with other federal agencies on which the arts might have a positive impact. The president had put crime prevention on his agenda, and so I arranged to meet with Attorney General Janet Reno to discuss after-school programs for kids caught in the judicial system. A visit to an outstanding facility in Pittsburgh called the Manchester Craftsmen's Guild had convinced me that arts programs were as vital to our youth as sports programs.

MCG was the brainchild of Bill Strickland, a member of the National Council on the Arts; he had invited me to visit after my first Council meeting. Bill grew up in a poor, African American section of the city and was fortunate to have a fine ceramicist as a teacher in his teenage years. This man, in addition to teaching him about clay, took him one day to visit the Frank Lloyd Wright house called "Falling Water." The design was an epiphany for the young Bill: he couldn't believe that water could flow through, and under, a house. His imagination was awakened, and he never looked back.

Manchester Craftsmen's Guild was a multitextured place, beautifully designed of brick and glass on the abandoned industrial banks of the Monongahela River. Late in the afternoon and into the evening, the building buzzed with students of photography, ceramics, jazz, computer technology, and cooking. The teaching was first-rate, the equipment the best, and the atmosphere serene. It was an oasis of light in lives that were often dark and depressed.

Bill and I went and visited the attorney general together. He spent twenty minutes telling his story to Janet Reno. Too long, I thought, and too late in the day of this busy woman. But she listened thoughtfully, and when he finished she said, "What can I do for you?" And thus began a most fruitful collaboration between the Department of Justice and the National Endowment for the Arts. Today there are a number of jointly sponsored arts programs that affect kids. Give a child a paintbrush or a clarinet and that child will be less likely to pick up a needle or a gun.

Another natural collaboration was between the Department of Health and Human Services and the NEA. I had long known of the beneficial use of improvisational theater to help people with either disabilities or addictions. My first husband, Robert Alexander, founded Living Stage, one of the most successful such companies in the world. His small band of actors and musicians had in their repertoire almost five hundred songs and poems to call upon in the course of their improvisations. They went into hospitals, prisons, and nursing homes, bringing joy into the lives of countless children who were disabled, disturbed, or disenfranchised. They would also have the children improvise themselves, acting out the issues that were uppermost in their minds in ways that might never surface otherwise.

Donna Shalala, secretary of HHS, knew what a positive effect the arts could have on the health of our citizens and communities. We soon were working together in the areas of domestic violence, teenage pregnancy, and alcohol and drug addiction. Plays that dealt with these subjects, music, the visual arts, and written materials were all helpful preventative measures.

The dynamic Henry Cisneros, the head of Housing and Urban Development, was the former mayor of San Antonio, Texas. He had seen firsthand the revitalization of his city through a cultural renaissance. The San Antonio River was now lined with fine restaurants, crafts boutiques, gardens, and flat-bottomed boats wending their way upstream. At night the lights glittered like stars in the water's reflection. Tourists came from far away to visit this former cow town. And the Spanish influence was everywhere, nowhere more vitally than in the Guadalupe Arts Center. Jocelyn Straus, a member of the National Council on the Arts, spearheaded the restoration of the old Majestic Theater, now the diadem in the city's crown. Henry needed no convincing about the importance of the arts to the life of a community, and he knew that good design was essential to good living. He sought to promote good design in every HUD contract.

The Department of Commerce was going to have a White House conference on travel and tourism. The marriage of tourism and cultural destinations was a natural, but the arts had never been invited to the table before, not overtly anyway. Secretary Ron Brown was enthusiastic about including both the Arts and Humanities Endowments. The result was overwhelmingly positive, and travel agents began looking at cities in a new way. New York of course had always had theaters and museums as cultural destinations, but was Cleveland ever booked as a place to visit solely because of its museums, theaters, or symphony, which were world-class?

The promotion of the arts and commerce next led to the idea of legacy—of preserving our important cultural history. The NEA started partnerships not only with Commerce but also with the National Park Service and the Department of Fish and Wildlife, proposing "heritage trails" throughout the nation that would follow historical paths where the arts had made a significant impact. There was a black heritage trail that followed the African American migration from the South to the North, the people bringing their unique music and stories each step of the way. There was a jazz heritage trail that led to New Orleans. There were Native American stories to be told in almost all our national parks. The possibilities seemed infinite.

Making partnerships in this way not only extended the reach of the arts in America and employed a lot of artists but also made the scope of the NEA more meaningful and recognizable to the public. Every project went through the same tough adjudication process of panels and Council approval, but the partnering entity paid the bulk of the cost. For a department like Health and Human Services, for example, with a budget of more than $30 billion and almost sixty thousand employees nationwide, these initiatives were not a burden.

The Department of Education was another behemoth compared to the tiny National Endowment for the Arts, and its secretary, Richard Riley, was a wonderful supporter of the arts. When, in the spring of 1993, the education bill "Goals 2000" was finally passed by Congress, Riley successfully saw the inclusion of the arts in the curricula. All education in the United States of America is controlled locally, but the federal government uses incentives to promote a national agenda. If a state signs on to the platform of Goals 2000, it is eligible for funds to implement it. Ultimately all fifty states signed on. I couldn't have asked for a better friend than Dick Riley. He was eager to collaborate with the Endowment, and we often appeared together at events promoting the arts in school curricula. His generosity and support were unflagging.

The NEA was in partnership with some strange bedfellows also, but then art can be found everywhere. The Department of Defense, for example, is the largest single contractor of design in the world. The Department of Transportation uses design and the visual arts in the building of highways, trains, and bridges. The Department of Agriculture uses painting, ceramics, and photography to promote products. The Arts Endowment forged partnerships with each of them. President Clinton and Vice President Gore were stressing interagency partnerships, and as a result, members of the cabinet were pleased to help.

My relationship with the most important player of all, the president, was mystifying. Although I never felt abandoned by the White House, I often felt neglected by the president's men. This was understandable considering the agenda the Clinton administration had set for itself and the chaos that I always felt was just beneath the surface over there. If I was flying by the seat of my pants with my small agency, I felt that they had to be winging it most of the time: lurching from crisis to crisis and juggling so many balls at once that some were bound to crash to earth. Still, the Endowment received a disproportionate amount of attention from Congress and the press relative to its size. I thought the president would have more to say to me about the agency.

It took me a very long time to realize that the NEA and I had been relegated to the office of the First Lady. I was well taken care of by Melanne Verveer, who advised the president on the arts and was intimately involved with the First Lady in the arena of policy. (In 1997 she became the First Lady's chief of staff.) Hillary Rodham Clinton really cared about the arts. She felt that the arts were as important to a good education and life skills as the study of history or mathematics. She may not have focused on it, as she did on health care in the beginning, but she increasingly spoke out for the NEA as the years went by and the pressure on the agency mounted.

Melanne was always responsive to my needs and consistently gave me excellent advice. She had formerly worked at People for the American Way, and we shared a similar liberal philosophy. She and another fine woman who also worked at People for the American Way, Barbara Handman, had initially promoted me for NEA chair. Melanne was the most gracious and loyal person I have ever met. Still, for all her remarkable qualities, and for all that the First Lady did, theirs was not the Office of the President. He was the one the people elected to office, and he was the one who engaged with Congress.

I do not know what happened to my letters or calls to the White House and the president. They went unanswered. Roger Stevens's words rang in my ear: "Always talk to the president." I couldn't even get on his schedule; his scheduler often never got back to me or to my chief of staff, Sandy Crary. Sometimes I thought that if I were simply Jane Alexander, citizen, I would have been able to get to him more easily; after all, he was a gregarious man and an impassioned letter about the arts, from an actress "on the outside," might have elicited a response. I did see him at social events, but only a few sentences at most were exchanged. Even sitting behind him in the presidential box at the Kennedy Center had been no guarantee of conversation.

He was always delightful when I ran into him, exuberant and boisterous. Bill Clinton is a seducer and a rescuer by nature. The combination is extremely attractive to most human beings. In a split second he can make you think you are the most important person in the world, and who doesn't want to think that? One time, as I was entering the doors of the West Wing of the White House for a meeting with the secretary to the cabinet, he startled me with a big bear hug from behind and an affectionate "Hello, Lady Jane!" We moved in tandem through the security check, leaving the officer at the desk and me dazed in the president's wake. "Does the president know you?" he asked, and then he quickly answered himself, "Well, yes, I guess he does! I've worked for five presidents, and I never had one so friendly with so many people. It's hard to keep up with him."

These fleeting moments were fun, but that was all they were. In time someone on the president's staff, probably Leon Panetta, must have urged him to be more presidential, because the hugs and kisses diminished and he stopped wearing shorts when jogging. Neither was missed much. In time too Melanne finally arranged a private meeting for me in the Oval Office, but by then a lot had changed: the 104th Congress was in power.

In retrospect I suppose the president's lack of attention to me and the agency was a blessing in disguise. I did not feel impelled to run things by the White House every time a crisis came up. I was free to govern as I saw best, and often fast decisions had to be made. It was also possible that the White House wanted distance from me in case there was a contretemps they needed to disavow. I continued to believe that their main expectation of me was to keep the NEA out of the papers. If that is the sole policy, I thought, so be it. I would try to fashion a more substantial one in the meantime if Congress gave us a break.

Congress so far, in the fall of 1993 and throughout the first months of 1994, had been fairly benign toward the NEA. There was the usual huffing and puffing by Jesse Helms and others, but they were clearly giving me a honeymoon period, maintaining a wait-and-see attitude. They kept nibbling at the agency's budget, but even the president was cutting government programs in order to control the deficit. Our Democratic president was beating the Republicans' balance-the-budget amendment to the punch. It was necessary, I supposed; the national debt had spiraled out of control. The president and the vice president were right to try to correct it. But the Endowment was losing purchasing power every year; if it had been keeping up with inflation, the budget in 1994 would have been $350 million, not half that.

Any cut had an impact on the nonprofit arts. It was the artists and the public in cities and towns all across America who were hurt. They were the people for whom the agency existed. I set out to meet them, to see their art, to listen to their thoughts, and to find out whether the NEA was doing well by them.

CHAPTER EIGHT

On the Road

Out-of-town tryouts were integral to the process of mounting new plays for much of the twentieth century. Before going to Broadway, the production would open in New Haven, Boston, or Philadelphia, where the writer, the director, and the actors would learn what meaning the play had for the audience, if any. Sometimes we bombed in New Haven and the production never went to New York, and sometimes the play was a triumph in Philly only to receive scathing reviews when it opened on Broadway. Going on the road demanded an ability to listen carefully to the audiences and the fortitude to dig in and do the hard work that was required. The company hardly split the sheets of the crisply made beds in the fine hotel rooms we stayed in out of town. Nevertheless, for all the weariness it entailed, taking a show on the road was an exhilarating experience. Going on the road for the National Endowment for the Arts had all the same elements. I was going to listen and learn—and give my audiences, I hoped, something to remember as well.

Our United States were not foreign to me. I had crisscrossed the country at least half a dozen times since the age of fourteen, when my dad took us on a camping trip out west. When I was nineteen my brother, my friend Susan Dowling, and I took off in our family's old Plymouth station wagon for almost three months, wishing we were Jack Kerouac. When we ended up in Mexico City with no gas and no money to our names we were resourceful enough to dress as poor Mexicans and beg for coins from American tourists at the Aztec pyramids. I guess I never left acting very far behind, and the ploy got us home. Later, in my professional acting career, I played in theaters and was on film location in over twenty different states. I had not visited every single state, however, and I certainly hadn't been to all of them in one year, as I intended to do as the head of the Endowment.

My first town meeting, in the autumn of 1993, was in Portland, Maine. "Why Maine?" someone shouted from the audience of four hundred. "As Maine goes, so goes the nation," I replied, eliciting cheers from the crowd. And I felt it was true. Maine may have had more individual artists residing within its borders than any other state, and perhaps more sympathy for the NEA, but the citizens generally were thoughtful and always had strong opinions. I had grown up in New England and knew what I might expect.

The meeting was held in an old department store that was being renovated to house the Maine College of Art. The Endowment had partially funded the move, not only because of the exceptional quality of the school but because it was part of a broader revitalization plan for downtown Portland. This was my first taste of a movement that was beginning to take hold nationwide: using the arts to lure people downtown again. The mass movement to the suburbs and the proliferation of malls had left desolate streets in the heart of cities as disparate as Detroit, Abilene, Tacoma, and Newark. Portland's downtown was shaping up beautifully again with fine new museums, restaurants, and other cultural entities. The folks at the town meeting let me know how important the NEA was to them and sent me on my way in good spirits.

The New Jersey Performing Arts Center broke ground on October 28, 1993. I remember it well because it is not often that you have a full symphony orchestra serenade you with "Happy Birthday." Governor James Florio, Mayor Sharpe James, and I joined others who plunged fancy brass shovels into Newark's soil before a large and diverse crowd of fifteen hundred. The dream was to build a rival to Lincoln Center across the Hudson and to engage the neighborhood through employment and art. Just down the street was the splendid little Newark Art Museum, which welcomed its gigantic performing arts neighbor. Today, just a few years later, NJPAC has fulfilled much of its mission, having presented a multitude of international performing events to over thirty thousand subscribers and patrons. Events are routinely sold out, and many New Jersey residents are drawn to Newark for the first time in decades.

Sometimes when a neighborhood or a community is hard hit by unemployment and lack of opportunity all that the people have left is art. The kids in Newark had rap and church music, and the kids in the mountains of western Pennsylvania sometimes had fiddle music and square dancing. The closing of the steel mills and coal mines had taken a real toll on parts of Pennsylvania. In America poverty is glimpsed in unpainted houses, collapsing porches and roofs, and rutted roads. The poor live side by side with vacant lots glutted with refuse, derelict buildings, and abandoned dreams. But dance and song can happen anywhere, and I saw it there in Johnstown and in many places I visited afterward. Art was a joy that was constant in lives that had little else.

I remember sitting next to Henry Cisneros one evening in Columbus, Ohio. We both had been asked to make remarks to the annual meeting of The Association of American Cultures. Henry, on behalf of the Department of Housing and Urban Development, had been traveling as much as I had. He told me how depressed he was by all he had seen, the broken-down neighborhoods, the broken-down spirits of the people, the drugs and violence. Since we had visited some of the same places, wasn't I feeling the same way he asked? "Oh no!" I replied. "Just the opposite: everywhere I go they take me to see the arts. I see people dancing or singing or painting or acting or making things with their hands. I see life, not despair."

The second time I visited Bill Strickland's Manchester Craftsmen's Guild in Pittsburgh I began to understand how profound his thinking was. He had raised $7 million to put up this serene and beautifully designed building in a derelict area. Give the kids something beautiful and they won't trash it, he thought. And it worked. They enter the building, where light plays on the floor as if in a temple. Sculptures, ceramics, and paintings are displayed openly in niches and on the walls. Give the kids something fine and they will know what excellence is, he thought. The lesson of Frank Lloyd Wright never left Bill Strickland. Wright's designs endure because they have the highest respect for human beings. Bill was passing on to new generations the idea of beauty, of design and art, and how it can change people's lives. Not just change but *save* people's lives. "The mass of men lead lives of quiet desperation," wrote Thoreau. Maybe art could mitigate just a little of that desperation.

I wanted to visit a school or arts program for young people in every place I traveled, to begin to know what was happening across our country for kids other than television and pop music. Noel Boxer did a yeoman's job of choosing the most interesting venues. I could hear him on the phone outside my office for hours at a time, asking detailed questions of everyone he spoke with. He was masterful. The scheduling was an intricate business, timed to the minute of my arrival. Sometimes I would be in a place for as long as three days, but usually just one. It was by no means a comprehensive picture of the arts in America, but as a snapshot it often told me a great deal. Communities were showing me the best they had in most cases, and their choices were revealing.

It was harder to reach the individual artists working in a community, but if my visit and town meeting were publicized sufficiently some of them would show up. Artists who work alone—writers, composers, and visual artists particularly—are holed up all over America doing their work. They are not usually organized to connect with each other, and to quote Tennessee Williams, they "depend on the kindness of strangers." They send their manuscripts, scores, or slides off to strangers in the hope of receiving a kind response: "Yes, we would like to publish, perform, or exhibit your work." It is a lonely endeavor, fraught with risks and rejection, but then it is something they feel they *need* to do.

They had been given a bum rap lately, and I wanted to talk to some of them if I could. In New York my friend Susan Sollins, who had founded a "museum without walls" called Independent Curators Inc., and Ronald Feldman, who owns a commercial art gallery in Soho, brought together about fifty artists and nonprofit arts administrators to discuss their problems with the NEA. These people were arguably in the avant-garde of the visual arts world in America. Nevertheless, the cutting-edge artists they exhibited in their "alternative spaces" were the butt of vilification and ridicule by members of Congress and some of the media. CBS aired a piece, for instance, in which Morley Safer made fun of the minimalist sculpture in a contemporary gallery.

I had often toured Soho, seeing the latest in art and performance in these spaces. Although there was much I didn't care for, I sometimes came across a work so arresting that it made up for everything else. Sometimes the only way to understand a piece is in its historical context. A work might be building on Duchamp or Man Ray in the 1920s or taking apart an entire school of painting from past eras. Labels like "conceptualism" and "deconstructivism" were invented by art critics and art history majors to describe certain schools of art, not to be used as terms of ridicule by those who have no understanding of the historical context in which artwork exists. I have never pretended to be a scholar of visual art, and I wouldn't dare say, "I don't know anything about it, but I know what I like," as some do. My usual approach is to observe quietly, keep my expectations low, and move on. I reserve judgment for those arenas I do know something about, like the theater.

Nevertheless, I am extremely sympathetic to the avant-garde. Those artists dare to take risks; they venture into terra incognita, often failing miserably on the journey, but then picking themselves up and venturing forth once again. How can anyone understand where they are going in their work when it *is* uncharted territory? Explorers are not ridiculed for seeking new paths, nor are scientists for conducting a thousand experiments in a test tube, yet artists receive little or no respect for new ventures into the unknown. Their anger was understandable. Their initial hostility and mistrust of me was also understandable.

For all the accolades I have received as an actress, there have been as many rejections; anger and hurt are not alien to me. The visual artists at the Soho meeting asked that they be understood, that they be fairly judged (probably an impossible request to fulfill because what they were doing was so new), and that they be funded. I did not disagree. They wanted me to speak out more for the contemporary artist—to make the case for new and even outrageous art. I tried to explain the politics of the situation. Nancy Kassebaum's remark ("You can't defend controversial art, don't even try") was foremost in my mind. There was no way that I was going to move the politicians to accept outrageous art. I could talk until I was blue in the face, and they would still not move one iota. I knew that; I am not sure the artists at the Soho meeting did.

I asked them to cool their own outrage for a while, not in their work but in their remarks about the NEA and the government. I told them it would be a long educational process for the Congress and to give me six months to a year. I had nothing in mind. Maybe I thought I could make a deal behind the scenes, but I didn't have a clue as to what it might entail. I knew that jumping up and down about the First Amendment and freedom of expression only made things worse, like waving a red flag at a bull. But I didn't tell them that.

By the end of the meeting, if they still didn't trust me, they were at least listening carefully. In the long run they gave me more than a year; they remained thoughtful and helpful for my entire term in office, showing a forbearance that certainly made it easier to salvage the agency. Perhaps these artists gave up on the NEA as they watched Congress hack away at it, but I know they were always grateful for what little funding did come their way. Most of all I did not want them to give up on their art. I wanted them to continue to produce and exhibit the art they needed to. This was harder to accomplish when the funds were low, and they knew that difficult or outrageous art might not get funded. The chill factor sets in, and the artist consciously or unconsciously begins to censor himself.

The theater community was going through similar problems. As costs escalated, as the amount of money it took to put on a show increased yearly, government funding decreased. As a result, more and more time was spent raising money or whittling the productions down to one set and two characters. I sat down one afternoon in New York with representatives from some of the four hundred nonprofit theaters in America. They were as concerned as the visual arts community about freedom of expression. The solo theater performers who played in their spaces had been vilified, just as the visual artists had been, and they worried about censorship. Many in the world of performing arts had followed the lead of Joe Papp and Bella Lewitzky and refused to sign the "loyalty oath" back in 1991. Stephen Sondheim had refused the National Medal of Arts for the same reason. Because I was one of them and had participated in my own share of controversies in the theater and in film, I think they trusted me to do the right thing.

Of more concern to them was the funding. How were we to increase the NEA's budget so that the theaters could receive healthy grants, proportionate to their budgets? And how were we to nurture new theaters when the pie was being sliced into smaller and smaller pieces? I didn't have any answers, and I was most sympathetic. I had watched my husband struggle as artistic director of the Hartman Theater in Stamford, Connecticut, in the 1980s. His board of directors, most of them corporate whizzes, did not understand the deficit that almost all nonprofit organizations live with. It was time-consuming to get money from them and from the community; the critical and commercial reception of a production was always a crapshoot, and it was exhausting to apply for funds from the government and foundations. There were only twenty-four hours in a day, and precious few of them were left for the art. Ed burned out after five years, meeting the fate common to most artistic directors in the nonprofit theater today.

The theater administrators were also concerned about the amount of money the NEA was allocating to outreach programs for the young, the disenfranchised, and others who might not have theater in their lives. The administrators were not opposed to outreach; it was simply that these programs were straining their capacities and resources. How were they to produce good theater *and* do all these adjunct endeavors with the budgets they had? The funds for outreach and arts education were rarely enough to enable administrators to hire a sufficient number of additional production people—actors, designers, directors, and so on. They wanted to build new audiences, but their primary mandate was to produce good theater, and they often couldn't accomplish both goals. With dwindling funds at the Endowment, they wanted the agency to understand that theater funds should first go toward the stage productions.

Again I was most sympathetic. In my twenties at Arena Stage I did double duty with an acting class in the local public school one semester as part of the theater's outreach. With performance eight times a week and rehearsal five days a week, and a two-year-old at home, the burden was overwhelming. The class I taught was rowdy, and the students probably learned nothing from the tired actress who was teaching them.

But as chairman of the NEA I was facing a dilemma. I knew that I could sell Congress on arts education and outreach programs, and by so doing perhaps divert them from the issues of controversial art that they were dwelling on. I wanted to increase the budgets for outreach and arts education to the point where these obligations would not be burdensome on the performing arts institutions. This never came to pass, but the focus on arts education and the arts as social welfare did take hold in the next few years. I cannot think this change of focus was a bad thing; in fact, I think it is a legitimate if not required occupation for a public entity like the NEA to serve all sectors of the population. Nevertheless, there was a great deal of grousing by the professionals that this was not what the NEA was created to do. I'm sure that if the NEA budget had been $350 million rather than $170 million—or the $99 million it became in my third year—outreach would have been championed by these same groups.

The Endowment's criteria for granting an award stipulated "artistic merit and excellence." Perhaps the hardest areas to judge were those involving the underserved or programs for youth. The panelists were required to adjudicate the worth of such programs not on the basis of the art itself but on the merit of the overall program. Sometimes the impact of the grant on the merit of the project would not be known for years. The NEA was again taking a chance, investing in a small group of citizens and trusting that it would pay off down the line. Sometimes I shuddered at the arts programs in schools I visited; the teachers didn't begin to comprehend the discipline and skill that learning an art form takes. It sufficed if the children played "Three Blind Mice" on the recorder or cut out construction paper turkeys at Thanksgiving. Fortunately I encountered many good programs too, and the difference was obvious and palpable.

In Chicago a dedicated and inspired woman named Dr. Rita Simo ran the People's Music School on the North Side. Children, the physically challenged, and others who couldn't afford it were given free lessons. And the instruction was first-rate because members of the Chicago Symphony Orchestra and other music professionals gave of their time several hours a week. Rita herself was a musician and knew that it took hard work and a lot of practice to begin to play a piece well. She expected this of the children, and they responded. She also gave affection and praise freely. Congressman Sidney Yates, First Lady of Chicago Maggie Daley, and I visited the school together and were impressed. Maggie pledged to help Rita build the larger facility she needed for her expanding roster of students, and by late 1995, with the city's help, Rita had her new building. As we were leaving that day, after a brief concert by seven-year-olds with diminutive violins, a young woman in a wheelchair stopped me to say that although her illness was terminal, the music lessons kept her alive and inspired every day. "This place is wonderful," she said.

The one-hundred-year-old Settlement Music School in Philadelphia told a similar story, as did NEA's own brainchild, the Rural Music Residency Program. An Endowment staffer, Eva Jacobs, had conceived of the idea of placing classical and jazz ensembles in rural communities for nine months of a year. The community's obligation was to house and care for the quartet in exchange for performances and teaching. No one could have guessed what a plus these residencies were all the way around. I caught up with one of our Iowa ensembles in Waterloo.

The Ying Quartet, three brothers and a sister, had extended their residency in Jesup, Iowa. They were beloved by the community, playing at high school athletic events as well as in concert. They had become an institution themselves there. One man at the Waterloo town meeting rose to thank the NEA. He said "Here I am in my fifties; all my life I have listened solely to jazz and pop music. If you had told me that I would become obsessed with Beethoven string quartets, I wouldn't have believed you. But I am because of the Yings, and I am very grateful." The young musicians were grateful too—for the appreciation of the community and for the opportunity to rehearse and perform their music so much. Tom, Phil, David, and Janet told me that the residency made them communicate more, which they had never had to do in the conservatory; the experience, they said, had made them not only better musicians but better people. By the time they left Jesup, the Ying Quartet was on its way to a secure future in the world of string quartets.

It was in meeting NEA's constituents in this way, the artists and their audiences, that I began to truly understand the magnitude of what the Endowment and state and local arts councils do. Without this kind of public funding it was doubtful that these artists would be seen by so many—and certainly not in smaller places like Jesup, Iowa, with a population of two thousand.

From left to right: "Buffalo Bill" Cody, my grandmother Helen Quigley holding my father Bart, Fred Garlow, Irma Cody Garlow, and baby Jane Garlow (for whom I was named)

My parents on their wedding day, New Year's Eve, 1938

Me doing an early dance step at almost a year old

The young mother with her darling son, Jace

The movie *Testament*, in which my nuclear radiation nightmare comes true

In the delightful play "The Sisters Rosensweig" with Christine Estabrook and Madeline Kahn

As a young Eleanor Roosevelt
in the TV film *Eleanor and Franklin*

Playing Calamity Jane
for a CBS special movie

With James Earl Jones during the
filming of *The Great White Hope* in 1970

NEA founder Roger Stevens (seated)
and his wife Christine (at far right)

With Attorncy General Janet Reno,
who spoke of the arts at one
National Council meeting

I always wore a big smile with these two
champions of the arts: Senator Alan
Simpson (left) and Congressman Sidney
Yates (right)

Greeting Congresswoman and friend Maxine Waters on the Hill. The NEA's congressional liaison, Dick Woodruff, is behind with staffer Marianne Klink

The finest politician of them all, Senator Ted Kennedy, and me at my confirmation hearing

Congresswoman Louise Slaughter and I try to convince Congressman Ralph Regula to save the Literature Fellowships at the zero hour

Being sworn in by Justice Sandra Day O'Connor while Ed holds the Bible

Visiting the Hand Workshop in Richmond, Virginia. One of the many NEA programs for children nationwide

At the Great Western Forum with back row: Kareem Abdul-Jabbar; front row, left to right: Herbie Hancock, Billy Dee Williams, Thelonious Monk, Jr, and Jerry Florence

The First Lady and I enjoy a moment of hilarity at the National Heritage Awards

In the Oval Office with President Bill Clinton

The President signs the Kennedy Center Bill
into law as I look on with political greats:
Senator Mark Hatfield, Chairman of the Center
James Wolfensohn, Senator Ted Kennedy,
and Senator George Mitchell

Some of those on my confirmation team:
Sandy Crary (to the right of me) and Melanne
Verveer (front row, right)

My family all dressed up for the Academy Awards in 1985. From left, Jon Sherin, Jace Alexander, me, Ed, Geoff Sherin, and Tony Sherin

A revelation in Africa

I had not been on the road for long when the first real controversy of my tenure exploded. The religious right had never ceased its diatribe against the NEA, but because I was new and still in a honeymoon period with Congress, no one had paid much attention to them. I was tested briefly in early March 1994 when the *Washington Times,* the city's conservative paper, printed an item saying that the NEA had funded the performer Annie Sprinkle in the film *Poison.* We hadn't, and she wasn't even in the film, but it took the efforts of several of us on the senior staff to address the issue. This was my first acquaintance with Annie Sprinkle, who had never received a grant from the NEA but had performed in venues that the NEA supported. It was a good test of my reasoning powers. Although I never saw Sprinkle on the stage, I did see one of her videotaped performances. At one point she invited the audience to come up and examine her private parts, as one's gynecologist might. She had a certain gymnast's fortitude and an ability to hold compromising positions onstage, but the excellence of her dramatic, or comedic (as the case might be), presentation would surely have been questioned by any panel had it ever come to that. If some theaters chose to present Annie Sprinkle, that was their business and the business of their community. If the NEA panel chose to recommend those same theaters for a grant for their entire season of work, that did not mean it was singling out Annie Sprinkle for a grant.

Endowment funding was a small proportion of any theater's entire budget, and never more than 50 percent. So I was comfortable with the idea that each theater presented a range of theatrical fare suited to its particular audience. There were going to be some things an NEA panel would endorse and others it wouldn't, but a theater's overall reputation for excellence and its ability to serve the community were taken into account in awarding seasonal support. The Sprinkle affair was good preparation for the big controversy to come.

On March 5, the Walker Art Center in Minneapolis presented the performance artist Ron Athey as one among one hundred events it staged in 1994. The Walker, arguably one of the finest museums in the country, was always awarded sizable funds, not only by the federal government but by the state of Minnesota and the city of Minneapolis, and the NEA grant had been awarded for a season of performances, not to Athey himself. I had never seen or even heard of Athey when the story broke three weeks later and I was asked by the *Washington Post* and other media to respond.

Athey, who was reportedly an HIV-positive gay man, drew designs with a scalpel on the back of a fellow performer (who was not HIV-positive), breaking the surface of the skin and causing superficial bleeding. He then blotted the designs on paper towels and strung the towels with clothespins on a line and pulled the line partially out over the audience eight feet above their heads. At one of the few performances that were given, a man apparently complained to the health department. My hurried conversations with my staff and people at the Walker revealed that all necessary health precautions had been taken, that latex gloves were used backstage in addition to bleach solution in case any mishaps occurred.

Athey, to my knowledge, had never applied to the Endowment for a grant. Although his work was certainly on the cutting edge (I guess the pun is intended, as this seems to define the meaning of the phrase), he probably was as surprised as the rest of us to be suddenly the center of attention. I felt that the Endowment's $104,500 to the Walker was easily absorbed by many of the other events they presented, but matters were complicated by the fact that the NEA's "seasonal" grant was in theory distributed proportionately to all of them. Accordingly, we had given the Athey production approximately $150. The NEA panel, in its deliberations almost a year earlier, had recommended a grant to the Walker as much on the merits of its fine past history as anything else. Any list of upcoming performers would not be comprehensive, since the institution rarely was able to contract with people so far in advance. This was normal procedure in almost all the arts fields, but now Congress was asking us to tell them exactly where the taxpayers' money was going. They did not want to buy a "pig in a poke," they said.

My hunch was that the rampant homophobia among conservatives was fueling the outrage over Athey. Scarification or bodily mutilation was certainly shocking onstage, but it was commonplace in the movies: bullets and knives ripped into flesh in almost every film that hit the local cinema. Teenagers all over the Western world were piercing their navels, noses, and ears and also spending hard-earned cash getting tattoos. Athey was ritualizing bloodletting in a way that some African or even Native American tribes did. As shocking as this was on the American stage, I was convinced that it was his HIV-positive gay status that riled people. I wasn't trying to defend the art; Kassebaum had told me it was not possible to defend controversial art with Congress. Besides, I hadn't seen it. But I was trying to make a point about discrimination, in this case against homosexuals who were HIV-positive. In 1994 the American public was not as knowledgeable about how AIDS is contracted as we are today. I was convinced that all appropriate precautions had been taken and that the man in the audience who complained to the health department exaggerated the scene by saying that blood was "dripping" from the paper towels, which was not the case, according to many witnesses. The Walker had also warned patrons that "viewer discretion is advised" and that the show was not for everybody.

I told this to the *Washington Post* reporter, Jacqueline Trescott, and added: "So what are we left with that was considered controversial? The scarification, the ritual-like aspect? Is it that the man is homosexual? I think those are areas that have to be carefully considered."

Kathy Halbreich, the museum's director, was quoted as saying: "We strive for a balanced and inclusive program and we feel it is our responsibility to present a diversity of artistic voices." She also recalled that in 1963 the museum was criticized for presenting the dancer-choreographer Merce Cunningham and the composer John Cage, both of whom were labeled anarchists at the time by the local media and are now hailed as greats of the twentieth century.

With a stroke of the pen, with a challenge thrown, my honeymoon with Congress was over. I thought it might be over for me and the White House too, but I made my points clearly and the voices of dissent retreated, at least for the present. I had violated the one tenet the White House gave me—to stay out of the headlines—but I hoped the president's men respected a fight against injustice. They could always disown me later if it didn't go well.

Museums had caused a number of problems for the Endowment since 1989, when the Mapplethorpe and Serrano contretemps had occurred. Ron Athey was also coming under attack as part of a seasonal museum grant to the Walker. Why museums? They were usually beyond reproach, their collections sacrosanct as we acolytes roamed the corridors of medieval art or stuffed birds, soaking up knowledge.

Museums began to change profoundly a decade or so ago. In an effort to meet the needs of a pluralist society that is expanding in almost every city in America, museums began to diversify their exhibits. Controversy was sure to result as different perspectives on an exhibit weighed in. For example, in 1996 the Smithsonian exhibited the *Enola Gay,* the airplane that had bombed Hiroshima in 1945 and effectively ended the war with the Japanese, causing massive death and radioactive fallout. Whose point of view was the Smithsonian to represent? That of the Truman administration? Or the soldiers who dropped the bombs? Or the World War II veterans? Or the Japanese? Or the anti-nuke activists? The answer perhaps is all of them, but it is a tricky business for any curator, and it is impossible to please everyone. After being attacked by veterans and members of Congress almost immediately, the Smithsonian decided to make some radical changes to the exhibit.

It is not possible to please all of the people—or as Abraham Lincoln said, even some of the people—all of the time. A museum director today can only hope that by consulting enough of the parties *before* an exhibit is mounted controversy will be minimized later. Education is the key: education of the public about the exhibit before they see it, and an interactive response available to them during the exhibit. This kind of forethought mitigates many impending disasters.

The good news about museums is that they are serving their communities in ways that they never dreamed of before. Museums are temples displaying great works of art; they are universities educating the masses; they are community centers, meeting grounds, and marketplaces. Their success today is unprecedented, and they are found in or near most communities in America. I was fortunate to be able to visit them wherever I went, and I marveled at such disparate pleasures as Richard Venturi's new design for San Francisco's vast art museum and a bandanna exhibit in the one-room museum in Jackson Hole, Wyoming.

The Athey controversy was stressful. My position required explanation to friends on the Hill and to the Endowment's employees, who looked at me anxiously, wondering whether this was the new contretemps that would cost them their jobs. I went back on the road, worried and anxious myself, about the upcoming congressional hearings. And my knee was beginning to kill me. On a trip to Colorado, finding myself with a rare free couple of hours, I walked the streets of downtown Denver in the chill blue air. The Rockies clung to the western horizon as if God had pushed the plains to the edge with a butter knife. I couldn't get enough of the view in one of my favorite cities and just kept walking. That night I felt a slight twinge in my knee but thought nothing of it.

A few days later, back in my apartment building's health club, I nodded to my usual colleagues in fitness: Feminist heroine Betty Friedan and Congressman Joe Kennedy from Massachusetts, the three of us dutifully working off the unwanted poundage. I watched Betty, at almost eighty, easily keep up a steady pace on the treadmill, and I admired Joe's graceful crawl in the pool as I trod the stairmaster, up and down, up and down, trying to negotiate the morning paper at the same time. The tension knob was broken on the machine, and so I stupidly exercised at a higher level. That did it. A swollen meniscus membrane plagued me for the next eight months, confining me in those initial weeks to a wheelchair.

It didn't stop me from going on the road anyway. But I began to resent riding airplanes in coach class because I couldn't extend my leg properly to give my knee the needed rest. All of us who were appointed by the president were required to travel economy-class. That included Donna Shalala, Robert Reich, Henry Cisneros, and Janet Reno. The president's men did not want the public to think we were in first- or business-class on the taxpayers' dime, so we were not even allowed to upgrade on frequent-flyer miles. This was understandable but extremely uncomfortable for people, like Reno, who were over six feet tall and people like me who had a bum knee. It was also annoying to be recognized and bothered after a long, tiring day. At least with a lousy leg I was wheeled around the airport.

In Wyoming I was wheeled around by no less a light than Senator Simpson. In Laramie, where he and his wife Ann had met as university students, Al pushed me on a tour of the new art museum, rising like a great tepee from the high plains. The design, by Antoine Predock, was provocative and the kind of bold statement in architecture that I loved to see.

There was a brief and small press conference at which the Athey controversy was brought up. The news had reached Wyoming already. Al surprised me by defending the Walker grant; even though he knew little about it, he put the media on the defensive by saying that sensationalism was all they ever wanted to discuss with the NEA. He won a friend in me for life at that conference; he was sure of his position and brooked no nonsense. I was impressed.

Visiting western states made me very happy. Part of my roots were there, and growing up with grandparents in Nebraska had made me feel at home with the plains, the mountains, and the great outdoors. In Cody, Wyoming, the Simpsons took me to the Buffalo Bill museum, which the NEA and NEH funded from time to time. There in a display of photographs of the great man was one of my grandmother holding my dad as a baby, next to Bill Cody. Also in the picture was Cody's daughter Irma, who was my grandmother's best friend, holding her baby daughter Jane, for whom I was named.

Ed and I had been to North Platte, Nebraska, where the photo was taken in front of my grandfather's house. We had visited Cody's ranch, Scout's Rest, and seen the vast railroad yards of the Union Pacific, which terminated in North Platte in 1867, before Wyoming track was laid. My grandmother's father came from Germany in the mid-1800s, crossed the country in a covered wagon, and ended up managing the railroad yards. Everything about the West is big, and the railroad yards even in the 1980s were huge, with tracks and trains as far as the eye could see.

When I arrived in South Dakota on behalf of the NEA I discovered that the arts council director had done some homework on my family. He drove me to the small town of Lennox, down a long dirt farm road and into the middle of a cornfield. There at the four corners of four farms was a graveyard shared by the families. It was a peaceful plot, well maintained, and there was the grave of my other great-grandfather, Thomas Quigley, who had emigrated with six brothers from Ireland in the 1850s. His was the most prominent stone of all. I learned that he had survived more Civil War battles than anyone else who came from that part of the Dakota Territory—seventeen of them. An item in a local paper of the 1860s told of his collapse on a southern battlefield, fighting under General Sherman on a hot summer day. Pits were dug for the dead, and dirt was about to be shoveled over the bodies when a buddy of my great-grandfather chanced by. He knelt by the hole and wailed for his dead friend Tom, whereupon my great-grandfather rose up from the dead and embraced him. He was a victim of sunstroke, not of Confederate bullets! (I am grateful to that buddy—without him I am nothing.)

The Endowment's presence was everywhere. In North Dakota, Cherie Simon, Stephanie Madden, and I were fortunate to be included in a circle dance with about twenty-five Lakota Indians, many of them teenagers. I was introduced to the group as the "head of the National Environment for the Arts," which seemed to me to be extremely apt given the pollution in Washington. Mary Louise Defender told the story of Standing Rock, the sacred hill we were on. A woman needed to get close to the creatures and plants of the earth and so turned herself into the rock in order to do so. We joined hands and circled round and round to songs chanted by the Lakota. One song we heard was rarely performed for outsiders, a rite-of-passage piece called "Sundance." The ritual for a young man was to have his chest pierced and to bear the trial of pain until he tore his flesh away. This mutilation of the body had been going on for thousands of years. The irony that there was great public support for the NEA's funding of the ritual dances, stories, and songs of Native Americans and none for the work of Ron Athey was not lost on me.

In nearby Fort Ransom we visited the Sarah Circle Quilters, elderly women who came together daily in the lone building of the town to quilt and keep the Norwegian traditions of tatting and lace cutwork alive. This was aided by a grant from our Folk and Traditional Arts program. I admired their delicate handiwork, thinking of my own grandmother from Nova Scotia and how her talents had not been embraced by my mother or passed on to me. As we were leaving and the women huddled together over a new quilt I said, "Keep up your wonderful work!" A tiny nonagenarian replied wanly, "No one will let us stop! We're so busy we wonder when we'll get a rest."

In Fargo a Lakota woman taught a third-grade class how to make monotypes. I sat at a wee table with two ten-year-olds, and we rolled out our four colors as we had been taught. Laura Heit spoke in a whisper, but the story was compelling. She told us of the colors of the four corners of the earth: black for the North, red for the East, yellow for the South, and white for the West. She told us of the four ages of man: infancy, young adult, adult, and elder. She asked us to make a simple picture on a piece of lucite with our red, black, and yellow paints, and then to press it out on white paper, creating a new print each time. The children at my table were far more successful than I with my smudges. As their clean landscapes rolled out, Adam, to my right, was dumbfounded. "This is awesome!" he declared. "This is the most awesome thing I have ever done!" And he pronounced his four prints "perfect."

I loved days like these in the Dakotas. The NEA's money was going a long way for a lot of people, introducing some to art, keeping ancient traditions alive with others. There seemed no end to the possibilities or to the delight encountered. Trollwood Park in Fargo had a performing arts program for four hundred kids in the summer, and the Rolling Plains Art Gallery toured the state in a semi, bringing paintings to people in town after town. In Sioux Falls the Northern Plains Art Gallery exhibited the work of contemporary Native American artists. The complex strands of tribe, nation, and the 1990s often came together in profound work. Francis Yellow's montages used Sioux pictographs and white memorabilia such as old bonds, treaties, and computer printouts of Indian names from the annals of anthropology to create insightful pieces.

Each state had its own stories to tell. The arts in America are as diverse and interesting as the people who make up our fifty states, and the arts in each place are informed by the land and the people the artists come into contact with daily. If the turkey sandwiches we were given for lunch everywhere we went were virtually indistinguishable, the same was not true for the art. There was no shortage of variation or excellence. If at one time good new art was found mainly on the coasts, that time had long passed. The visual arts panels at the NEA, which did blind judging of the submitted slides, said in 1994 that for the first time they could no longer tell from the paintings alone where the artist came from. Good art abounded in cities across America, and I had a hard time restraining myself from buying paintings or sculpture in most of the places I visited.

Out of many exceptional visual arts centers we saw on our travels, the Bemis Center for Contemporary Arts in Omaha was unique. Ree Schonlau, its director, leases out huge spaces in old warehouses downtown to artists for use as studios and apartments. If you are working in giant pieces like installations or sculptures twenty-five feet tall, this is the place for you. The Wright brothers could have built dozens of airplanes in these spaces. Artists come from all over the world to spend a few weeks' residency here, and the exchange between them is stimulating as they create next door to each other. Omaha was smart; what better use could there be for old warehouses? Omaha also had the good sense to hire the great architect Norman Foster to expand its fine Joslyn Art Museum recently. And the multimillion-dollar Omaha Playhouse, where such stars as Henry Fonda and Marlon Brando got their start, is one of the oldest and grandest community theaters in the country. Now who would have thought of Omaha as a cultural destination?

The citizens I met in towns and cities all across America told me how valuable the NEA and their state and local arts councils were to them. In town meeting after town meeting they shared their concern about decreased funding and the loss it meant to them personally when community arts organizations suffered. The subject of controversial art rarely even came up, and when it did another audience member usually responded to the query of the first by saying that their community could handle it themselves, through education and discussion. They also pointed out that community standards varied from region to region and that what might be commonplace in Soho might never be exhibited in Louisville, Baton Rouge, or Tulsa.

There were only two town meetings disrupted by protesters. The first was in Fort Wayne, Indiana, where a well-organized and courteous religious right group co-opted the entire question-and-answer session. They brought up Mapplethorpe, Serrano, and all the usual suspects. I responded as I usually did: the artworks in question were part of museum exhibitions, not direct grants; the Endowment does not discriminate on the basis of race, creed, gender, or sexual orientation; and a handful of grants out of more than one hundred thousand had been considered problematic by some people since 1965. This did not satisfy the group, however, and they continued to dominate the Q-and-A. The ploy won them no sympathy from the rest of the audience, who, finally tiring of their harangue, softly "booed" them into sitting down. The mayor of Fort Wayne was chagrined, but I was not at all surprised by the group's presence. These were the people who had elected Dan Coats senator of their state. It was good to see them in action and to hear what they had to say.

The other protest of any significance occurred at the town meeting in the gorgeous San Francisco Opera House. I looked out over the vast house and up into the balconies where people sat in scattered bunches. I made my opening remarks for about thirty minutes, talking about all that the NEA was doing in San Francisco and in northern California and praising the art I had seen in the city. The arts are deeply embedded in the history of San Francisco. Its opera, theater, and museums are world-class, and the city is hailed far and wide for its rich culture. When I threw the meeting open to questions I wasn't expecting the artists in the audience to be so critical of me. They told me that I was not speaking up enough for artists and homosexuals, and that I should let Congress know, in no uncertain terms, that I would not tolerate violation of First Amendment rights. It was hard to see my accusers in the huge dark space. I held my hand to my forehead to block the light and sputtered some inadequate response. How could I tell them what politics was like? That it did no good to rant and rave because no one in Washington would sit down with you again if you did? That gains were made incrementally and involved compromise and patience? I defended myself weakly, protesting that they were not being fair to me, and left the stage shaken by their adamance. The West Coast was three thousand miles away from Washington and New York. For all their volatility, it could have been another country.

San Francisco has one of the highest concentrations of homosexuals in the world, and the city's population had been hit hard by the AIDS scourge. The NEA had been concerned about AIDS from the very beginning because so many artists were vulnerable, and those in San Francisco more than most. In 1994 the Names Project housed the legacy of the twenty-eight thousand men and women who had died of

the disease and were immortalized on squares of "The Quilt." When
The Quilt last visited Washington it lay spread out on the mall, all the
way from the Washington Monument to the Capitol Building. No one
who saw it failed to be moved. As a piece of cultural history it has no
equal. The sadness of death is conquered by the indomitable spirit of
remembrance in each stitch of the cloth, in every photo and poem
woven into the squares. When the Quilt, or a portion of it, is not on
the road it is carefully housed in a climate-controlled building in San
Francisco. The NEA has helped pay for its conservation.

Down the California coast, outside of Monterey, the huge base
called Fort Ord was converting from military to other uses. Part of it
had been a sacred area for Native Americans who wished to reclaim the
land of their ancestors. Also vying for space was an equestrian center,
the police department, which wanted a training institute there, a state
college, and artists, who viewed the stables and other large buildings as
perfect studios. After visiting the site, which was larger than the entire
city of San Francisco, I came away with dreams of turning "swords into
plowshares" all over America.

The Endowment had been extremely successful in a partnership
with The Mayors Institute in bringing mayors together for colloquies
on design in their cities. Visionaries like Joe Riley, the mayor of
Charleston, South Carolina, had been so influenced by what he learned
that he urged mayors nationwide to take part. The concept of the Institute on City Design was simple: bring a small group of mayors together
for a few days with some of the leading architects and designers of our
time to discuss a particular problem, such as roadways, the inner city,
or parking facilities. The mayors were guaranteed to think about their
cities with new perspective after such a weekend.

I thought the base conversion of Fort Ord was a perfect candidate
for the NEA's design program. Its lively director, Samina Quraeshi, was
asked to mediate what was becoming a testy dispute in Monterey. With
her usual vigor and foresight Samina held meetings with the different
parties, including local politicians, U.S. Congressman Sam Farr, and
major architects such as Hugh Hardy, a member of the National Council on the Arts. The results were encouraging. The architects did a
"charette" showing how the land might be parceled out and designed to

the satisfaction of most. I was very proud of these kinds of endeavors of the NEA. It was working in the best interest of the public all the way around and resulted in a design concept that would please future generations as well as present contenders.

Some of the other ways in which the Endowment helped local communities were efforts that only the national government could undertake. Los Angeles was rocked by a major earthquake in 1994. The NEA had responded to disasters in the past by providing funds for arts organizations that suffered damage from hurricanes, fire, and floods. We had also aided Oklahoma City after the bombing of the federal building in their city with funds for the symphony orchestra to play at memorial services, and visual and literary artists to assist victims in the healing process. These were special chairman's grants that did not need to go through the lengthy process of peer review. As chairman I could also intervene on the organization's behalf with the Federal Emergency Management Agency (FEMA). This was a perk of the job I welcomed; I liked being able to pick up the phone and get right through to the head of another government agency. The Endowment had provided relief after Hurricane Andrew, and now we helped a few organizations that were wrecked by the Los Angeles earthquake.

The Lula Washington Dance Company in South Central Los Angeles was left with an uninhabitable building after teaching a generation of African American kids how to pirouette and *elevée* in ballet as well as all manner of traditional and modern dance. Lula's school and her performing company were a vibrant part of the community. The boys and girls who graduated from her classes did not go on to drugs or guns. Lula had a motto: "Do dance, not drugs." With a little money and a few phone calls we helped her get back on her feet again.

There was hardly time to breathe when we were on the road, there was so much to do and see. Cherie or Stephanie and I were whisked from an art museum to a press conference to a town meeting to a school and maybe to an evening theater, ballet, or opera performance if we were lucky. The days and the states rolled by: Rhode Island, Nevada, Illinois, Mississippi, Alabama, Michigan, Minnesota, Florida, New Hampshire, North Carolina. Anyone might think they would have blurred in my mind, but no, each was singular in its art, and the state and cities remain distinct in my memory to this day. I remember the prison writing class I visited in New Hampshire and the wild imagination of the students at the North Carolina School of the Arts. I remember vividly how a young fifteen-year-old dancer took my breath away in Miami, and how the designs of the teenagers at YaYa in New Orleans did the same. I counted myself lucky to be a witness to the plethora of creativity in America at the end of the twentieth century.

Another distinct impression was that each and every program, from the Lyric Opera in Chicago to the Cowboy Poetry Festival in Elko, Nevada, never had enough funding to do all that it was capable of doing. For some arts organizations it was a pitiful struggle from year to year until they finally gave up and folded. Every time that happened a neighborhood lost a little bit of its light. My heart was beginning to ache for them. There was so much possibility, and so much myopia in the echelons of power. I didn't know how I could make the case for more funding for the arts in America at the same time that I needed to defend freedom of expression for those arts. I needed to think. It had been a nonstop whirlwind for nine months at the Endowment, and for over a year before that with *The Sisters Rosensweig*. A long-scheduled vacation with friends, river rafting in Idaho, was calling. In late June 1994 I took a break for two weeks.

CHAPTER NINE

Intermission

The Selway River in Idaho, one of our nation's most remote waterways, is located in the largest contiguous wilderness of the lower forty-eight states. Our friends Alan Rabinowitz and Howard Quigley, leading zoologists, and their wives, Salisa and Kathy, a geneticist and veterinarian, were accompanying Ed and me on this adventure. I had known Alan since the early 1980s when I traveled to visit him in Belize. He was tracking jaguars in that small but ecologically rich environment, and I had written a screenplay about a female zoologist studying jaguars. The Bronx Zoo suggested that I contact Alan as part of my research, and so I hopped a plane immediately and spent a week with him in the Cockscomb rain forest, hearing the telltale jaguar cough at night and searching for scat during the day. The screenplay was never produced, but our friendship grew. Ed and I later journeyed with Alan to visit the Lacandon Indians in the rain forest of southern Chiapas and climbed jungle heights to glimpse the rufous-necked hornbill in Thailand. He and Salisa trekked part of the Annapurna Himalayan range with us too. We had planned this river-rafting trip for over a year and were excited about hitting whitewater for the first time.

I felt a small bit of anxiety leaving the Endowment as the appropriations bill was about to go through Senator Byrd's committee, and Dick Woodruff looked at me as if I were about to jump ship when the sea might roil. But it was all new to me, and since the rafting trip could not be rescheduled, I blithely went ahead. Howard Quigley was president of the Hornocker Wildlife Institute, which studies tigers in Siberia, cougars in Montana, and many other species. My maiden name is

Quigley, but Howard and I, surprisingly, could find no common ancestry.

The Institute owned Running Creek Ranch, which was situated in the middle of the Bitterroot Wilderness, an hour's flying time in a small twin engine from the town of McCall. As we put down on a grassy oasis in the sea of trees, founder Maurice Hornocker welcomed us. He was visiting this remote outpost of the Institute to see how some of the studies were going. The river burbled near a low-slung log ranch house, and birds graced the branches all about. After a fine meal and hours of talk about endangered species and the reluctance of Congress to fully support efforts to save them, we fell into bed and I slept more soundly than I had in years. No phones, no roads, no people but us.

Deep in that forest in late June 1994, tension left me as quickly as water evaporates on a hot stove. I was back in the milieu I loved best, the great outdoors. I really was a nature girl at heart, and for twenty-five years birds had been my passion. It was a hobby that I could take with me anywhere in the world; all it required was a pair of binoculars, some curiosity, and a lot of patience. It had served me well on film locations and out-of-town tryouts. In fact I loved the outdoors so much that I never understood how I could have picked a profession that kept me inside and working mostly at night when I loved the day and the dawn. But the theater *had* made it possible to have my mornings free for birding walks with my trusty golden retriever, Cody. I missed those hikes in Washington. Now I was back in the wilderness and as happy as I could be.

The next morning we were picked up by a flotilla of four rafts and met our companions and travel guides for the trip downstream. The Selway was allowed only one group of rafters daily, so we virtually had the river to ourselves. I was content not to paddle and usually took up the docile position lying on the stern of the raft, gazing at the treetops and sky between bouts of whitewater, when I had to hold on for dear life. At one point I saw Ed and Howard totally submerged at the bow twelve feet in front of me as we raced down a waterfall, then paddling like hell to bring us up again. Those few minutes were exhilarating, like riding the roller coaster at Nantasket Beach in my youth. Most of the time we drifted downstream quietly. I mused in the rear, soaking in the sun and the oxygen and counting the Townsends and MacGillvray warblers, the osprey, harlequin ducks, and spotted sandpipers. Occasionally I'd catch sight of a golden eagle gliding in the circle of a thermal high above.

My musing took me over the trajectory of the past year—what had been accomplished and what was yet to be done. I felt good about the relationships I had developed. The Endowment was now in partnership with other federal agencies to expand the reach of the arts and institutionalize them in communities across America. We were reaching young people "at risk"—of dropping out of school, of getting into trouble, of taking drugs. As one educator told me, "All kids are at risk—just being a teenager puts you at risk anywhere in America." Some neighborhoods, however, were riskier than others, and those with strong arts and sports programs for young people were less likely to have problems. The president's focus on crime prevention had resulted in the creation of a commission, composed mainly of cabinet members, to deal with the issue from all angles. Attorney General Janet Reno proposed that I join the committee, and the secretary of the cabinet assured me that I was soon to be named. I don't know who dropped the ball, but regrettably, it took over three years for me to receive the final authority.

The president created a new domestic Peace Corps called AmeriCorps; I sat down early on with its director, Eli Segal, to figure out a way to involve the arts. The NEA eventually applied for AmeriCorps funds and was rewarded with a partnership for young writers in the cities of San Francisco, Washington, D.C., and the Bronx called WritersCorps. It was the only arts project given a grant by AmeriCorps that first year. Writers worked with young people, the elderly, the indigent, and the incarcerated to help them develop expressive skills through the written word. The program was an immense success almost immediately, and today these cities are filled with student poets and storytellers.

On another front, it pleased me that the NEA, arts service organizations, and lobbyists were working in solidarity to promote the value of arts in communities and to increase the Endowment's budget. I had spoken at the annual conferences of the National Association of Local Arts Agencies (NALAA) and the National Assembly of State Arts Agencies (NASAA), and to Dance America, the American Symphony Orchestra League, the coalition of nonprofit theaters called Theater Communications Group, the American Association of Museum Directors, Opera America, and a dozen other major organizations. We were all promoting the same message, and turf wars had radically diminished. Although collectively we may not have had the clout of the American Association of Retired Persons (AARP) or the National Rifle Association (NRA), I felt we were moving in the right direction.

At the Endowment my senior staff and I had successfully weathered a retreat at St. Michael's on the eastern shore of Maryland when an ice storm blew out the power on the second day, marooning us. It was all to the good: we enjoyed each other's company and came up with plans for some needed restructuring. The staff kindly did not criticize me, but it became clear that I was not managing things internally very well. Although I had hired some excellent people, I was not delegating efficiently and tended to create strategies outside the agency with a great deal of enthusiasm but little or no follow-up. We determined that I needed a chief of staff, and I appointed Sandy Crary on the spot. Sandy's easy way with people, his extensive knowledge of past events, and his organizational abilities were perfect for the job. In addition I promised to run my ideas by the staff before I acted on them and always to be accompanied by a staff member when I attended meetings outside the agency.

As an actress I had no intrinsic knowledge of how things get accomplished and was familiar only with the audition process, which is usually a one-on-one meeting with a director. I had been a producer of several films, but that process too involved pitching ideas to a potential source of money—a relatively uncomplicated yes-or-no situation. The day-to-day work of shooting a film was left to the "line" producer. Government was definitely a much slower and more complex process, with everything having to pass through committee after committee. I could not stand the amount of paperwork that shuffled across my desk and insisted on being read before I could sign off on it. The agency was small enough that I was responsible for virtually everything that went on, from grants to employee discontent to clutter in the halls. I applauded Vice President Gore's dictums for "reinventing government," one of which stated that an official should try to put all information on three typewritten pages at most. Hah! Not a chance in the corridors of bureaucracy! I was happy to assume responsibility for all that occurred in the agency and proudly subscribed to Harry Truman's motto, "The Buck Stops Here," but it was exhausting. Because I was female and signed off on every single award, my motto was "The Dough Starts Here."

On the home front I was feeling the strain of separation from friends and family. There is simply no substitute for being there. Ed never complained, but I knew he missed me as I did him. He was the one who got back to our empty house at night, which suffered from lack of attention too. I kept in touch with the boys and my girlfriends by phone but was often too tired to attend events on the weekends when I was home, and I usually had at least six hours of work to do anyway.

Geoff and Hope had arrived back from India and Sikkim before Christmas, but it was clear to us right away that something was wrong in their marriage. Slowly their pain unraveled. They were star-crossed lovers, caught in an irresolvable dilemma. Hope, who had the beautiful look of the Himalayan princess she was, had found that the ties to her birthland were stronger than she had imagined. As Geoff reported to us, the people loved her wherever she went, some of them bowing down, forehead to the ground, as she passed by. Her elder half-brother had assumed the throne and did not treat her kindly, but the people of Gangtok still loved her as their princess. She would never inherit the throne—her brother Palden was next in line—but it was unlikely that India, which had taken over Sikkim in the 1970s, would ever relinquish this important gateway to Tibet and China. Hope Leezum, who had spent most of her young life in the United States, attending boarding school when she was not with her mother in New York, could still remember her first years in the palace and the beauty of life in the highest mountains of the world. She felt the need to return. Geoff was in agony. As much as he loved her, he could not imagine life as a prince consort, nor as a chef of Sikkimese cuisine, which still used yak milk and dal as staples.

The two of them were so blue, as sad as sad can be. Geoff moved back in with us temporarily, while Hope went to her mother and stepfather's house in Brooklyn, making plans to return to Sikkim and start a mountain trekking business. Geoff was eager to begin his career. He was a wonderful cook; even as a little boy he would inhabit the kitchen with me, whipping up sauces with gusto. He fell in love with fishing at an early age and became a master fisherman in his late twenties, learning the secret places of trout and salmon, especially in the Rockies, where he wanted to live. Meanwhile he was working in a fine restaurant in New York and preparing for a trip to Italy to apprentice in one of the great Tuscan kitchens. I thought of all the changes that had occurred in his life in the last twelve months, and I ached for him and for myself that I had so little time to give to him or the others.

The other boys were doing well at their chosen professions. Jace was about to graduate from the American Film Institute, steadfast in his desire to be a filmmaker; Jon was excelling in neurobiology, working on his Ph.D. in the labs at Harvard. And Tony was going from one film to another as an editor in Hollywood, while at home he marveled in his son Evan as he learned to walk and talk. They were all doing well, grown and on their own. The river trip made me realize how quickly it all goes by: babies, childhood, college, and then . . . I always loved the speech in Thornton Wilder's *Our Town* by Emily, who has died in her twenties and, looking back at the living, says:

> It goes so fast. We don't have time to look at one another. . . . Good-by, Good-by, world. . . . Good-by to clocks ticking . . . and Mama's sunflowers. And food and coffee. And new-ironed dresses and hot baths . . . and sleeping and waking up. Oh, earth, you're too wonderful for anybody to realize you.

Ed and I did not take life's brevity for granted, and we were making the most of these sylvan days in Idaho together. We were with good friends for ten days and far away from civilization where no one from our offices could contact us. In the evenings the four rafts would pull ashore on little sand spits and we would erect our tents. A quick plunge in the icy water would be our bath for the day, and drinks by the fireside and roasted meats over the grill would warm us in the cool night air. If the bugs weren't too bad, Ed and I slept out under the stars and listened to the shuffling of nocturnal creatures making the rounds of the campsite. The next morning, after a leisurely breakfast, we'd gather our gear together and move on downstream. The trout were huge and plentiful in the deep pools. Geoff had promised to teach me fly-fishing one day; I knew I would love it. Now I was content to spot birds, revel in the glory of the river, and drift.

Of all we had accomplished at the agency in my first year I was perhaps proudest of the first national conference on the arts ever held by the federal government. Olive Mosier, Rosemary Cribben, and Cherie Simon managed to pull it off in record time, and on April 14, 1994, we had convened "ART 21: Art Reaches into the 21st Century." More than one thousand people attended from all over the United States. We gave modest financial help to some of those who could not afford the trip, and the conference was funded with the generous help of foundations and private donors. I wanted the event to be held in a city that supported its arts well and also had the wherewithal to contribute to a conference like ours on short notice. Chicago was the natural choice. Not only was it a mecca for the arts and a leading American city architecturally, but it was also the home and district of our congressional champion Sidney Yates. In addition, Mayor Richard Daley and his wife Maggie vigorously promoted the arts and arts education. Maggie had begun an arts program for young people in the summer. It was so successful that some of the art they created was now sold in a room called Gallery 37 in a historic city building. Brightly painted chairs with designs of moons and stars or basketball players like Michael Jordan adorned the space, while paintings and fabrics for sale covered the walls.

We divided the conference into four themes: "The Artist in Society," "The Arts and Technology," "Expanding Resources for the Arts," and "Lifelong Learning Through the Arts." Olive and I had chosen the topics ourselves, knowing that there was little time to go through committee to reach consensus. They were themes I felt needed airing, and my travels in the first few months on the job had introduced me to a number of people who could make significant contributions to these subjects. The staff at the Endowment made additional suggestions, and all in all I think we ended up with a diverse and interesting group of panelists. The four main speakers, who were each asked to address one of the themes, were people I contacted personally.

This was a natural for President Bill Clinton, I thought. When John F. Kennedy gave his memorable tribute to Robert Frost in October 1963, just a few short weeks before he died himself, his words were some of the most potent a president had ever given on the arts. President Clinton declined the invitation to be a speaker at the conference, sending instead a brief video. His comments were not inspired but nonetheless welcome at this parched time for artists:

> The work you do over the next few days is extremely important. Your deliberations will begin an ongoing dialogue about the role of the arts in the twenty-first century. . . . I don't view the arts as an isolated cause. The arts are fundamental to our history and our culture. And in this administration support of the arts is part of a broader social agenda that speaks to our very essence as Americans. . . . That's why exposure to the arts must be a part of every child's schooling. . . . As part of our "Goals 2000" legislation the arts will become a core subject in the school curriculum, along with English, math, science, history, civics, geography, and foreign language. . . . I assure you of the ongoing commitment and support of this administration.

The president's pledge to the NEA was a great psychological boost to the opening of our conference, especially since he had already eliminated over one hundred government programs because of his commitment to reducing the deficit. The vice president was my second choice to keynote, but although he returned my call promptly, Al Gore also declined. I wondered whether the boys in the back room of the White House felt we were still too much of a political hot potato to touch at this time, or whether there were too many other important things to do. I decided to continue my pursuit of high officials and called up HUD Secretary Henry Cisneros, after sending a written invitation a week earlier. He claimed never to have received my invitation and told me that, regrettably, he had a conflict. Days passed; we were getting down to the wire and needed to be able to announce our speaker. Just as I was about to pick up the phone and ask yet another VIP, Cisneros called back and said somewhat breathlessly, "Do you still want me?" "You bet!" I almost shouted into the receiver.

He was a galvanizing speaker:

I came to this job because I believe our country is in deep trouble. . . . Fifteen months later I am absolutely certain. . . . We have a big job to do. And it is a job of the spirit, it's a job of tolerance, it's a job of understanding. . . . It requires real communications. And that's where the work you do comes in. . . . We can communicate the things that bring us together—our common sense of humanity. We can't afford to lose another generation of our young people. I'll tell you, if I sit in one more meeting where I hear people say—intelligent, mature, thoughtful, educated people—say, "Well, why don't we concentrate on the four-year-olds 'cause we've already lost the fifteen- and sixteen-year-olds." My friends, no society can afford to decide it has lost its fifteen-year-olds!

Cisneros had been a remarkable mayor of the city of San Antonio. He was on the road to being a remarkable leader of HUD before he was brought down by zealous conservatives seeking to expose the underbelly of his personal life. In a short time he was embroiled in a battle over the legality of his confirmation statements to Congress. His extramarital affair, now ended, cost him his job and a lot of his income. That he tried to hide the fact that he was sending money, for the noblest of reasons, to his former paramour was enough for those who wished to bring him down. But at ART 21, on that spring day in Chicago, this handsome, thoughtful man was at his best, and the arts crowd loved him.

When Ernest Boyer took the podium the following morning, the huge ballroom hushed immediately. Boyer was a major educator and in 1994 was president of the Carnegie Foundation. He was in demand constantly as a speaker but had made a special effort to be with us because he felt so strongly about the arts. He continued Cisneros's theme of the importance of art for all people and eloquently talked about it as one of our oldest forms of language:

In most respects, the human species is far less equipped than other creatures on the planet: we are no match for the lion in strength; we're outstripped by the ostrich in speed; we can't outswim the dolphin; we see less acutely than the hawk. And yet, as humans, we excel in the exquisite use of symbols which empowers us to outdistance all other forms of life in what we see, and feel, and know.

For our arts and technology theme I asked Richard Loveless to be our speaker. Loveless was the director of the Institute for Studies in the Arts at Arizona State University. I had met Richard several years before in Oklahoma, where he told me of the many research environments in the arts they were conducting at the university, including interactive media and human performance, visualization, sound and text composition, telecommunications, and interdisciplinary projects. This was so new in 1994 that it was difficult for many at the conference to grasp the possibilities. But technology in the service of art, particularly as a tool for compiling information and promoting an organization, was becoming a reality. CD-ROMs were looked on as a boon for museums in particular. The creative possibilities, the storytelling possibilities, were still unrealized for all but a handful of artists, but there was no doubt in my mind that as soon as the informational cycle of the new technologies was exhausted, we would move directly into creative art, just as the radio and television industries had done in decades past, moving from all-news broadcasts to comedy and drama as well. Loveless gave us a good introduction to the subject.

As powerful as the men were, it was our first speaker, Thulani Davis, who brought the house down. A playwright and librettist, Davis had a storyteller's gift for enthralling her listeners:

We live now in a society that denigrates art and those who make it, a society that places a premium on the artist's ability to make money, not on her relationship to the society. . . . We live in a society with more capacity to provide communication between human beings than at any time before, and yet we have an ever-narrowing access to the varieties of expression. We live in a world where the places you might find artists are closing down. . . . Art does not happen to society as a whole or all at once. Art happens one mind to one mind. One person hearing or reading, at a time, even if we all sit in the arena together. In a society where children have no books in the school library or classrooms, such as schools in my neighborhood ten years ago, where children do not put the awkward paintings of home and trees and family in the schoolroom windows, or go to museums, or see Shakespeare, or hear the sweet music of all kinds of people they will never know, chaos should be expected. . . . We study our despairing, endangered, and unschooled youth, noting the lack of structures for socialization and the teaching of ethics, self-esteem and crisis management, and yet we refuse them the tools of art. Tools which teach self-discipline and wonder, which encourage liberty of the spirit and the right to self-definition. Let's give them art as at least one tool with which to challenge their exile from us. . . .

I think of the artist as the person who is asked to express the inexpressible, what cannot be expressed. I say the artist is asked to do this because it was my first experience of artists that he or she was often the person in my community who was called upon at the awkward moment before an important ritual to find the words for a union, a birth, or separation from life. The poet was asked to find the poem to say what cannot be said about life's meaning. . . . Because our families have so little connection left to the spiritual life our ancestors knew, so little connection to the comforts of ritual in times of turmoil and during rites of passage, we need more than ever those living people who can express what cannot be expressed. The Vietnam Memorial first woke people up to this craving for art that communicates one mind to one mind and invites our response to despair and praise, confusion and celebration.

Thulani went on to talk about the erosion of serious art in our society and the rise of selling as the be-all and end-all. She discussed the closing of small publishing houses and literary presses: the ripple effect doomed in turn the corner bookstore and small journals. And still she had hope because she saw art everywhere, and art being produced, despite the odds, by all kinds of people.

I have never feared for art. Like seeds in a concrete sidewalk, art will find a way to flower. In New York those small seeds sometimes grow to be substantial trees clinging to the small beds of soil that nurture them and breaking the bonds of stone that contain them. Art is like that—always finding a way to survive. But in a healthy culture nourishment helps create unimagined beauty and diversity and can sustain vision on a grand scale. After all, it is only government or religion that has the wherewithal to create huge monoliths like pyramids, cathedrals, or aqueducts. The United States could use more of that. And the United States could have a better understanding of the need to protect the vast range of art forms that exist, past and present. Even the seeds that sprout in New York's concrete are the hardiest of species, not the vulnerable or exotic species that need more care and cultivation.

Our ART 21 speakers were the highlights of the morning breakfasts and the afternoon lunches. In between we held four concurrent panel discussions on an aspect of one of the themes. Some of them were provocative, such as the panel called "Facing Society's Censure," which explored censorship, prejudice, and excoriation. I had selected artists who had experienced society's censure in one way or another.

Luis Jimenez hailed from New Mexico and was a well-known visual artist. His large public sculptures in colored fiberglass sometimes caused problems for people. After his "Vaquero" went up outside the American Art Museum in Washington, a mile from the Capitol Building, to great fanfare and with NEA support, it stood contentedly in place for thirteen years. Then a local politician running for office demanded that the statue be removed, claiming that the cowboy with the gun in his hand promoted violence. Jimenez pointed out that there were statues of George Washington, Robert E. Lee, and Sam Houston in town that were also armed, and that perhaps the real issue was that the gun was in the hands of a Mexican. The rearing horse with the vaquero and his gun was finally moved to another site behind the museum, and the furor died down.

Luis Jimenez had learned through the years to listen to the voices of a community before he created his sculpture. He found that working with a city on his public art was ultimately far more satisfying than trying to push something on them. After all, they were going to be the caretakers of his artwork, and he wanted it to be welcome where it stood. He did not feel that partnership with a community compromised his work in the least.

Public art has historically been problematic for citizens who must live with a piece daily, and contemporary work is usually the most contentious. But mores change with the times. The nineteenth and early twentieth centuries did not share our current distaste for nudity in public art, for example. Washington, D.C., is full of statues of armed soldiers and of nude and semiclothed men and women representing myth or metaphor from bygone days. Outside the Department of Justice sit colossal figures in various states of dishabille, holding scales or babes to their breast, and looking immensely important. One of my favorite public sculptures in Washington is on Pennsylvania Avenue just down the hill from the Capitol Building, in full view of all who pass by. It is a larger-than-life piece of Civil War General George Meade. He is circled by nude men and women who cling to his uniform and to each other as if a harsh wind might blow them all away. The metaphor is totally lost on us today. Imagine if we had erected a similar statue of General Norman Schwarzkopf after the Gulf War, with nubile, topless gals clutching at his military medals in broad daylight in the nation's capital. Not a chance. What was acceptable, even welcomed, a hundred years ago would not pass muster in today's climate.

Public art, like the architecture of buildings that seem so bold initially, eventually finds acceptance with the next generation, who grow up with the work in their city. In 1967 the very first grant that the NEA awarded for public art was to Alexander Calder to create a sculpture for the city of Grand Rapids, Michigan. "La Grand Vitesse" incorporated forty tons of steel, was painted a vivid red, and rose from the central plaza of the city forty feet into the air. There were many who protested the stabile, calling it a monstrosity dominating their once quiet cityscape. When I visited more than twenty-five years later the Calder had become as integral to the town as the moniker "the Big Apple" is to New York. "La Grand Vitesse" was the logo on stationery from City Hall, decorated the side of every garbage truck, and was the signatory spot for people to meet. I spoke in front of the giant piece during the annual Calder Festival to a crowd that numbered in the tens of thousands. Men cradled beer cans and babies in the crooks of their bare arms on that hot summer afternoon; when I asked whether they loved their Calder, they hooted their assent. Like many sculptures and buildings nationwide, Alexander Calder's remarkable work for the citizens of Grand Rapids illustrates that today's controversy often becomes tomorrow's classic.

Others on the panel for "Facing Society's Censure" were Brian Freeman, founder of the performance group Pomo Afro Homo, which explores race and homosexuality, and Nedra Darling, a Native American filmmaker who had encountered prejudice and difficulty getting her work funded. Freeman said that his biggest challenge was the misperception or anticipation of what the work was really about. People's fears when it is announced that a black gay group will perform far outweigh the reality of the work, which is often taken out of context. Appearances by Pomo Afro Homo had sparked near riots in Alaska and on the campus of Morehouse College, a black university for men. He added that his grandmother made it through the performance.

Nedra Darling made the public television film *Surviving Columbus,* which celebrates the indigenous peoples of North America, most particularly the Pueblo Indians. She completed the on-camera interviews and handed the film over to editors at PBS only to discover later that they replaced the Pueblos with 156 images of Plains Indians because they thought the Pueblos did not look "Indian" enough. She finally was able to restore the film to reflect accurately the Pueblo experience and ended up as a frequent consultant to the station on Native American issues. It has not been any easier for her to get work, however, despite the numerous awards that *Surviving Columbus* has won.

I had experienced a small degree of censure in my work on stage. James Earl Jones and I were the first interracial couple to lie on a bed together in a play. We had clothes on and were talking romantically when the scene closed with a kiss. *The Great White Hope,* coming as it did during the height of the black power movement and on the heels of the civil rights marches in the 1960s, was a volatile piece of Broadway theater. I received hate mail regularly and two death threats from October 1968 to October 1969. It was unnerving, but I knew that the white bigots who sent it were way off in their thinking. The stage manager screened my mail after a while, and although I was careful about the path I took home at night, I thought no more of it.

For most artists criticism hurts; even when it comes from those you disdain it is like a slap in the face. At first you don't understand it; then you get hurt and angry. Sometimes that hurt lives with you for years, because it is deeper than you as an artist: it is an indictment of the society we live in—the prejudice, the hate, and the violence. Artists would like to believe that they will always be understood, and perhaps loved for what they do, but that is rarely the case. Most of us stay in the game because we have to do what we do despite anything we may encounter. Luis Jimenez, Brian Freeman, and Nedra Darling represent just three of thousands upon thousands of dedicated artists in America.

The panel called "The Working Artist" illustrated just how very difficult it is to make a living as an artist in America. Even when you get a job or sell a painting or a book, the income is unpredictable and health insurance and pensions are difficult to obtain. There is still a deeply ingrained suspicion of artists, not only in the United States but also in many parts of the world. I remember visiting Ireland once with a friend of mine who was also an actress. We tried to rent a car at Shannon Airport only to be told, "Sorry, we don't rent to theatricals." "How about secretaries?" we replied, knowing that most of our supplemental income came from moonlighting in clerical positions between jobs. Yes, that was fine, said the clerk, and we were off on our tour of Ireland. Car rental is one thing, but health insurance, or any kind of insurance for that matter, is quite another, and there is real but subtle discrimination against artists in general.

Lisa Thorson was disabled when she was in her early twenties by doing a flip onstage that left her a paraplegic. Her singing voice was undiminished in its beauty, however, and she built a successful career for herself in the world of jazz, where a wheelchair mattered little as long as she could negotiate the usually inaccessible terrain of theaters and nightclubs. Still, Lisa noted, the average annual income for jazz and classical musicians is $15,000. There is a classic irony, she added, in the fact that people seem to value great art of the past yet fail to value artists working in their communities today.

The panelist Dale Chihuly, a world-renowned glass artist, challenged artists to use their creativity in creative ways to make money. He said that visual artists, for example, have trained eyes and specific talents that museums, collectors, and corporations value. Chihuly parlayed his own significant talents and a $2,000 grant he received in the 1970s to found the Pilchuk Glass Center outside of Seattle. The area went on to spawn more glass factories than anywhere in the world outside of Venice, Italy. As major museums worldwide began to exhibit his work, glass art, long seen as a craft, was reclassified as high art.

Twelve additional panels over the course of our three days in Chicago focused on education, community activism, technology, and funding the arts. In between sessions we were treated to performances by local dancers, singers, and musicians, and Mayor Richard Daley and Maggie Daley hosted all one thousand of us at a gala dinner one evening on the Navy Pier. The conference closed with rousing gospel hymns, bringing us all to our feet, swaying and clapping our hands. As we left Chicago sentiment ran high with hope and goodwill.

My NEA colleagues and I returned to the agency charged with a new sense of mission and a long agenda of issues to tackle. We had learned that the Endowment should take the lead in helping artists traverse the new technologies; that we should stress arts education to those within government and outside of it; that we should explore new resources for funding the arts in America; and most especially that we should champion the individual artists and help create viable structures to assist them.

We wasted no time. Within weeks Scott Sanders had a plan to bring together leaders in the arts and in education to find ways to implement "Goals 2000" so that the arts were part of the core curriculum in schools everywhere.

When I first arrived at the Endowment it was clear to me that we had to be "wired" as soon as possible. In 1993 most government agencies were behind the private sector in computer technology. At the NEA we all had PCs, but we had no e-mail or shared databases and files. Finding out simple facts, such as how many performing arts organizations reached communities other than their own through touring, was painstakingly tracked manually by two staffers dubbed "geography detectives." The information they gave us was extremely important to members of Congress, who wanted to know where the money awarded in their state ended up. Sometimes it was days or even weeks before we could tell them. In the future I wanted us to be able to call it up on the computer screen at the touch of a key. That future, although begun during my tenure, was regrettably not realized until a year after I left office. The wheels of government grind very slowly indeed.

There was a lot to be done, but the future looked bright despite the one or two controversies that had surfaced. I thought Congress would vote an increase in our appropriations as the bills emerged from the House and Senate committees in those summer days of 1994 while I drifted blithely downstream.

Our idyll on the river was coming to an end. We had passed only two signs of civilization in the pristine wilderness. The first was the forest ranger's home, and the second was a rustic resort for fishermen, glimpsed through the trees as we glided by on the last day. Yet even in this remote area there were declining species of birds and animals. Howard Quigley's work with the Hornocker Institute was all about protecting the habitat for these species for the future. Alan Rabinowitz's work with the Wildlife Conservation Society on the great cats of the world was also concerned with preserving habitat and convincing governments that it was in the long-term interest of society to do so. My work for the National Endowment for the Arts involved saving species of another kind, to be sure, and preserving habitat for artists, but I perceived it as no less important to the next generation of homo sapiens.

Despite worry over the future of our causes, we felt good—burnished by the sun and blissfully satiated with the heady effects of the great outdoors. We said good-bye to our guides, climbed into the vans that would drive us the last twenty-five miles out of the forest, and promised, of course, to return to that River of No Return someday. The vehicles bounced along the dirt road and emerged within an hour onto a paved two-lane highway, still isolated on the edge of the park. Up the road a small sign read "Lowell, Idaho, population 23," and just beyond it a lone general store was bathed in the late afternoon light. As I stepped from the van, a woman hurried toward me from the store. "Are you Jane Alexander?" she said. "Call your office immediately!" Intermission over.

CHAPTER TEN

Act II

Senator Byrd was agitating, and the senior staff at the NEA was frantic. Where was the chairman? Get her off the river! I was grateful that Dick, Noel, and Stephanie decided *not* to send in the National Guard. They seriously considered it, helicopters and all. Outside the Lowell, Idaho, general store was one isolated pay phone; I tied it up for the next fifteen minutes and got the scoop. The Appropriations Committee chairman, Senator Robert C. Byrd, had sent a bill out of his committee that cut the NEA's overall budget by 5 percent, specifically targeting the Theater, Visual Arts, and Presenting and Commissioning programs. This was a serious body blow, and all the more so since it came from a leading Democrat. Et tu, Brute?

Byrd apparently thought he was taking care of the problem of con-troversial art this way, since most of it emerged from grants awarded in those three programs. I'd known he was conservative in his thinking, but I had no idea he was in league with Jesse Helms.

Dick thought we had some time, at least until the Fourth of July recess was over on the eleventh or twelfth. He suggested that I marshal my forces by contacting other leading senators immediately before they left town. For the next three days, as Ed and I and our friends made our way from Missoula, Montana, to Glacier National Park, I made calls from gas stations, local parks, and restaurant restrooms to Senators Kennedy, Simpson, Boren, Kassebaum, Hatch, Durenberger, Inouye, and Metzenbaum. Of course I called Byrd too, for about the fifth time in a month. Byrd played a game of cold shoulder if he didn't like what you were doing. He simply was always "out" when you called and never got back to you. Because he was such a powerful senator, chairing the most important committee, I had been trying to set up a meeting with him for a long time. At least this time I succeeded with his aide in getting an appointment, but it was *after* the horse had left the barn. That was the way the man operated. He would do something that showed everyone how powerful he was, leaving you to grovel in his path. Our meeting was set for July 12, when Congress reconvened.

Byrd was particularly disgusted by the Walker Art Center grant to the performance artist Ron Athey. He and Senator Don Nickles of Oklahoma, the ranking minority member of the Interior appropriations subcommittee, had written me on June 17 expressing their concern about the Athey "bloodletting" performance. I had answered them immediately and included the facts about the museum and the performance. I told them that I supported the Walker Art Center in its distribution of our $104,500 grant to help finance a season of more than one hundred performing arts events. I did not need to support the single Athey performance to be supportive of the Walker. I had also sent a letter to every member of Congress explaining the facts.

When I managed to reach the other senators by phone from road stops in Montana, they were most helpful. I explained my thinking to each of them. Durenberger, a Republican from Minnesota, knew how prestigious the Walker was and also knew that the Walker's performing arts events were funded by the state arts council as well as the federal government. But he complained that organizations like the Walker didn't seem to know how hard controversies like these made it for members of Congress, and that they were not apologetic. I replied that Kathy Halbreich, director of the Walker Art Center, had seemed most apologetic for all the trouble the event caused the Endowment. I put the two in touch, and their telephone conversation seemed to ease the senator's concerns. Paul Wellstone, the other senator from Minnesota, a former hippie, and arguably the most liberal of all the Democrats, said he also would speak up for the Walker as one of the finest institutions in Minneapolis, even though he found the description of the performance very troubling. I didn't disagree with him, but we both knew it was a principle we were upholding, not a single event. Metzenbaum told me that in order to make my case fully I needed to reach Mark Hatfield of Oregon and Claiborne Pell of Rhode Island, thoughtful and influential men who were not the liberals that he, Wellstone, and Kennedy were. Ted Kennedy, as always, never asked questions about the art but renewed his commitment to me by being as helpful as possible. He suggested I come up to the Hill and speak to all of the senators at a luncheon. We were never able to organize it because of the senators' many conflicting schedules, but I appreciated his efforts. Nancy Kassebaum also jumped right in with support, even though I knew she had to be appalled at the art in question. She told me that later in the summer, when the House and the Senate were trying to balance their appropriations, she and other senators would try to hold off any cuts the House committee might try to make in the NEA budget. Her faith in my judgment touched me, and I vowed not to let these fine people down.

Byrd and Helms were talking, I knew, but what I was beginning to understand when I spoke with David Boren was just how involved his colleague, the junior senator from Oklahoma, was in the 5 percent cut to the NEA budget. Don Nickles and I had already had a falling out in his office six weeks earlier. He was a handsome, engaging young senator, shiny as a river stone and about as hard. He told me in the presence of some Oklahoma arts advocates that his problem with the NEA was that we had just given grants again to Holly Hughes and Tim Miller, two of the infamous NEA Four, and now to Ron Athey. It didn't seem to matter to him that the peer panel had ranked Hughes and Miller highly or that Athey's grant was not a direct grant to him but to a museum. Nickles was clearly homophobic. He stood in his white shirt-sleeves that warm May afternoon, circled the center of the room playing to his small audience, and just when I thought he would end his diatribe by blurting out "those homosexuals," he stopped himself short, leaned over, and grabbed his jacket, as if to make a swift exit. I said I saw no reason to turn down their grants and have the taxpayers of America back in court again at a cost of $250,000 or more. Nickles was irritated with me, but I was discouraged that a U.S. senator could behave in this way, flouting First Amendment rights with such a cavalier lack of concern. I became convinced that he was strategizing with Helms and Byrd about how to control the agency, if not bring it down altogether. Fortunately Oklahoma had formidable arts advocates in Betty Price, head of the state arts council, and Mary Frates, founder of the Arts Institute, and their senator was not going to get away with it. David Boren told me that Nickles was a rising Republican star who was positioning himself to be head of the party one day and that he wanted to be the next Dan Quayle. He acted like it.

The White House was getting nervous. The top brass closest to the president felt that I should not be defending the Walker Art Center. Even Melanne suggested that maybe I should find *something* to disavow. I stubbornly refused. No. Period. We had done nothing wrong, nor had the Walker, which fulfilled the needs of its community *at large*. If I had been at the political game a bit longer, perhaps I would have understood that putting the agency in jeopardy was putting my boss, the president, in jeopardy, but I didn't catch on. There was no one I held in higher regard than Melanne, and I certainly listened carefully to her advice, but I thought we could win this one on legal and perhaps moral grounds. Whether she trusted my thinking or simply took a wait-and-see attitude I never knew, but she did not bring it up again.

Congress was in recess, and I was still on vacation, if not in mind then in body. The six of us rode the "Going-to-the-Sun" highway up and up to Logan Pass high in Glacier National Park. Forty years before my father and mother had taken the family here, and we had camped out at Two Medicine Lake for over a week. I remembered the bite of the glacial water as we kids waded in, screaming with exhilaration when we got just waist-deep. In those days the glacier itself reached all the way to the information center, and we had a rip-roaring snowball fight at its perimeter. Now we walked almost a mile to touch the ice. Was this the result of global warming, I wondered? Mountain goats licked salt from the pavement, a muledeer browsed near the center, and masses of big mammals called human beings drove us to seek quieter venues.

My mind was on other things even as I birded the trails in the early mornings. Two days later we quit Montana and returned to Idaho, traversing the rolling clover fields and hillsides covered with dusky wheat in the late afternoon light. Alan, who had spent much of his zoologist's life negotiating with political entities for wildlife protection, told me that I must play Byrd carefully, that he was not going to change his position; I would have to negotiate with him, not antagonize him. We flew from Pullman, Washington, to Lewiston, Idaho, to Boise, to Denver, to LaGuardia Airport in New York, and on July 5 I was back in my D.C. office ready for combat.

Ron Athey's performance at the Walker had hit the media with full force. There were pro and con editorials from many of the major papers. On radio Rush Limbaugh was predictably slamming the NEA again, but fortunately we were spared TV coverage because there were no pictures and no video of the performance—at least none that had surfaced yet.

Jesse Helms, as usual, had been distressed about a number of grants, but particularly Athey's presentation, which had the added fillip of bodily mutilation to arouse his indignation. The senator and I had visited together in his office earlier in the year, and we had corresponded a number of times. I was careful never to criticize him publicly, and our dealings were always cordial. I had even invited Helms to speak to our Council meeting in February 1994. He had initially accepted with alacrity but then sent regrets the day before the actual meeting. This was one of those situations where we won either way, and Helms must have known it. If he had shown up in alien territory he could have been subjected to ridicule through the questions asked by Council members. If he did not show up, the NEA maintained its integrity and Helms looked like the scaredy-cat. We did not capitalize on his excuses, but the newspapers had taken note of his absence anyway.

I reread our correspondence of the past month, certain now that Helms had shared it with Byrd and his Republican colleagues. I wanted to be sure that the NEA's position, as stated in my response, was sound. His letter to me of June 9, 1994, defines pretty clearly our relationship and his thinking. I quote it, and my subsequent response, in toto to give the flavor of the congressional correspondence that crossed my desk with some frequency. Helms's letters were more detailed and florid than most.

Dear Madam Chairman:

I genuinely appreciate your kind comments that have appeared in a number of publications. I have done my best to reciprocate during several interviews—in fact, one newspaper down my way suggested that I have a "crush" on Jane Alexander. (I have pleaded nolo contendere.)

You and I have agreed to be candid with each other. In that vein, I feel obliged to say that I am greatly disappointed in the NEA's recent decision to award—again—taxpayer funds to groups and individuals widely known for their prurient, offensive, and/or absurd "art"—including:

1. *Tim Miller,* who has heretofore used NEA funds to disrobe and sexually stimulate himself on stage (and among the audience) during his so-called "performance art" presentation titled "My Queer Body";
2. *Holly Hughes,* whose previous awards of taxpayer funds were devoted to her writing and performing in such sewer "performances" as the "Well of Horniness";
3. *Karen Finley,* whose past grants were used to deliver anti-religious and radical feminist harangues on stage while nude and covered in chocolate syrup;

(Of course, you are aware that Hughes, Finley, and Miller sued the Endowment for denying them the chance to raid the federal treasury in 1990.)

4. *Kitchen Theatre* (THE KITCHEN-SIC), which had previously used taxpayers' money to pay Annie Sprinkle to invite the audience to examine the inside of her genitalia with a flashlight.
5. *Frameline,* which has used taxpayer funds to reorganize and run the pornographic offerings of the Gay and Lesbian Film Festival in San Francisco each year;
6. *Marlon Riggs,* who used taxpayer funds from both the NEA and Public Broadcasting to produce the pornographic, profanity-filled, and pro-homosexual documentary titled "Tongues Untied" (which even many PBS stations refused to air because of its content);
7. *Walker Art Center* in Minneapolis, where Karen Finley first came to national attention and where Ron Athey recently sliced designs into the flesh of another man's back, soaked the blood up with

paper towels, and then sent the blood-soaked towels winging over his audiences' heads—all with the help of taxpayer funds (News reports speculated that the blood from the man might have been HIV-positive);

8. *Franklin Furnace Archive* in New York, where Karen Finley, Holly Hughes, Tim Miller, and numerous others have been given yet another taxpayer-subsidized venue to shock the public with their so-called "performance art";

9. *Highways Inc.,* in Santa Monica, another taxpayer-subsidized venue where Tim Miller develops his homosexual "shock" material and serves on the Board of Directors;

10. *Centro Cultural de la Raza,* which was responsible for using NEA grants to give away tax dollars to illegal aliens on the U.S./Mexican border last year.

Madam Chairman, inasmuch as the NEA has *again* approved *all* of these groups and individuals to receive NEA funds, I believe the taxpayer is entitled to know what these grant recipients propose to do for the taxpayers in exchange for NEA grants this time around. The same goes for three other grant recipients—how do these grantees propose to merit the taxpayers' money they will receive from the National Endowment for the Arts:

1. *Brava! For Women in the Arts,* which has said it will use taxpayer funds to support "an after-school writing and performance program designed for gay and lesbian teens of African, Asian, and Latino descent"—will there be a tax-paid advocacy of sodomy?

2. *Caveh Zahedi,* who has said the tax dollars will be used to support a "seriocomic narrative film meditating on the vagaries of sexual obsession." (Please translate that "job description" for me.)

3. *Visual AIDS for the Arts,* which proposes to use its taxpayer grant to support "a series of artists' projects, public programs, and services to increase public awareness about AIDS and its impact on the art world." Here again, I will be grateful for further explanation of what all of that means.

I will appreciate the NEA's providing me with the applications, supporting documentation, award letters, and whatever other documentation was considered pertinent to the aforementioned awardees, as well as to the attached list of groups, individuals, grant numbers, awards, and contracts.

It is essential that I be provided with a detailed response to the enclosed request for information relating to the NEA's three-year, $3.2 million "consulting contract" with Melanie Beene—from which she has apparently paid herself almost $350,000 while spending almost $700,000 on "travel and per diem."

As you know, the Endowment's Chair is not bound by the decisions of the arts panels, nor those of the National Council for the Arts, to fund any particular application. In that regard I hope you will review the propriety of requiring the American taxpayers to provide funds—as opposed to voluntary private funding—for these, and perhaps other, recent beneficiaries of NEA grants—whose established track records have offended or insulted the vast majority of taxpayers required by law to foot the bill.

I write in good faith as a Senator who feels a responsibility to know how the taxpayers' money is being spent. I am confident that you will respond in good faith with frank and candid answers to my questions.

Sincerely,
Jesse Helms

It took us some time to amass the documentation he requested, and so I had stalled a week in my reply. On June 16 the *Washington Times* beat me to the punch by publishing excerpts from Helms's letter to me; the article was headlined: "Helms Denounces NEA's Awards, Noncooperation." Leaking correspondence was a common tactic with our critics in Congress I had discovered—common and underhanded. I was in California as part of the fifty-state tour but dictated a response to the senator the next day:

Dear Senator Helms:
    I know we share common ground with regard to the arts as a pos-

itive element in society. After all, what would the world be without music, dance, drama, painting, literature, and architecture? I have reflected that understanding between us in interviews and when people ask me about you. It pleases me that we continue to communicate with one another, and we are working to compile the material you requested as soon as possible.

Please keep in mind that the taxpayer in the United States is as diverse as the art that is created by the many kinds of people who make up this great country of ours; and that we at the Endowment, like other government agencies, do not discriminate on the basis of race, creed, ethnicity, gender, or sexual orientation.

I would be happy to discuss these questions further if you so wish.

Sincerely,

Jane Alexander

Not only was discrimination illegal, but it annoyed me that Helms referred so consistently to "the taxpayer" when in fact every working citizen in the United States was "the taxpayer," and that included an estimated 10 percent who were homosexual.

The senator wrote me again on June 27, saying that he:

was not certain that I fully understand what was being said to me when the June 17 letter bearing your signature was composed. I hasten to assure that I don't want to do or say anything to offend you personally, but I do hope that the June 17 letter was written by staff and not you. . . . The U.S. taxpayer(s) are indeed "diverse," but I am confident that only a minute percentage of them are sufficiently *per*verse to approve the use of their taxes to fund such "art" and such "artists." . . . There may, as some explain, be "only a few of them," but it takes only one cockroach to spoil a pot of soup, whether it falls into it accidentally or is gratuitously put there by someone who ought to know better.

The "cockroach" bit was too good, and in some perverse way I was beginning to enjoy this correspondence. I replied that sometimes a cockroach could spoil the soup but bring pleasant surprises in other ways, as when a French restaurant gave my husband and me a free meal after we found a cockroach in my onion soup. The full-course free dinner was worth that one little cockroach. That seemed to stop the senator for a while.

NEA staff members, under the supervision of Karen Christensen and Dick Woodruff, compiled all the documentation, which involved pulling old files and panel tapes, interim reports, and even original applications. Karen checked that everything had been handled legally and was in good order, and Dick composed the response to Helms's inquiries, which we mailed in early July 1994:

PART 1

Tim Miller: The Endowment's $9,375 grant to Tim Miller was based on the exceptional ranking of his application by the citizen review panel. The panel, which included the artistic director of the Yale Repertory Theatre and head of the Yale Drama School, the director of the New England Puppetry and Family Theater, as well as other artists and a layperson, ranked Tim Miller number twelve among seventy-one applications for funding. Mr. Miller's application was subsequently recommended unanimously by the National Council on the Arts, all of whom, as you know, were appointed by either Presidents Reagan or Bush. While Mr. Miller's performances occasionally include nudity—a component of art that dates back centuries—at *no time* has he ever "sexually stimulated" himself (nor anything remotely similar) during a performance.

Holly Hughes: As with Tim Miller, Holly Hughes was recently awarded a $9,375 grant from the Endowment, her application being ranked number one in the same category. I would take issue with your characterization of her work as "sewer performances." As evidenced by her panel ranking and her critical reviews from performances across the nation, Ms. Hughes's work, albeit provocative at times, is well respected by critics and audiences alike.

Karen Finley: Karen Finley has not received a grant from this agency since her application was rejected in 1990. As a result of a court ruling that found that the Endowment used improper procedures in rejecting that application, she was awarded an out-of-court settlement in 1993.

Kitchen Theatre: The Kitchen, whose grant in 1993 was $50,000, had its funding reduced to $10,000 for the current fiscal year. While Annie Sprinkle, whose work in my estimation holds no artistic value, did appear at the Kitchen in January 1990, she did *not* receive any funding from the federal government.

Frameline: Frameline received a $10,000 grant from the Endowment, not to support the International Lesbian and Gay Film Festival, but to fund the organization's distribution of films and videos of excellence, which we mutually determine with the organization. While you appear to equate artworks which depict gay and lesbian themes with "pornography," it would be wrong—and contrary to constitutional guarantees—for an agency of the federal government to do likewise.

Marlon Riggs: The late Marlon Riggs, who passed away this past April, received a $5,000 grant from the Rocky Mountain Film Center as part of the American Film Institute/NEA Regional Fellowship Program. Mr. Riggs's film "Tongues Untied" received wide critical acclaim, including the top prize at the Berlin International Film Festival, a Blue Ribbon at the American Film and Video Festival, and a Special Jury Award at the USA Film Festival. Your description of the film as "pro-homosexual" is in striking contrast to its depictions of the anguish and pain endured by the gay community. Of the 270 PBS stations, more than two-thirds broadcast the film. In 1993, Signifyin' Works of Berkeley, California, received a $50,000 grant to support the production of a documentary by Mr. Riggs exploring the matters of color and identity within the African-American community.

Walker Art Center: Irresponsible news reports have contorted what actually occurred at the Walker almost beyond recognition. The

Walker Art Center, whose reputation for excellence in contemporary art spans more than a century and is certainly a deserving recipient of Endowment support, used less than $150 of its seasonal grant toward a performance by Ron Athey. The performance was based on African tribal traditions in which some surface blood (akin to a shaving nick) was raised. The blood—which was *not* HIV-positive—was blotted with paper towels and affixed to clotheslines. At no time did blood drip from towels, nor was the safety of the audience in jeopardy at any time. The Minnesota Department of Health has indicated that the Walker took prudent safety precautions.

Franklin Furnace Archive: Franklin Furnace received a $5,000 grant to support its 1994 performance season. In keeping with the diverse nature of Endowment grants, the organization presents emerging artists whose works are often experimental or cutting-edge in nature.

Highways, Inc.: The $18,000 fiscal year 1994 grant to Highways supports a performance season of over two hundred solo performers, theater ensembles, music ensembles, poets, and dance companies. Support for organizations such as Highways helps to ensure that for those taxpayers whose tastes may not run toward the opera, symphony, or ballet, their tax dollars are supporting aesthetic styles more to their liking.

Centro Cultural de la Raza: Centro's $15,000 fiscal year 1994 grant will support its season of performing arts, particularly works which tell the story of Chicano, Latino, and Native American experiences. The organization also received a $41,000 grant through the Expansion Arts Program and a $28,000 grant through the Visual Arts Program to support its exhibitions, literary programs, and associated events. Centro was only peripherally involved in the "Art Rebate" project last year. And need I reiterate that absolutely no Endowment funds were used as part of this project.

PART 2

Brava! For Women in the Arts: During the 1993 fiscal year, Brava! received a $10,000 Expansion Arts Program grant through its Arts Education Initiative to support the WRITE ON! ACT OUT! Theater project, an after-school writing and performance project for students who have been disenfranchised because of their sexual orientation or ethnic background. The pieces used in the program, for the most part, do not contain themes or subject matter related to sexuality.

Caveh Zahedi: Mr. Zahedi received a 1993 Film/Video Production grant in the amount of $20,000 to support a narrative film. His was one of 29 applications recommended for funding out of some 382 applications that were reviewed by two rounds of panels. The film explores the lessons learned from the filmmaker's own personal struggle with his sexuality.

Visual AIDS for the Arts: Visual AIDS received a $12,000 grant through the Visual Arts Program to support, as you note, a series of artists' projects, public programs, and services designed to increase public awareness about AIDS and its impact on the art world. Annual programs will include "Day Without Art," a national day of mourning in tribute to those who are living with, or have died of, AIDS, which is held in conjunction with "Night Without Light," a fifteen-minute blackout of skylines across the country; the creation and distribution of artists' posters or "broadsides"; the "Ribbon Project," which encourages the wearing of a red ribbon to express support for those living with AIDS; traveling exhibitions; and related activities.

Karen Christensen and her Office of General Counsel answered the senator's questions about Melanie Beene. Ms. Beene was a consultant who oversaw the Endowment's advancement program, which provided technical and management assistance to over forty-five organizations needing organizational stability. The cost for her services was entirely competitive in the marketplace, and the travel expenditures were related to the visits she and her staff paid to the grantee organizations. Our challenge and advancement programs offered some of the most sought-after grants the Endowment awarded. The challenge grants were given to institutions in need of large funds for capital improvements or other major projects. The advancement grants usually aided the smaller organizations that had been formed on a wing and a prayer, then found themselves thriving artistically but badly in need of long-range planning and management training to survive. The rate of success of the organizations that had been through the rigorous two- and three-year programs was very high.

.   .   .

Our response seemed entirely satisfactory to me at the time. In retrospect it was foolish of me to capitulate to the witch-hunt fervor by stating that Annie Sprinkle's work held no artistic value. It was unnecessary and in violation of my own code of ethics: as chairman I was to withhold my personal opinions. Fortunately our critics were not focused on Annie Sprinkle, and I didn't make the same mistake again. But the slip was indicative of the pressure I was feeling—along with everyone else at the Endowment.

In the summer of 1994 we had about 250 men and women working for the NEA. They had been through controversy before, and it was never easy to experience. They feared for their jobs with good reason: even a 5 percent cut to the agency budget could mean a small cut in staff, as it had the year before. I tried to reassure them that the setback by Byrd and the press was just one battle in a big war that was being waged throughout society over values. I said that we might lose the battle but we would not lose the war. The troops were becoming demoralized nevertheless. We were facing the possibility of almost $9 million in cuts, and I wanted the program directors to tell me what might be dropped. The tension was palpable. I knew I had to offer something to Byrd when I met with him to enable him to move away from his specific cuts to Theater, Visual Arts, and our Presenting and Commissioning Program, which could amount to 41 percent of their budgets.

The possibility of restructuring the Presenting and Commissioning program was on the table. "P&C" was a vital part of the performing arts component. The program had a budget of $5.272 million in 1994 and funded everything from the Center for Puppetry Arts in Atlanta to the Colorado Dance Festival in Boulder to a jazz workshop at San Francisco State University. Although a few of the funded spaces booked blatantly commercial performers, they also booked nonprofit fare as well. Most were struggling to get by and depended on the NEA grants. They could apply in several different categories, and often the very best of the presenting organizations, like the Brooklyn Academy of Music (BAM) or the Walker Art Center, would be awarded multiple grants. I understood the need for presenters; they were producers essentially, and my entire career had been dependent on producers. Actors, dancers, and musicians do not, after all, perform in a vacuum. Playwrights, composers, visual artists, and filmmakers are all dependent on presenters, producers, exhibitors, and distributors to present their work to an audience. Without them we have no substantial career because there is no interface with the public.

As much as I respected presenters, the Presenting and Commissioning program at the Endowment was a hodgepodge, funding a bit of everything. It was a very fine hodgepodge usually, but it wasn't always clear that the NEA grant was going to end up funding the most excellent art. I wanted to explore the idea of dispersing the components of the presenting program throughout the disciplines of Dance, Music, Opera and Theater as it had been done in the early days of the Endowment. Dance presenters would then apply to the Dance program, theater presenters to the Theater program, and so on. In this way I believed the peer panels would be able to focus more clearly on the excellence of the applicants. I was talked out of this idea, however, by some very persuasive presenters who convinced me that they were the most important tier in the process of creation to presentation, and that artists were in fact hungry for places to perform. In addition, they pointed out, many of the events seen on the stage today include multimedia elements—dance, theater, opera, and music mixed together. I couldn't argue with their thinking, but I still had to find some demonstrative change in the way the NEA did business to take to my meeting with Byrd.

Commissioning was the other half of the P&C program. It was one of my favorite awards given by the agency because it nurtured new works. The staff felt that we could reinstate commissions within the programs for each discipline (Dance, Music, and so on) without doing much harm. So at least I had something to offer Byrd when I saw him, as slight a change as it was.

With all the press attention I was grateful when Dotson Rader showed up in my office on July 7 to interview me for a cover story for *Parade* magazine. Although it would not be published until October, the issue would reach 73 million people in their Sunday papers. I would have a chance to tell the story of the NEA as I saw it. As remarkable as Cherie Simon was in the public relations arena, she had a staff of only six people and was bucking the vast and well-oiled machine of the religious right. Dotson came along at the right time. He said he had been dining with Ted and Vicki Kennedy and Ted's sister Pat Lawford when Ted suggested that he interview me as one of the president's best appointments. I had one of our leading senators to thank for this most important interview.

Dotson wanted to help. He fielded me softball questions, intended to introduce the readers to me as a sympathetic person and also to educate them about the NEA. He described me in the article as "polite and without a hint of vulgarity or self-promotion," as if only vulgar people would appreciate vulgar art, which is hardly the case. The first paragraph addressed the religious right, although they were never named as such because they made up a sizable share of *Parade*'s readers:

"I never doubted that I'm under attack," said Jane Alexander, the chairman of the National Endowment for the Arts (NEA). "We're part of a very large discussion that's ongoing among certain forces in America—political, philosophical, and cultural. So I never doubted that we would be under fire. But I was surprised by the intensity of the attack, the distortions and false accusations, the questioning of the endowment's commitment to American values, the questioning of even my own deeply held Christian values. I resent it, I resent it terribly, because I grew up a Christian and I'm very spiritual, very religious."

This last bit about my being "very religious" was a stretch. Yes, I had grown up a good Christian child. My mother moved from one church to another in an effort to find a more acceptable denomination for the Brookline society matron she had become, leaving the simple Methodist girl behind in South Boston. After exploring the Unitarian religion of New England intellectuals past and present, and the Congregational Church, which introduced me to the organ recitals of the great E. Power Biggs, my mother settled us at the Church of Our Savior as Episcopalians.

When I say "us" I mean primarily my mother, my sister, and myself, except at holidays, when my brother and father sometimes joined us. Dad was a lapsed Catholic, and Tom invariably found something else to do on Sunday mornings, like tinkering with his Model A Ford. I loved the story of Christ and the ritual of liturgy, but I was beginning to explore other religions as well, Buddhism in particular. By the time I went to college I had some real philosophical questions churning in my mind and noted that most of the wars throughout history had been fought because of religious differences. My own hypocrisy finally got the better of me, and I stopped going to church entirely.

I still considered myself a spiritual being, however, and roamed the canon of religions from Zen Buddhism to transcendentalism like a starved nomad. Ultimately I found the wonder and serenity I was searching for in the daily world of nature, which I entered with increasing frequency as I got older. Birding became a passion, and jogging was displaced by long walks in the woods. God was always there in the flutter of a wing. No more questions asked.

The *Parade* interview also allowed me to give a little history lesson about subsidizing the arts. I pointed out that governments, kings and queens, and the church have always subsidized the arts, and that "most of the great old-master paintings in museums in the world today were supported by the church. So, in a sense, people taxed themselves, in their offerings to the church, to support artists." At the same time I said this I was trying to imagine what kind of art the religious right was currently supporting and was hard-pressed to come up with anything that might rank as excellent.

The *Parade* article, when it was published in October 1994, did a great deal to humanize the Endowment and me. I had been doing interviews on an almost daily basis since assuming chairmanship of the agency, with the hope that ultimately the good news about the NEA would filter throughout society. Cherie had also set up meetings with the editorial boards of major newspapers in the cities we visited. We never knew when these meetings would pay off, or whether in fact I made a good impression on these tough journalists. The *Boston Globe,* for example, was a harsh critic of ours. Then one day, late in 1994, just when we needed all the help we could get, the paper came through with a lead editorial in support of the agency; the writer concluded: "Grants came to people as they were struggling to create their art. A country that fails to encourage this loses its genius and its soul." Such editorials, however, as fine as some of them were, often preached to the converted; despite their mass circulation, none of them could reach as many people as had Dotson Rader's article in *Parade.*

Our three-pronged strategy of touring America to see artists and their communities, talking to the press, and meeting members of Congress to increase confidence in the agency had been unexpectedly derailed by Senator Byrd. It was one thing for Jesse Helms and his Republican colleagues to attack the Endowment, but quite another when the attack came from the leading Democrat in Congress. My brief time with Byrd would be one of the most important half-hours of my four-year tenure at the NEA. I prepared for it as if I were going up for a major part in a play.

The week prior to July 12 I read as much about Robert C. Byrd as I could, and I spoke with a number of people who knew him. Sharon Rockefeller told me that he was "old-fashioned" and that I should just listen to him because I was not going to change his mind about anything. Rachel Worby, who was the conductor of West Virginia's Symphony Orchestra and the wife of the state's governor, had just come on board the NEA's Council. She warned me that Byrd would brook no more controversial grants and that I should be careful because he was so powerful.

Raised in the hardscrabble coal country of southern West Virginia, Bobby Byrd graduated at the top of his high school class but had to wait twelve years before going to college because he couldn't afford it.

Largely self-educated, his mastery of the great books and of history is legendary; he quotes freely from the Romans, the Bible, and Shakespeare on the Senate floor. His vocabulary is unparalleled and confounds his colleagues, whose aides must regularly consult dictionaries when Byrd is speaking.

It was Byrd's fiddle playing, however, that propelled him into politics, drawing out voters in the hollows who came to hear him play and then stayed on to listen to his speech. In 1946 he was elected to the state's legislature, and to the U.S. House of Representatives in 1953. He has an abiding love for the Senate and, as the primary guardian of its traditions and procedures, even wrote the definitive history of that body, in several dense volumes.

Robert Byrd was feared by his fellow senators. His power was so great and the IOUs he had accrued so plentiful that few dared cross him. As chairman of the Appropriations Committee he ensured that his beloved West Virginia received a generous portion of "pork" yearly, for which he made no apology, claiming that the people expect that from their senator and that what is good for West Virginia is good for the nation. Sometimes his efforts on behalf of his constituents seemed downright absurd to me. I grew up on the Atlantic coast of Massachusetts, where naval bases and the Coast Guard were familiar sights. When Senator Byrd in 1995 began politicking for a new Coast Guard Academy in the state of West Virginia, I laughed out loud. But Byrd was apparently quite serious, noting that Harper's Ferry was only one hundred miles upriver from the ocean. When other legislators also took his efforts seriously, because of who he was, I began to think I was in a scene from *Alice in Wonderland.* In 1996, however, when Byrd was no longer chairman of Appropriations—having been replaced first by Mark Hatfield and then by another king of pork, the redoubtable Republican Ted Stevens of Alaska—West Virginia's bid for its Coast Guard Academy went unrealized.

Two days before my meeting with him the heat turned up a notch. A filmmaker named David Russell cavalierly stated in a *New York Times* interview that even though the NEA had disallowed the use of his $20,000 grant to make a film different from the one for which it was awarded, he had gone ahead and made the new film anyway. The film,

Spanking the Monkey, was about self-gratification and incest and was doing nicely at the box office. Congressman Romano Mazzoli from Kentucky called immediately, instructing me to demand the money back in no uncertain terms. This was not a difficult incident to field. Russell was in clear violation of the terms of grant acceptance, and it was simply a matter of reaching him and then letting Congress know we had taken care of the issue swiftly. Russell was hurt more than anything else when the staff spoke with him. He thought we should be proud of the film, since it received such fine reviews, not disavowing it. He did understand, however, that he had changed the scope of the project, and he returned the money to us within the year. Dick let Congress know what we had done, and the entire issue blew over within a matter of days. Nevertheless, we could have done without the publicity at an extremely sensitive time; to our critics it seemed like a case of "here they go again."

I made one last call to the White House before my meeting with Byrd. A staffer told me that the senator might be defensive with me because I'm a woman; he didn't like conflict with women at all, because it was so much harder for him to be tough with a woman, and perhaps I would do best to show deference and make the senator feel relaxed and not cornered. The word was that Byrd was getting "pumped up" for this meeting with me and that he was probably more anxious than I was! Maybe it would smooth the way if I reminded him that I had played Eleanor Roosevelt, the staffer suggested, or presented him with something Shakespearean. I thought of doing a soliloquy for him, knowing that he and I were possibly the only two of hundreds in the Capitol Building who knew Shakespeare's words by heart. Perhaps Portia's "The quality of mercy is not strain'd, It droppeth as the gentle rain from heaven . . ." from *The Merchant of Venice* would be appropriate for this meeting. No, too much grandstanding, I thought.

I had played characters so often in my auditions for directors and producers that it was no hardship to play the gentlewoman to this old southern gentleman, and that's what I decided to do. I asked Karen Christensen, who was pretty and petite as well as a crackerjack lawyer, to accompany me, rather than Dick Woodruff, who might be more threatening to our senator. I could be as sexist as the next person when need be. I also decided we would dress accordingly.

Karen and I showed up looking like summer flowers in a southern garden, all soft and pastel. I brought him a tape of fiddle music from one of our Heritage Fellowships, which he accepted with pleasure, and we spoke briefly of his fiddle playing and the folk arts, which he loved. His office was the largest and most spacious in all of Congress, the walls and ceilings ringed with murals and moldings. We sat at the end of a huge conference table in one of his many rooms, accompanied by his aides Sue Masica and Jim English. The senator was slight of build, with snow-white hair and sky-blue eyes that fixed me with a sideways stare. He spoke measuredly in the lilting tones of his people.

He had been briefed on some of the NEA's grants to West Virginia: the bulk of the $973,700 awarded for fiscal year 1993 had gone to the symphony, to the Huntington museum, to the folk and traditional arts, and to Public Radio. I told him that we had instituted some procedural changes at the agency: grantees had to give us interim reports on how they had spent their money before they could draw down the entire sum; commissioning had been moved back to the disciplines; and I was working to ensure greater diversity on the panels. He seemed satisfied with this and went on to say that he sided with Jesse Helms not because he himself was a "right-winger" but because he objected to the same kinds of grants that Helms found objectionable. He did not want the NEA to award money to "those kinds of art." Neither he nor I mentioned Ron Athey or any of the others. I did not venture into the fruitless territory of how to keep controversy per se from art but rather talked of the importance of our grants to the theaters of the United States and to the visual artists. I also dropped the idea that perhaps with such limited funds the Endowment might place a cap of two fellowships a lifetime on individual artists. He scrutinized me obliquely, weighing the possibilities. I think he liked me, although we concluded nothing in the twenty minutes we spoke.

Before we left he showed us a painting he had done as a young man, one of two he claimed to have completed. It was a small oil of a millwheel on a stream, a summer sky, and conifers. He had it lithographed for his closest colleagues and intimated that someday, if I were still in his favor, I would be graced with one too. The work was good, representational and careful, and there was nothing exciting about it at all. As a curio it would have had some value, something to talk about when friends asked about it on my wall. I never received one but chanced to see a copy a few years later in a distant state, where it had been banished to a corner in the basement bathroom of a former senator. Robert C. Byrd was held in high regard, but his art had sunk pretty low.

Six weeks later Stephanie and I visited West Virginia for two days. It was a beautiful state, difficult to traverse because of the hilly terrain, but replete with pockets of art. The most magical time I ever experienced on the road was helicoptering into remote Calhoun County, landing in a large field, and being surrounded on that sunny August afternoon by fifty brightly costumed students of the Heartwood Dance Center. I felt like Titania in *A Midsummer Night's Dream* traipsing through the knee-high grass with her retinue of fairies—"Lull'd in these flowers with dances and delight." Even there, in the heart of coal country, the children came from all around to release their creative souls. I wished that Senator Byrd had been with me to see it. I also wished the senator had seen the only erotic art I encountered on my travels, in an exhibit of West Virginia's folk art. The woodcarving was about eight inches high; a man was standing in back of a woman, and when you moved a lever he entered the woman from behind. It was a harmless enough piece, but I am sure the young people who toured the exhibit came back for another glimpse, just as I had done decades before when I spied an erect penis on the ancient Greek vases in the Boston Museum of Fine Arts. It was ironic that this bit of erotica was not a photograph by the "decadent" Robert Mapplethorpe, from the lower depths of New York City, but a piece of the "innocent" folk art beloved by Robert Byrd in his own state. Some things remain the same throughout history and all strata of society.

After my meeting with Byrd, Dick and I made follow-up calls to his aides and other senators to test the idea of implementing a lifetime cap of two individual awards in exchange for an amendment that would lift Byrd's cuts to theater and the visual arts. I did not feel I was compromising the Endowment with this suggestion. The truth was that there were so many applicants for individual awards in all the arts fields that it seemed only fair to spread the largesse around. Two grants in one lifetime seemed reasonable when overall funds were so low.

I had also been considering the elimination of subgranting in all programs except the international program. Subgranting was commonplace throughout the agency: it allowed the grantee organizations to form their own panels and regrant the NEA's money, thereby saving time and effort on the part of the Endowment and spreading the funds more widely. It was a good idea in theory, but in practice the Endowment's criteria of artistic merit and excellence were often vitiated. I had enormous faith in the NEA's panels and believed they were the best in the country, pulling together as they did the most knowledgeable people in their fields and also the most diverse, geographically, racially, and ethnically. Some of our subgrantees simply did not apply the same standards or have the expertise in a given field that the NEA panels had.

My guru, Sid Yates, listened carefully to the report of my meeting with Byrd, and to my ideas about procedural changes. He was supportive of eliminating subgrants but reminded me that for some organizations, like the American Film Institute (AFI), it would mean the loss of an enormous amount of money.

The American Film Institute had been born of a bold new dream for the arts in America. In 1965, when President Lyndon Johnson signed the executive order creating the Endowments, he surprised everyone by stating that national institutions would be established in each of the arts fields, beginning with a film institute. In 1967 the first National Council on the Arts, including high-profile celebrities like Charlton Heston, Gregory Peck, Sidney Poitier, and George Stevens Sr., founded the AFI to preserve and develop the nation's artistic and cultural resources in film. Of the Endowment's $8 million budget that year, $1.3 million went to set up the AFI as a nonprofit, nongovernmental organization. Every succeeding year AFI received the largest NEA grant given. I admired the Institute and its many programs. It was a leader in film preservation, helping to restore, catalog, and screen old films. AFI also gave seminars and conducted a world-renowned film school in Los Angeles that my son Jace attended in 1994 and 1995 on his way to becoming a director. It subgranted to other media entities for film preservation and to directors for their film work. One couldn't quarrel with its agenda or accomplishments, but I questioned whether a single organization should still be receiving such a disproportionate share of the NEA's funds at a time when the agency was not gaining ground financially.

The dream of a national symphony orchestra had been partially realized, if only in name, when Roger Stevens was chairman of the Kennedy Center. The National Gallery of Art had been around a long time, thanks to the Mellon family, who donated their own vast art collection and funded it substantially. The establishment of a national opera company had been more problematical. The already famous companies, like the Metropolitan Opera in New York or those in San Francisco, Houston, and Chicago, objected to the designation of a single "national opera." The same held true for nonprofit theaters, which saw themselves collectively as our "national theater." The NEA gave grants to all these institutions, but hardly in the amounts given the AFI annually.

The American Film Institute was one of a number of organizations devoted to film and media. The University of California in Los Angeles, the University of Southern California, New York University, and Boston's Emerson College had fine film schools and archives. And there were a dozen or more media centers from Portland, Oregon, to Minneapolis, Minnesota. It would have been more equitable to spread the wealth more evenly among them, but if possession is nine-tenths of the law, then AFI's entitlement was deeply entrenched. I could only hope that the Institute's director, Jean Firstenberg, would understand the rationale of my argument when the time came.

Sid Yates and I spoke further of other changes the Endowment might have to undergo. We both understood that with the hostility in Congress and a president committed to reducing the deficit, we could anticipate a reduced NEA budget of between 2 and 7 percent in September when the House and the Senate reconciled their individual bills for the upcoming fiscal year 1995. I suggested moving our museum program's conservation grants to another government agency, the Institute for Museum Services (IMS), whose $28 million budget did not seem to be in jeopardy. I was grasping at straws, trying to figure out how to maintain the best services at the Endowment and prevent cuts in staff. Sid considered all of this, and we parted with his kind confidence in me: "Whatever you want me to do, sweetie."

On July 13 I was invited to the vice president's home with about thirty others for a discussion of "Metaphors in Science and Technology," one of three evenings devoted to the topic of metaphor. I was exhilarated by the speakers and the ensuing discussion throughout dinner. The machine metaphors of the early twentieth century had transitioned to the information metaphors of today. We had lost our community knowledge and its metaphors, and with it the sense of culture we used to honor. "What is honored in a country will be cultivated there," William Sloane Coffin once said. Today we honor our strong economy and the stock market that cultivates it; we honor a strong defense system and cultivate the weapons to back it up; we honor the new technologies and cultivate their dissemination throughout society. We do not honor the arts or humanities, or even our educators, in the same way. We do not protect them by cultivating their welfare for the good of society as we do the economy, defense, and technology. Does it matter? Is this in the evolutionary scheme of things? "Culture is a pyramid to which each of us brings a stone," wrote Wallace Stegner. It is hard to know what kind of pyramid is being built now.

As the evening of metaphor musing came to an end, Al Gore and I talked briefly about the NEA's struggles, and he reassured me of the administration's commitment. He then told me about a *Washington Times* article concerning North Korea in which the writer wished I had been kidnapped by North Korea's new prime minister, who loved movie stars. "Outrageous!" I laughed. "Yes," replied the VP about the conservative newspaper. "In the past they accused me of beating my dog!" Gore told me he read six newspapers every morning while on the treadmill. I admired his skill and stamina. I could barely get through the *Washington Post* and the *New York Times,* much less on a treadmill.

The press nationwide was sounding off about the Endowment on almost a daily basis. Still, for all the negative coverage on the front pages, we seemed to be gaining the high ground in the nation's editorial pages. The *Atlanta Constitution* wrote that soldiers bought *Playboy* and *Hustler* on their military bases and that there was no public complaint;

maybe the Department of Defense should be brought to task as a smut peddler. The comparison may have seemed a welcome one for the NEA, but regrettably, for soldiers, shortly thereafter conservatives *did* complain about magazines like that being sold on the bases and got rid of them.

We were gaining friends in other high places as well. At one of my VIP lunches that summer, Jim Jeffords of Vermont began telling us what he was going to do for the Endowment on the Senate floor when the bill came up. He, a Republican, was going to buck Byrd, arguably the most powerful man in Washington after the president! I was delighted. Jeffords's decision was entirely his own and indicative of his independent ways as a Republican. Cokie Roberts, an ABC correspondent and sometime critic of the Endowment, laughed and listened wide-eyed to Jeffords. She, David Brinkley, George Will, and Sam Donaldson had stunned me a year earlier on the Sunday morning *David Brinkley Show* when they blithely claimed that the NEA wasn't needed anymore because the private sector picked up the tab for art in America. Tell that to a kid in Appalachia or the Bronx, I wanted to shout at them. Maybe Jeffords's enthusiasm about the agency would move Cokie and the ABC gang off their position.

The next day I was invited to the Oval office as the president signed into law the Kennedy Center's release from the National Park Service, on which it had been dependent. It was now free to raise necessary maintenance funds on its own. The few of us present included Ted Kennedy, James Wolfensohn, the dynamic chairman of the Center, Melanne Verveer, and Senators Hatfield, Mitchell, and Leahy. Ted was always extremely generous promoting others, and he proceeded to embarrass me in front of the president and senators. He knew our bill would reach the floor soon and told these influential men what a fine job he thought I was doing. They said nothing, but his compliments were welcome at a time when my president must have wondered what I was doing showing up in the papers so often.

Fortuitously, other important senators promised to help as the appropriations bill neared the Senate floor debate. In mid-July, Ed and I drove to Waterford, Connecticut, in torrential rains, to celebrate the

Eugene O'Neill Theater Center's thirtieth year. George White, its founder, was also an NEA Council member. The event and the weather proved to be providential because I was seated next to Senator Christopher Dodd. We had to yell to be heard over the deluge on the tent ceiling above us. Dodd's Irish humor made for good company, and his quick mind rescued us a few weeks later when the NEA needed to be defended vigorously.

While Dodd, the other Democrats, and a few Republicans continued to be totally supportive of the Endowment, other senators were panicking. Proposal after proposal was being written to mollify the NEA's critics and redefine the agency. Kay Bailey Hutchison, a Republican from Texas, wanted to redirect much of our funding to the states and honor only "national treasures." Spencer Abraham, a newcomer from Michigan, also Republican, wanted to privatize the agency. Everyone thought they could "fix the problem." I stood my ground, knowing that what I thought wouldn't matter anyway when the bills and amendments were introduced on the Senate floor.

In the dog days of summer, before the long-anticipated congressional recess in August, when everyone else in Washington could finally take a break too, we knew that Jesse Helms would again propose amendments against the agency, but we didn't know exactly what they were. In midafternoon on July 25 Helms asked for an amendment prohibiting funds for any art that involved mutilation, invasive bodily procedures, and bloodletting. The Democratic leadership told Chris Dodd and the others that the amendment was okay and to let it go; either it would be defeated, as usually happened with Helms's amendments, or, if it passed, it was unlikely to pose any hardship for the art that the NEA normally funded. Dodd thought otherwise. He jumped up and said, hold on a minute: this amendment would preclude all art involving Saint Sebastian, the head of John the Baptist, and the crucifixion— in other words, most of the Christian art of the world. In addition, he said, it precluded the funding of paintings depicting military battles, many of which ringed the walls of the Capitol's corridors. Helms defended his position, showing pictures of a pierced Ron Athey, but to no avail. The vote to table his amendment was 49–42. It was a shock when Al Simpson voted against tabling Helms's amendment, after all his support of the agency and me. I couldn't believe it until Dick Woodruff pointed out that it was a purely political move on Simpson's part: he knew that the amendment would be defeated and that he could buy points with Helms by throwing his vote his way—a "free vote" it was called. It was a common strategy in Congress, and a kind of politicking I was beginning to understand, but it still hurt when a friend said one thing and then voted another. Simpson redeemed himself a few minutes later during a discussion of mining in the Interior bill. The Endowment had nothing to do with mining, but he brought the agency up anyway and spoke of it in glowing terms. In any case Simpson's negative vote on tabling the Helms amendment could not dim my pleasure. It was my first Senate victory for the NEA, and I was thrilled.

The Senate proceeded to the appropriations bill itself. Minnesota's Dave Durenberger spoke in wonderful terms about the Walker Art Center, as did his colleague Paul Wellstone. Jim Jeffords offered an amendment to restore the 5 percent cut that Byrd's committee had given us. Finally Senator Byrd rose, and the chamber quieted. He spoke of meeting me and of being impressed with my plans for the agency. He quoted Shakespeare, about the need to cut out "the noisome weeds," and then did a turnabout, saying he would seek only a 2 percent cut in conference, going along with the 2 percent the House of Representatives had given us. It was not Jeffords's suggestion of zero cuts, but it was a triumph nonetheless. We had moved the great leader Robert Byrd from his previously stated position.

The battle for the year was almost over. We could expect a 2 percent cut for fiscal year 1995—that is, if we could keep controversy at bay in the next two months, before reconciliation of the House and Senate budgets in September. I should have guessed it wasn't possible.

A week later I greeted five new Council members, the latest appointments by our Democratic president. They had been put through the same grueling procedure I had endured, including Senate confirmation, before being sworn in. Sometimes just one senator would put a hold on someone, and the process would back up for months at a time. Although I had plenty of liberal thinkers on the Council already, appointed by Republicans Reagan and Bush, I looked forward to these new faces and minds.

Rachel Worby from West Virginia was one; Barbara Grossman, an assistant drama professor at Tufts and a staunch Democratic contributor, was another. A third was Judith Rubin, the wife of the president's economic adviser and soon-to-be treasurer, Robert Rubin; she was also a board member of Playwright's Horizons and the New York State Council on the Arts. Colleen Jennings-Roggensack, who was the executive director of Arizona State University's many presentations, was the fourth. And the fifth was Ron Feldman, a dedicated Democratic fundraiser, advocate of First Amendment rights, and gallery owner in Soho.

I had chaired two prior Council meetings, but I knew this one in August was going to be a rip-roarer. Andres Serrano had been recommended by the panel for a visual arts fellowship. Before the meeting I had called as many of the twenty-six members as I could to alert them to the recommendation. Perusing the huge book of applications thoroughly was difficult at best, and I didn't want them to be caught unaware at the public meeting. I asked them all to attend the working groups of the program directors the day before to acquaint themselves with the applicants' materials.

There was one Council member I especially hoped would attend. Father Leo O'Donovan, president of Georgetown University and a leading Jesuit spokesman, had been appointed by Clinton a year earlier. It was remarkable having a spiritual leader of his magnitude adjudicating grants to artists. As a Jesuit, Father Leo had a keen philosophical mind and could articulate the most difficult predicaments in thoughtful and incisive ways. He had great respect for artists and wrote fine essays on art. I longed to hear what this Catholic priest and educator would say about the photographs of Andres Serrano, who had grown up Catholic and whose work was often suffused with Catholicism. Regrettably Father Leo's busy schedule didn't allow him to attend the meeting. He told me, only half in jest, that maybe he ought to leave town for a few weeks, in case the press wanted to talk to him.

Another Council member boldly exclaimed, when I called, that a grant to Serrano would finish the agency and that "we must be squeaky clean for a year." Many asked me what I wanted. I told them that I was

not going to tell them what to do; I simply wanted them to be prepared, to read the panel's recommendation carefully, and to vote their
conscience as to the excellence and merit of each work.

I didn't tell them that I was not going to reject a grant to Serrano if
they approved it, no matter what the political climate. After careful
thought I had decided that if I went the way of John Frohnmayer it
truly would be the end of the Endowment. The artists of America
would be compromised. As long as the panel process was honest and
the jury by one's peers was nonpolitical, as I believed it to be at the
agency, I would uphold the system. But I was between a rock and a
hard place. If I signed off on a grant to Serrano the House and Senate
could decide to give us zero appropriations. The president would then
veto, but the Senate might well override the veto with a two-thirds
majority vote. The Endowment might cease to exist. If the Council
decided to reject the panel's recommendation of a grant to Serrano, we
would be accused of caving in to Congress. There was no way to win.

All of this was causing me palpitations, literally. I would be jogging
away on the treadmill in my building's health club and little stabs in my
heart would force me to stop. I consulted a doctor a few days before the
Council assembled, fearing the worst. Maybe this was a way to make it
all go away: "NEA Chairman Collapses as Council Deliberates Controversial Art." My doctor assured me, after a battery of tests and an EKG,
that I was quite all right, that the pain was heartburn (aptly named)
and that I was under stress (no kidding). Just knowing I was not about
to have a heart attack relieved my anxiety somewhat.

Even though I suspected that Sid Yates had heard that a possible Serrano grant was coming before the Council, he and I did not discuss it;
to do so would have been unethical. But I asked him whether he felt
that politics and art were antithetical. He replied that as support for the
arts gained ground across the country, the cry for accountability of
public funds would increase as well; the tension between "high culture"
and democracy, he believed, was inevitable. Garrison Keillor had told
me something similar when he said: "There is an inevitable tension
between art and politics."

The Council deliberations were quite extraordinary. The members wrestled hard with the Serrano grant. In the photography program thirty-one out of seventeen hundred applicants were selected. The Council member Louise McClure, whose husband Jim was a former Republican senator, said with disappointment: "This is the best of photography today?" The assessment was echoed by many of the members as they discussed the applications prior to voting. The work of three photographers in particular was in question: Andres Serrano, whose application was accompanied by slides of large color portraits depicting people and church iconography; Merry Alpern, whose submitted photos were from the perspective of a voyeur and involved prostitution; and Barbara DeGenevieve, whose pictures explored feminism through the depiction of hands, faces, lips, and other body parts.

Bill Bailey, a painter and teacher at Yale, felt that the selections were simply not good enough. Roger Mandle, the president of the Rhode Island School of Design, and Ron Feldman defended the selections on principle: a panel of peers had forwarded them to the Council for grants, and their recommendations were sound. A profound and meaningful exchange took place between the newcomer Colleen Jennings-Roggensack and Bill Strickland, the visionary founder of the Manchester Craftsmen's Guild, both African Americans. Colleen described a painting of slaves that had hung in her school when she was a child, and the daily pain it caused her when she walked past it. She said that the important thing was that it was well painted, and that she would give the painter a grant today. Bill responded that he could not vote for any work that humiliated a child.

Their dialogue was the crux of the issue of art and the viewer: yes, art has a right to exist, but can it harm? Should funds be given to work that will harm? I believe that some art can harm human beings psychically. Just as great works of art can influence us positively, so the reverse is true. As a child I was terrified by science fiction and horror movies; some of the images live with me today as if they were real and not celluloid. Hollywood has always known that the movies can move us to fear, to laughter, and to tears. And the advertising world has always known that art can influence the viewer; a good print ad or television commercial is a marriage of artfulness and persuasive propaganda. Pornography is often extremely humiliating to women, even though some pornography is extremely artful. When does a work of pornography or propaganda become art? And who decides?

Although the art of the three photographers was not obscene, pornographic, or in any way overtly harmful, its content partially obscured the discussion about technical excellence, which was the main requirement. Did the works have "artistic merit"? Yes. Were they "excellent"? On a scale of one to ten where did each body of art rank in excellence? I had my own response to the work of the three photographers in question, but I remained silent. As chairman it was my job to foster debate and a principled vote, not sway opinion.

When all the votes were tallied, the three photographers did not measure up to the standard of excellence the Council wished to maintain. Out of so many worthy applications for individual photography fellowships, it was not surprising. Their rejection was interpreted by some to be politically motivated, but the Council had strong opinions about the work itself. At many subsequent meetings the members rejected works in other fields because they did not consider them good enough. In addition to determining the "artistic merit and excellence" of each application for a fellowship, the Council was also asked to consider whether "the applicant's work reflects a serious continued investigation of important or significant aesthetic concerns . . . during the proposed fellowship period." The Council did not believe that any of the three photographers met this criterion.

It would be disingenuous to say I was not relieved. It was a dramatic finish to an agonizing deliberation, and to say that I did not count the political points that would accrue for me and the agency with Congress would be dishonest. But my heart is always with the artists, not the politicians. I felt sick to my stomach when I received the following letter from Jesse Helms on August 11:

My dear Madam Chairman:
    When I was about ten I landed a job in the composing room of a semi-weekly newspaper in our little town. The foreman was a gentleman named Mr. Cadieu and all of us learned the wisdom of reluctance in unduly intruding upon the foreman's time; he would

generally inform us that he was "busy as a one-arm paper-hanger with the itch." I didn't understand at that time how busy that was because I had been blessed not to be one-armed, nor a paper-hanger. And I've never had the itch, but the presumptions prevailed that this must be some sort of dangerous malady.

We've not been *that* busy in the Senate in recent weeks but we have been a trifle preoccupied with various matters, possibly known to you. All of this is a lead-in for my apologizing for not having earlier commended you for what I am confident was the most effective way you handled the recent awards matter. (Jim McClure told me of the report he was given by Louise.) In any event Mr. Serrano was passed over in his bid to be further subsidized by the taxpayers.

I am fully aware that yours is a job that can never be performed in a manner that will please everyone. As I asked Jim to convey to Louise—I'm proud of Chairman Alexander, and I wish you well.

Sincerely,

Jesse Helms

In September the House and Senate passed the appropriations bill for fiscal year 1995. The National Endowment for the Arts was given a final budget of $162,311,000, which reflected Senator Byrd's final compromise of a 2 percent cut plus the administration's recision to reduce the deficit. It was Sid Yates who saved us in the final conference with the Senate. He saved us from those who still wished to impose a 5 percent reduction, but he couldn't save us from Byrd's slap on the wrist.

The honeymoon was over, but the marriage was still on.

CHAPTER ELEVEN

The Critics

"I'm shell-shocked," Tipper Gore whispered to me through clenched teeth as we smiled for the cameras. We were being honored by *Glamour* magazine as its "women of the year," along with the tennis great Martina Navratilova, Health and Human Services Secretary Donna Shalala, New Jersey Governor Christine Todd Whitman, the actress and singer Vanessa Williams, the Olympic skating champ Bonnie Blair, the TV talk show host Mary Matalin, the writer Naomi Wolf, and the Citadel cadet Shannon Faulkner. We were in great company, but it was difficult to concentrate. Two days earlier, on November 8, 1994, the Republicans had taken control of the House of Representatives and of the Senate. For the first time in forty years the entire Congress was in the hands of the GOP.

The Clintons, the Gores, and those of us appointed by them hadn't seen it coming. We had known that the Republicans might pick up a few seats, but hardly a majority. The electorate that had put Clinton in office in 1992 neglected to show up at the polls in sufficient numbers in 1994. The conservatives and the religious right worked hard to make gains, and although little more than one-third of the population bothered to vote, it was enough to sweep the Republicans into office.

Newt Gingrich, the House minority leader, immediately ascended to the exalted position of speaker, two heartbeats away from the presidency. The jubilation among his colleagues was as boisterous as that of fans at a winning home team stadium, and about as statesmanlike. "Politics is like football," someone once said. "You have to be smart enough to play the game and dumb enough to believe it's important."

It seemed immensely important at the time. I sat next to Harold Varmus, the director of the National Institutes of Health (NIH), at dinner the night after the GOP took over. He said, "There goes my fetal tissue research"—an area that had promised enormous advances in the world of medicine.

For those of us in the world of arts advocacy, the GOP victory was like a death knell. The Republicans wasted no time in letting the world know what they intended to do. They stood in phalanx on the Capitol steps and presented their guiding principles, which they called their "Contract with America," and the list of what they intended to accomplish in the first one hundred days of the new session. The Contract sought to:

> transform the way Congress works. That historic change would be the end of government that is too big, too intrusive, and too easy with the public's money. It can be the beginning of a Congress that respects the values and shares the faith of the American family. . . . We intend to act . . . to restore accountability to Congress. To end its cycle of scandal and disgrace.

Above all, the new House under Newt would "balance the budget."

President Clinton's economic policies were already reducing the deficit on our country's massive debt. And Vice President Gore was ensuring that government worked more efficiently by having us all "streamline" our endeavors. The NEA had taken its cut along with all other government agencies in fiscal years 1994 and 1995, and the senior staff was implementing our internal "streamlining." But balancing the budget meant that the nation would not spend a penny more than it received in taxes. In that event all federal agencies were in for massive cuts in their budgets and some would be totally eliminated. Since 25 percent of the Republicans who voted claimed in exit polls that they were Christian conservatives, it was clear where the pressure was going to be applied.

A new breed of Republican had been elected to the 104th Congress. They weren't the Rockefeller Republicans of my youth, who had been prompted by their guiding principle of noblesse oblige to found and patronize great institutions of culture and learning and always to give a hand up to anyone who needed it. No, this new breed had the notion that if everything were stripped down to nothing, the nation could rebuild itself as a pure and noble society free of violence and abiding by prayer. The religious right had triumphed, and in return for helping to elect the new Congress, it had extracted certain platform promises. One was to rid the country of the NEA.

Newt Gingrich, as minority leader, had been making Bill Clinton's life hell since 1992. He was a master Democrat basher and bill(Bill)-slayer who had successfully steered the House Republicans toward a more combative style in an effort to redefine the party. Now, as speaker of the House, he was in charge of an unruly mob of firebrands out for total revolution. There were seventy-five new Republican congressmen—a number that gave them a fifteen-seat majority in the House but not the overwhelming mandate to lead that Gingrich made it out to be. In thirteen of the narrowest elections the total Republican margin of victory was only 39,000 votes. Fewer than 39 percent of registered voters turned out at the polls, and 16 million women who voted in 1992 stayed away in 1994. In spite of these facts, the revolution was being played as if the majority of the people in the United States wanted everything that Gingrich wanted.

Newt Gingrich's mind was far more facile and complex than those of his followers. He was sincerely interested in reducing the size of the federal government, an agenda that included the elimination or reduction of the cultural agencies. Gingrich was not primarily concerned about suspect grants, although he used such controversies to his advantage whenever he could. He was an extremely clever politician but as sloppy in his homework as he was zealous of his agenda. On C-Span's *Inside Congress* on January 3, 1995, he said of the Endowment:

> I would like to find some way to maybe look at block-granting to the states some money for the arts at the state and local level. I'm for the Atlanta Ballet. I'm for the High Museum of Art or the Metropolitan, maybe the greatest art museum in America, in New York City. But I'm against self-selected elites using your tax money and my tax money to pay off their friends—this guy who was slashing his AIDS-

infected performer so that they would drip AIDS-infected blood on the audience as performance art. I don't think that's performance art. I think that's grotesque. And I think you have every right of free speech. And if you want to go and slash yourself and drip AIDS-infected blood, that's under free speech. Free speech is not subsidized. There's a big difference. I don't think there's an automatic right to coerce the taxpayer so we can finance people to do weird things.

If he had done his research he would have known that the NEA already distributed more than one-third of its funds in the form of block grants to the state arts councils and also funded local arts councils that applied. The NEA gave grants regularly to the High Museum and the Metropolitan Museum, often for arts education so that the public schools could bring children to visit them. And in referring to Ron Athey, Gingrich's inflammatory language (using words like *slash* and *drip*) was simply irresponsible. The performance was not put on by "self-selected elites . . . to pay off their friends." It was a performance, like it or not, put on by a major museum and attended by a diverse population of Minneapolis citizens.

Gingrich's remark "If you want to go and drip AIDS-infected blood that's under free speech" is just as distorted as everything else he said. Free speech is not protected when it causes panic or substantial harm. The First Amendment does not allow anyone to falsely shout "Fire!" in a crowded theater or, by extension, to "drip AIDS-infected blood" on a captive audience, although that is not even what Athey did.

In Utah, two weeks after the election, I vicariously experienced the force of Newt. Governor Mike Leavitt had just returned from a governors' conference in Virginia when I was ushered into his office. He'd had an epiphany. He had been walking at dawn in Williamsburg when who should appear from the mist but Gingrich himself! The two strolled through the old town as Newt, the history professor, detailed the colonial past of each building. Leavitt was still glowing from the experience when I met him. As chairman of the Republican Governors' Council Leavitt had found himself charged by Newt with the task of forging a state "package" to reduce the burden on the federal government. Decentralization was the new cry of Congress, and Leavitt was eager to outline what states could take care of on their own without federal help. When I pointed out that a state actually gained two dollars from the NEA's federal grant when a single dollar was matched in their state, Leavitt turned without hesitation to his arts council director, Bonnie Stephens, and said: "We can do that." I knew then we had our work cut out for us: we had to prove that the federal grants were worth as much, if not more, than either state grants or block grants of all NEA money to the states. Governors wanted control of the money that the federal government gave them, to do with as they saw fit, whether it was transportation or agricultural funds. The mayors, on the other hand, knew that they had a better deal if their cities received funds from both entities, and they weren't subject to the vagaries of a state's political agenda, which might vary from year to year depending on who was in power. They also knew that a grant from the National Endowment for the Arts was a highly prestigious award for their community. The mayors were always the NEA's friends, but the Republican governors were thrilled with the possibilities the new Congress offered their states.

Newt Gingrich was the man of the hour. If folks were not currying favor with him they were quaking in fear of his awful retribution or ridiculing his power. Garrison Keillor penned an ode to him for his weekly radio show *Prairie Home Companion:*

I took me a trip down to Capitol Hill,
I came to the door and I felt the chill.
It was changed so much from two months before.
They had a liberal detector set up by the door.
You had to take an oath you had never known sin.
I had to lie pretty bad before they let me come in. . . .
Newt, Newt,
He doesn't give a hoot.
He's gonna bring in the crackers and kick out the fruit. . . .
Oh it's Newt, Newt—
He's kinda cute.
His hair is shaped like a parachute.

And on and on for seven or eight verses, as only Keillor can do it.

The Republican takeover had resulted in major changes for the NEA's friends in the House and Senate. Ted Kennedy was succeeded by Nancy Kassebaum as chairman of the prestigious Labor and Human Resources Committee. He and Nancy worked well together and expected to continue to pass important legislation, but losing the chairmanship also reduced Kennedy's immense staff to about twenty-five. A narrow election had not lost him his seat after thirty-two years, but it had cost him valuable personnel. Fortunately Kathy Kruse, the senator's remarkable aide for arts and humanities issues, was not one of them.

Jesse Helms gained great power in the Senate in 1995, as chairman of the Senate Foreign Relations Committee. Although he continued to flail the Endowment with his annual amendments to the appropriations bill, he had his mind on other things, such as holding presidential appointments hostage until he got his way with foreign relations issues. Just as Robert Byrd had held all the cards as chairman of the Senate Appropriations Committee when the Democrats were in power, now Jesse Helms and the new Republican leadership—Strom Thurmond (Armed Services), Orrin Hatch (Judiciary), and Mark Hatfield (Appropriations)—were in full control.

Hatch was a long-standing supporter of the Endowment and reiterated his support, even telling me not to take up my time visiting him again but to concentrate on the fence-sitters. Mark Hatfield was a grand statesman and a centrist on many issues; I knew he would be fair with us. In some ways it was a relief not to have to deal with Robert Byrd as chairman of Appropriations anymore. Thurmond would vote with Helms and couldn't be counted on to run a meeting well, much less know our agency's issues, but if Thurmond and Helms had seemed like toothless old lions before, they were now roaring and full of bite.

Al Simpson was happy, at least for the time being. The Senate Republican victory was sweet, and all that he sought to accomplish for the western states, like ranchers' rights, was within reach. Two years later, however, he suffered a wounding blow. Although he had seniority and was a natural leader, his moderate stance on issues cost him the position of majority leader when Bob Dole left the Senate to run for president. His colleagues narrowly voted in conservative Trent Lott. Simpson's wife Ann confided in me that in some ways it was for the best; at least he could freely speak his mind about issues and not toe the ultra-conservative party line.

In the House of Representatives, Sid Yates, the lion of the arts, won reelection as easily as he had so many other times since 1949, but the GOP victory cost him the chairmanship of the subcommittee on Interior appropriations, which he had ruled for decades. His reelection made him the oldest member of the House, but it was an ignominious honor under the circumstances. He remained my guru still.

Ralph Regula was now the chairman of the subcommittee. I got along well with Ralph and had visited him at his farm in Ohio a few months before, in July 1994. He and his lovely wife, Mary, hosted a breakfast for me in their home overlooking an undulating pasture and a herd of cattle that Ralph and his sons tended personally. Ralph was a good, salt-of-the-earth man with his feet squarely on the ground and little desire for contentiousness. It had not been a sure bet that he would become the subcommittee's new chairman—not until he swore allegiance to the Newt agenda. Ralph was a stalwart party man, but it must have been hard for him to swallow all of the new party line, particularly with regard to the NEA and the NEH. Swallow it he did, however, in order to gain his advanced position.

There was a lot of work to be done when the new Congress would convene after the Christmas break. I was eager to wrap up my tour of the states and the districts beforehand. Noel had scheduled me for Hawaii, Guam, and the Northern Mariana Islands, but the Republican victory put a crimp in the plan. Sandy, Cherie, and Dick felt strongly that a trip to the Pacific at this time would smack of indulgence on the part of the NEA and be used against me. I was loath to break my promise to the arts communities of Guam and the Marianas; they were rarely visited and had earnestly been preparing for my arrival. But I succumbed to the better judgment of my colleagues and made Puerto Rico and Hawaii my final stops, forgoing the Virgin Islands as well. First I had a few more continental United States to visit.

Stephanie and I flew to Kansas, which was especially important to the NEA now because of Nancy Kassebaum and Bob Dole, who had become majority leader. The flight was long, and it was difficult for me to concentrate on my reading. I gazed out the plane window at the reflection of a full hunter's moon, bright in the sky. It slithered across the land, its silver light catching hold in patches of field water, along streams, rivers, and pools. Sometimes it ran ahead of the plane, and sometimes it lagged behind, depending on how we lined up with the moon.

Kansas itself was not nearly so magical. As always, there was good art to be found. There were some stunning paintings in Wichita's art museum. In the Northeast Magnet School of the Arts and Technology a brilliant teacher of ceramic and fabric art was transforming the lives of kids. One boy had kicked drugs and made ceramics his new habit; he gave me a finely turned raku pot. In the town of Wamego, population thirty-five hundred, an NEA grant to restore large paintings from the 1893 Chicago World's Fair had resulted in the complete restoration of the Colombian Theater and brought the community together as it had never been before. The hardware store, the pharmacy, and the bank, as well as individual citizens, all helped match the NEA grant and now took special pride in the restoration they had collectively brought about. Community theater had sprung up as well, bringing a mini-renaissance to Wamego.

In Topeka, while riding up to the Museum of History where our Folk and Traditional Art Program sponsored a cowboy boot exhibition, we bumped up against the ugly side of the religious right. The road was lined with people holding signs that said "FAG-JANE-NEA" or "WHORE-JANE-NEA." I was sickened to see that some of the carriers were small children, maybe five or six years old. The group was not large, maybe several families, but it was beyond me to understand how they could inculcate their children in such venal ways.

The museum had canceled Maya Angelou's visit two weeks earlier because of these people, but we moved intrepidly on and entered through the back door of the building where they did not attempt to follow us. These zealots were sorry figures and in no way representative of the people of Kansas. The town meetings we held were filled with enthusiastic arts supporters and only an occasional dissenter. Still, for all the great people in Kansas, there was a traditional fundamentalist core. Being in the middle of the country can do that to a state, a kind of hunker-down, "we'll get by and don't you easterners try to tell us what to do" philosophy. I knew it from my own father's Nebraska background. He had astounded me at times with a deeply conservative viewpoint, conveying a sense that indecency could creep up behind you and take over the world if you weren't careful. My brother Tom inherited the same backbone, whereas my sister Pam and I were "laissez-faire," preferring to believe that people find their own moral compass given enough freedom, education, and compassion. I certainly never loved my father or brother less for their rectitude. And it served me well in trying to understand the motivations of a state like Kansas in veering substantially to the right. The state was passing more and more reactionary legislation, bringing back creationism in the school curricula and electing extremely conservative officials.

The Christian Right had only begun to make inroads with its agenda for a moral nation when they decided to get involved politically. They seemed to forget that separation of church and state was a founding tenet of our democracy. Or maybe they believed that with a Congress dedicated to conservative Christian ways they could change or even subvert the laws of our nation. The Christian Coalition's bright young leader, Ralph Reed, escalated the strategy to Christianize the Republican Party by Republicanizing the Christian Right. In the 1990s Reed more than anyone led the charge for expanded political involvement by the religious right, which now took on a broader range of issues than those encompassed by "family values" (primarily homosexuality, abortion, school prayer, and sexual content in media and education). By electing their own to school boards, local and state legislatures, and federal positions they calculated that in a few generations the nation would be theirs. They were not wrong. Communities all across America today have significant numbers of elected officials who subscribe to a Christian Right agenda for their schools and cultural entities.

What the Moral Majority did not count on was their own leaders' fallibility, which had helped reduce the impact of the religious right by 1989 (when Ralph Reed and the Christian Coalition came on the scene). For every bastion of rectitude like Pat Robertson or Pat Buchanan there was a repentant sinner like Jimmy Swaggert or Jim Bakker whose fall from grace would set the movement back. The liberal does not hold the monopoly on sexual errantry after all. For many these setbacks put the lie to the possibility of human beings ever achieving a moral nation, but for others they were reason to step up the effort. Behind every sinner who fell on the path stood a saint ready to take his place.

The conservative Christians also didn't count on the factionalism that ensued as the various organizations and leaders attempted to nestle under one umbrella. The National Right to Life Committee was not terribly interested in NAFTA or crime agendas. Most of these groups *were* interested in the elimination of the NEA, however.

The Endowment was cited regularly in the newsletters of the Christian Action Network, the American Family Association, the Family Research Council, the Liberty Alliance, the Eagle Forum, and Pat Buchanan's campaigns, among others. Several of us on the senior staff asked our husbands to contribute a few dollars to the organizations so we could keep abreast of their attacks. The newsletters and fund-raising pleas reached millions and millions of homes across the United States on a regular basis. Often they were cited in Sunday worship services by church leaders and preachers, who would thus reinforce the distortion or lies about the Endowment inherent in such appeals. One man in Texas confided to me that his mother was going broke because she sent money weekly in response to these incendiary newsletters.

"Dear Friend," a typical letter would begin. (This one is a 1993 missive from Jerry Falwell's Liberty Alliance). "They're back and the perverted art they are funding with our tax dollars is worse than ever before! The President and Congress respond only to public pressure— *so they must hear from thousands of citizens.* . . . Your gift of $100, $50, $25, or even $15 will help pay for printing, postage, radio airtime, and production."

The letter would always catalog the egregious grants given, hyperbole taking precedence over fact, as in this May 1994 fund-raising appeal from the Christian Action Network:

This is "ART"? ***DRIPPING BLOOD ON THE AUDIENCE?*** . . . My friend, I don't know about you—but this makes me *SICK!* . . . *THE ARTIST WAS INFECTED WITH HIV*—the virus that leads to the deadly AIDS disease. Would you want this fellow dripping blood on you? . . . THE CLINTON ADMINISTRATION IS

FUNDING THIS KIND OF GARBAGE! But Bill and Hillary don't care—because they appointed their good friend, actress Jane Alexander, as Chairman of the NEA and she told them she wants:!! **AN NEA BUDGET OF $50 BILLION TAX DOLLARS!!** . . . Doesn't Jane Alexander and the NEA know that the deadly HIV virus is transmitted through blood?

Martin J. Mawyer, president of the Christian Action Network, saw members of Congress directly on the Hill when he could. In July 1993 he had mounted a show called "A Graphic Picture Is Worth a Thousand Votes" in a room of the Capitol reserved by Representative Philip Crane, a foe of the Endowment from Illinois. It lasted only fifteen minutes before Representatives Sidney Yates and Dan Rostenkowski decided the exhibition violated House rules on lobbying in the Capitol. It didn't matter: Mawyer and his organization got the coverage they wanted. The next morning's *Washington Post* declared: "An Open and Shut Case of 'Offensive' Photos—House Sends Anti-NEA Exhibit Packing." It was always necessary for the NEA to set the record straight. In this instance the American Arts Alliance and the National Association of Artists' Organizations were present on the Hill to pass out fact sheets to members of Congress and their aides and to the press. We often wrote to every representative and senator directly. Dick Woodruff spent hours on the phone with congressional aides giving them our side of the story. And if that wasn't enough I would place calls myself to members of Congress. Cherie Simon and others in the communications office spent an equal amount of time speaking with members of the press. Cherie always gave them a thorough briefing on the facts well before I was interviewed. And she schooled me also before I got on the phone. An undisciplined remark on my part could have ramifications for months to come, and so I made sure I did the homework required.

A few evangelical leaders were sympathetic to the Endowment and supportive of government funding for the arts, but their promises to broker a meeting between me and conservative Christian leaders like Gary Bauer or Ralph Reed never came to pass. I'm not sure it would have mattered anyway; none of these leaders was about to change his mind, not when a new Congress had just been elected on a platform that called for the elimination of the NEA.

As if we didn't have enough critics to contend with, the Endowment was hearing negatively from those in the arts world. November 1994 was a tense month for the agency. The American Civil Liberties Union, the National Campaign for Freedom of Expression, and the Center for Constitutional Rights had filed an appeal asking that the agency reconsider its rejection of the three photographers from the August meeting. Marjorie Heins, the director of the ACLU's Arts Censorship Project, was concerned that since the National Council's working groups were closed to the public, decisions were being made in private. This was not the case. Karen Christensen and her two staff lawyers at the Endowment sat in on all the working groups and were strict about keeping their sessions informational, not deliberative. It took a while to convince the organizations of this and made us suspect in the eyes of our grantees.

In addition my decision to eliminate subgranting was causing a furor. Jean Firstenberg of the American Film Institute, which had the most to lose, was gracious and understanding when I informed her. The Rockefeller Foundation and the Andy Warhol Foundation were less sanguine. Together we supported numerous artists through a partnership called "Artists' Projects: Regional Initiative." Our joint funds certainly expanded opportunities for many artists, but because it was a subgrant, I could not support the repaneling that the initiative entailed. Moreover, the initiative was not cost-effective; in some cases it was 50 percent more expensive. Mainly, I wanted to raise the bar and make an NEA grant the finest award given. I felt that a grant from the *National* Endowment to a local group or artist should confer distinction above and beyond what a local or regional grant conferred, because the deciding panelists were a nationwide jury of one's peers. Some of the art that the regional initiative supported was provocative, and therefore it was assumed that I was eliminating subgranting in order to rid the Endowment of possible problem grants.

Arch Gillies, the director of the Warhol Foundation, took me to task in a *Newsday* op-ed piece on October 30, 1994, claiming that the NEA was bowing to political pressure in its decision making and that we were abandoning our duty to nurture new art. I couldn't argue about the presence of political pressure; whether or not I was "bowing" to it, however, was in the eye of the beholder. I was certainly walking a fine line, but I hoped I was still dancing rather than bowing. The accusation that we were departing from our support of new art because some of it was controversial was simply not true. In fact, when we eliminated sub-granting I increased the NEA's direct funding of individual artists' fellowships by $750,000 in order to avoid a loss to new creations.

Alberta Arthurs of the Rockefeller Foundation was more understanding of our position, saying in the *Village Voice* on November 15: "Regranting is a methodology they have . . . questioned. That's a different kind of 'political' than trying to distance yourself from controversy. I don't see it as censorious. Jane and her staff may think they are making things procedurally more defensible."

The *New York Times,* in an article on November 3, tried to make the case that the subgrant cuts were to control controversial work and then ended the article with: "Oddly . . . the Athey grant wasn't under this category." Oddly, virtually *none* of the controversial work was under the subgrant category.

The negative press and uneasiness about the future of the agency made the November Council meeting difficult. My staff had received word that there might be protesters at the meeting. Whether they were from the right wing or the left, I was the focus of many people's ire. Plainclothes detectives watched over me throughout the two days until it was clear there would be no harm done. Some of the Council members were up in arms about the changes I was making. One went so far as to say that maybe the Endowment should be done away with so we could all undergo "purification." It was certainly a possibility and closer to realization than he believed. I had traveled to most of our United States by this time. I was as weary as anyone of the attacks on art by Congress, the attacks on me by some in the art world, and the constant questioning in the press, but there was no way that I was going to let the agency go under. It meant too much to too many. I went back on the road, where, despite the occasional dissent, I could always see some wonderful art and meet enthusiastic people.

My final state was Hawaii. What better way to end a fifty-state tour and a tumultuous year than in paradise? I had spent glorious weeks in Hawaii several times before and knew all of the islands. In the 1980s I had been in a four-hour TV movie called *Blood and Orchids,* which was shot in Honolulu and elsewhere on Oahu. Kris Kristofferson and a young Madeleine Stowe also starred in the true story of a racial incident in the 1930s. We filmed in old mansions, and I spent my leisure time swimming, snorkeling, and hiking the volcanic trails looking for a white-tailed tropic bird, with its three-foot-long swallowtail and narrow angel wings lofted behind. One cloudy day I was finally rewarded. High over the sea, and buffeted by strong winds, she came in, hovering like the Holy Ghost before landing on an ancient lava cliff to tend her lone egg. These were the sights I lived for.

This time, visiting on behalf of the NEA, I was treated to awesome sights of a different nature. Most memorable was Halau O' Kekuhi, a group of Hawaiian women who danced and chanted to the goddess Pele as their ancestors had done, a tradition kept alive by NEA help. Stephanie and I visited the International Longshoremen's and Warehousemen's Union Building to see an extensive mural painted in 1952 by Pablo O'Higgins, an apprentice of Diego Rivera's. NEA's Design program had awarded $50,000 for the restoration of this historical painting of immigrant labor.

The town meeting we held in Honolulu was so jam-packed that an overflow audience watched on monitors in other rooms. Hawaii is replete with culture, the result of centuries of different peoples coming together on the islands and bringing something of their own to the mix. The state backed its arts well in 1994, spending $10 million for a population of one million people, surpassing all other states. I told them how pleased I was to be among friendly faces, and how sometimes on the road I had encountered a different attitude. Once, I said, I walked into a little shop to buy a Coke and the fellow behind the counter said, "Anyone ever tell you that you look like Jane Alexander?" "Yes," I replied, "They sure have." Whereupon the man said, "Makes you kinda mad, doesn't it?" This always got a laugh. The story was untrue; I had stolen the joke from Washington's best jokester, Al Simpson, but it was a foolproof sympathy-getter in the current climate.

On Maui, on the final day of my tour, we were hosted by one of Hawaii's visionaries, the octogenarian "Pundy" Yokouchi. As an eleven-year-old boy Pundy, the son of Japanese immigrants who worked in the cane fields, would walk daily by the beautiful house he now lives in. Built in 1936, it stands on a rise amid green trees and small pools. Spacious and full of light, even Frank Lloyd Wright told Pundy that *he* would like to live there. Our host loved fine things and believed in the importance of drama and music to a community. He led the effort to create Maui's Cultural Center, with a grand 1,400-seat theater that stands as testament to his vision.

It was a few days before Christmas. I picked Ed up at Maui's airport, and we drove through the late-afternoon light over the spectacular winding road to the Hana Ranch on the east coast. A pasture tumbled below us to the ocean, and in the distance we glimpsed the snowcapped peaks of the volcanoes on the "Big Island," Hawaii. We had rarely been away from our home at Christmas, but I could not face the holiday chores this December after the tumult of the previous months. Ed was exhausted too from a long season on *Law and Order*, and so we found peace and quiet together at Hana.

I had a massage on the first morning of our holiday. It felt lovely, but at the end of the hour, when I started to rise off the table, I couldn't move. My back seized; the poor masseuse thought she might have ruined me forever. No, I assured her, the Congress of the United States did that. The problems with my knee, which had plagued me for the better part of the year, had finally healed only to be replaced by an out-of-whack back. Politics was ruining my health. I managed to move slowly through the Hawaiian days and nights, but the interminable flight home on cramped coach seats finally did me in. By the time I was back in my office on January 3, 1995, my back went out completely. I lay immobile in my apartment for five days.

The program directors paid visits to my bedside to give me the annual review of their fields. Cherie and I conducted press interviews by telephone, and I managed to strategize with Nancy Kassebaum when she called to talk about our Senate reauthorization hearing on the twenty-fourth. Nancy wanted to be sure I had accomplished real reform at the agency. I told her of the procedural changes in place and of those I was going to have to implement during the year. I had asked the staff to start thinking about restructuring the agency, based on a 50 percent budget cut for fiscal year 1996. We'd barely recovered from all the tension of controversy and appropriations when we had to dig in and rethink the entire agency. The senator said that there were only two Republican votes we could count on from the subcommittee: hers and Jim Jeffords's. It did not seem to me that we were going to advance the cause of reauthorization one iota given the current Congress, but I was pleased she wanted the hearing anyway.

As soon as I was up and about, Dick and I began making daily visits to the Hill. There were many new faces in power and newly elected congressmen who needed to hear the NEA story. Speaker Gingrich would not schedule a meeting with me. He was a very busy man; everyone wanted to see him. We kept our request in but concentrated on others close to his inner circle.

Representative William Goodling of Pennsylvania was now chairman of the House Economic and Educational Opportunity Committee. He was a bland fellow who said that he was for us but that the budget had to be cut, so it would be a fight to keep us in existence. Bob Livingston, a congressman from Louisiana, was now the chairman of the Appropriations Committee. He too seemed like a nice enough guy but was slightly patronizing. His remark "You're certainly an excellent advocate for the agency" reminded me of Hatch's first comment to me: "You're sincere, you're a lovely person, people on the Hill will respond to you." Maybe I was too sensitive, but would they say such things to a man, I wondered? I just wanted the truth, and no one was coming out with it directly. I had to read between the lines with Livingston. When he kept repeating that private contributions to the arts amounted to $9 billion a year, I assumed he was telling me that we didn't need public-sector participation.

I didn't bother to try to schedule a meeting with the new majority leader, Dick Armey of Texas. He had been against the NEA for so long it would have been fruitless. But I saw him across the room at a crowded reception one evening. Dressed to the nines in an evening gown, I was being trailed by an ABC-TV crew at the request of Peter Jennings, who wanted to do an hour special on the NEA. General Colin Powell came up to me, chuckling sympathetically about the battle I was in; he told me that he could give some advice about the trenches, but then spying the camera crew, he quickly exited, whispering, "Live mike, live mike." It gave me the idea that introducing myself to Armey with the tape running might be interesting. My tactics were beginning to disgust me, but if I was going to play the game of politics to win, I couldn't stall.

I introduced myself to Armey, who smiled cheerily and said: "Well, we should talk." Paying no attention to the camera, he said he would like to move the debate from the issue of controversial art, which would come and go and always be there, to the question of whether public funding should support the arts. I agreed, adding, "The controversial art debate is a red herring." "Yes! A red herring," he agreed. "I'm glad we agree on something," I said as we shook hands and parted. Like the Cheshire Cat, I was grinning ear to ear, delighted to have caught Newt's top man in a tacit admission that the issue wasn't controversial art at all, but something else entirely. I thought of the millions who would see it when ABC aired the hour, but regrettably, a few months later, Jennings and his producers jettisoned the story. I never knew why.

A leading Republican on the Economic and Education Committee, which had jurisdiction over our reauthorization in the House, was Randy "Duke" Cunningham, who hailed from San Diego, California. A "top gun" Navy flyer, he was a big robust fellow who seemed inclined to put his arm around this little lady in a gesture of goodwill and bonhomie. Duke Cunningham and I had one of the more bizarre talks of my visits to the Hill. His record in support of the NEA was nil, but he too was wreathed in smiles. What was it with our enemies, I thought? Killing us with kindness? He began coaching me in ways to win on the issue and ended by telling me that I should study *A Book of Five Rings* by Miyamoto Musashi. Perhaps he was attempting to reverse an inherent sexism, or maybe his twenty-year stint in the Navy had gotten to him, but we moved from a discussion of the arts to a discussion of the art of war, with which he was far more comfortable.

Of course I ran out and bought the book immediately, then read it from cover to cover that evening. I was mystified. I am all for spiritual and metaphorical aids to the difficulties of life, but try as I might I couldn't relate this 350-year-old book on the martial arts to my battle for the NEA. For example, in the section called "A Stand Against Many Opponents" the author states: "A stand against many opponents is when an individual fights against a group. Drawing both long and short swords, you hold them out to the left and right, extending them horizontally. The idea is that even if opponents come at you from all four sides, you chase them into one place."

I couldn't even get this to work on a symbolic level. I turned to the passage on "Upset": "Upset happens in all sorts of things. One way it happens is through a feeling of being under acute pressure. Another is through a feeling of unreasonable strain. A third is through a feeling of surprise at the unexpected." So far so good.

In large-scale military science, it is essential to cause upset. It is critical to attack resolutely where enemies are not expecting it; then while their minds are unsettled, use this to your advantage to take the initiative and win.

In individual martial arts also, you appear relaxed at first, then suddenly charge powerfully; as the opponent's mind changes pitch, it is essential that you follow what he does, not letting him relax for a moment.

I imagined myself being sweet and demure and then charging powerfully at Jesse Helms or Dick Armey, lashing out about the value of the arts to society. Would this win the day? Would they just think I was a crazy woman and relegate me to the status of "Mad Dog" Dornan? I put the book on a shelf. This must be a "guy thing," I thought. Months later I received an eight-by-ten photo in the mail from Duke Cunningham, inscribed to me in gold ink, as if we had gone to the prom together. We are standing happily together, the promise of good times to come in our eyes. Duke never voted for the NEA once, not then, and not now.

Another House member I made no inroads with was Barbara Vucanovich from Nevada. Vucanovich said flat out that she was going to vote to abolish the agency, that her constituents were very conservative and they didn't like the art we funded. "Which art?" I asked. "Oh, you know," she replied, "the Christ in urine." "That was five years ago!"

I said. "Doesn't matter, it's the perception of the agency that counts," she stated with finality. I almost gave up then and there. Fighting perceptions was akin to sparring with ghosts: the target could always be moving and you wouldn't know it. Congresswomen were usually behind the Endowment no matter what their party affiliation, but Vucanovich was a new breed altogether. Or was her seeming lack of intelligence indicative of the level of many of our legislators?

Our visits to the Hill were focused mainly on the House of Representatives, but there were a few senators I needed to meet. Slade Gorton, from the state of Washington, was now in charge of our Senate appropriations subcommittee. Our first meeting was something of a disaster. He began by saying, "I understand you've done some acting," and it went downhill from there. He called artists "90 percent lefties." The pejorative tag irritated me, but I didn't argue with him. Ninety percent of artists *were* humanists, as the human condition was their primary focus, and if humanists tend to be left of center, so be it. Gorton was supposed to be a financial whiz. He quickly shot down my argument that the Endowment leveraged eleven dollars on average for every dollar it granted in a community because so many individuals, corporations, and foundations matched the award. He said curtly: "Then the private sector can pick up that twelfth dollar." I thought the man was full of himself and full of hot air. He reminded me of a crane, tall and taut and slim with a big eye moving around looking for a target. It irritated me, too, that he didn't know who I was and hadn't bothered to learn before our meeting. When I returned to my office I shot off my four-page résumé listing my one hundred stage roles, my forty films for TV and the feature market, my Tony and Emmy Awards, and the four Academy Award nominations.

The new junior senator from Tennessee was a smart lawyer turned actor named Fred Thompson. The last film I had done, in 1991, was a miniseries for television called *Stay the Night,* a psychological thriller based on the true story of a Georgia woman who finally nails the killer, who was played by Barbara Hershey. Fred had done a large supporting role in *Stay the Night.* I remember thinking happily that he was going to be a piece of cake. Of course he was going to support the Endowment, he knew what the arts were all about firsthand. I was wrong. Fred had made it into the realm of movie actors without a struggle. He had never gone the route of nonprofit theater and independent film to get there, as so many of us had done. His own story of representing a woman named Marie when he was a lawyer had been made into a movie with Sissy Spacek. Fred played himself in the film, which marked the beginning of his career as an actor. Now he was finding stardom in the Senate, and although he was always cordial to me, he barely had the time to give me five minutes.

At least he was better than Sonny Bono, the 1960s pop music star and newly elected representative from California, who immediately adopted a stand against the Endowment, saying he had never met any-one who received an NEA grant; ergo, what good was it? I guessed he didn't get around much.

Ralph Regula held preliminary hearings on the NEA and NEH. His main witnesses were William Bennett and Lynne Cheney, two archcon-servatives who had previously chaired the Humanities Endowment and now called for its elimination, and Charlton Heston and Frank Hod-soll, who both said the NEA could do a better job, Frank intimating that under his chairmanship the NEA *did* do a better job. He neglected to tell everyone that the grants that had gotten the Endowment in trou-ble back in 1989 and 1990 had all been awarded on his watch.

I had a dream about Ralph Regula a few nights later. I dreamed I was conducting a staff meeting with ice skates on. Then I walked on the skates to Ralph's farm, where I found him half-bearded and scruffy in overalls. There were masses of people all over his place, and exotic ani-mals in cages. He was selling endangered species, tigers and others, to circuses and those who wished to buy them. The dream was clear to me: Congress was choking the arts, their uniqueness was not valued except as entertainment, and I was on thin ice.

My president, my boss, gave a long State of the Union address, which I watched on television, unlike the year before when I had stood cheering in the House chamber. This 1995 speech was a rousing one too—for a Republican. Even Clinton was moving to the right. There was no mention at all of the attacks on culture. The president took a cheap shot at Hollywood: "We recognize your creativity, but . . . you've got to stop this violence on TV and in the movies," and received a long standing ovation from both the Democrats and the Republicans. As much as I abhor gratuitous violence in film, this seemed particularly hypocritical since most of these guys, like the rest of America and the world, adored Stallone and Schwarzenegger.

President Clinton, for all his charisma, was a bit of a mystery to me. He seemed to espouse all the causes I believed in, but then he made no seminal speeches about them. There was no ringing call for the reduction of weapons of mass destruction, there were no quotable remarks on the glory of art in our civilization or the meaning of technology in our society. Personally he was warm and supportive, but his reach didn't seem to extend beyond the next handshake. I wanted a vision for the next century that was more than "building a bridge."

When I visited Tennessee and nearby Arkansas, spending a day in Bill Clinton's hometown of Hot Springs, some of the pieces of the puzzle came together. The modest house where he, his little brother, and his ebullient mother, Virginia, had lived was perched on the rise of a hill along a main street out of the town center. Below were the famous baths frequented by Mafioso back in the 1950s and 1960s. I pictured young Bill riding his bike down the hill past the baths into the heart of the town. It was a pleasant place, dependent on tourists who brought in revenue.

Not far away was the thriving metropolis of Memphis, Tennessee, where another hometown boy, Elvis Presley, had been king of the pop charts. Bill Clinton must have watched the way Elvis enthralled people with his walk, his eyes, his lips, and his throaty voice. There were worse role models certainly, and little Billy, growing up in Arkansas, may not have been exposed to many better ones, except the president of the United States, John F. Kennedy, from a distance. Clinton did not follow the path of Presley, but he retained some of his signal qualities. And he can still do a knockout imitation of the crooner at the drop of a hat. When I heard the president sing "Love Me Tender" once at a small party, I was transported back to my teenage rock-and-roll days in the 1950s.

Bill Clinton was clever, likable, and knowledgeable in how to get ahead. He carried his boyhood aptitude for high achievement to Georgetown, Yale, and Oxford, and then into the highest echelons of politics in Arkansas and Washington, D.C. If John F. Kennedy was his idol, it was Elvis Presley with whom he identified. Not the pill-popping addict but the sexy down-home boy who indulged his senses and knew his seductive charm could get him anything he wanted.

Hot Springs, I conjectured, was one reason why my president never really took on the issue of the Arts Endowment in a public way. He had learned tangentially about painting, literature, and theater, and he played the saxophone, bopping to the music with his band; but the arts were not his passion. Most of all, he loved people, and art was one step removed from direct contact. Although I still could not get a private meeting with the president, and he did not give ringing speeches about the arts, I was grateful for the support he did give the agency. Even in the face of the "Contract with America," the president's budget asked for an increase to the NEA of $5 million, for a total of $172.4 million, a nice vote of confidence. Money was, after all, the bottom line of politics, and there was no one who played the game better than William Jefferson Clinton.

Sandy Crary, my chief of staff, and I met with the First Lady and Melanne Verveer in the basement War Room of the White House one December morning. It gave me a thrill to think of FDR poring over the maps in that very room, learning the positions of the troops during World War II. My years of involvement with Roosevelt history, the research and then the filming for the TV series, had given me a deep appreciation of Franklin and Eleanor. Here I was sitting with another impressive First Lady, one who had not been given her due. Knowing her interest in the welfare of children, I wanted to talk to Hillary about the power of the arts for at-risk youth. She suggested we visit a school together to bring attention to the subject.

Her frustration with the Gingrich agenda was palpable in her feistiness. She said she would be out every day responding to his attacks. The latest one to arouse her indignation was his allegation that one-quarter of all White House staff had taken drugs in the past. The First Lady began to analyze specifically the NEA's needs and how to get what we wanted. She said that op-eds in the newspapers wouldn't be all that effective because our response to lies and distortions would come too late. She said we needed to find big campaign donors to Gingrich and the others and ask them to place a call on behalf of saving the Endowment. In other words, cut him off at the money source. I began working on that strategy that very afternoon, calling friends in Georgia, and I watched it slowly pay off two years later. I was learning the ropes. Politics is about giving money in great quantities to candidates who will then do your bidding, and it is about candidates finding money sources for their constituents in the form of home-state "pork." The gilded idealism with which I'd been suffused on taking office was tarnishing fast.

The First Lady was the honorary chairman of the President's Committee on the Arts and Humanities (PCAH). Ellen Lovell, its director, brought together influential people appointed by the president from the private sector, such as Harvey Golub, CEO of American Express; Lerone Bennett, executive editor of *Ebony* magazine; and Harold Williams, president of the Getty Foundation. PCAH was immensely helpful in its advocacy for the NEA and NEH, and we needed such help more than ever. John Brademas, former congressman from Indiana, president emeritus of New York University, and arguably the leading arts advocate in America, chaired the PCAH. I listened as the First Lady stressed the need to preserve the arts and humanities for all citizens and watched as subcommittees were formed for "arts and kids" and for "cultural tourism."

Independently, Brademas, William Luers of the Metropolitan Museum of Art, Andrew Heiskell, my mentor and the former Time-Life chairman, and Richard Franke, CEO of the Nuveen Corporation, were putting together a group of national, bipartisan CEOs who would publicly support the NEA and NEH in the media and through phone calls to their congressmen. They called their effort Americans United to Save the Arts and Humanities. All four men devoted a great deal of time to preserving the arts and humanities in the United States. Their lives were very busy, but they tackled the cause unasked and without hesitation. Republican CEOs had a great deal of clout on the Hill. We were building coalitions.

The new Congress thrust most of us in the federal culture community together. We were all nervous about the future of our institutions and traded notes, phone calls, and lunches to strategize. I met regularly with Sheldon Hackney of NEH, Ellen Lovell of PCAH, and Diane

Frankel, who was director of the Institute for Museum Services, at a "four corners" luncheon hosted in one of the four corner offices we each occupied on the fifth floor of the Old Post Office Building. It was good to commiserate together; if I wasn't the current object of attack, it might be Sheldon and the Humanities Endowment. These luncheons gave us an opportunity to shore each other up and share some gallows humor, as well as to strategize. Now the circle was enlarging. No one seemed safe anymore. Mike Heymann of the Smithsonian said that the GOP members of Congress were making threatening noises to him, and he later experienced the wrath of the military and Congress when the Smithsonian opened its exhibit on the *Enola Gay,* the bomber that had devastated Hiroshima. The bomber meant different things to different people, and the critics would not accept any curatorial editoralizing in the exhibit. They threatened to close it unless some language was excised, and so the exhibit was revised. Jim Wolfensohn said that if Congress cut off the programming funds for the Kennedy Center, he would simply close the doors. Earl "Rusty" Powell of the National Gallery of Art was being attacked for how he was handling a leaky roof that threatened the artwork in the museum, but he was subsequently rescued by a blockbuster Vermeer exhibit, which the public lined up in droves to see. We all wanted our own "Vermeer" to come to the rescue. Nobody argued with the public or with great dead masters.

Ervin Duggan, the president of the Public Broadcasting Service, was embroiled in "BarneyGate," which was threatening to destroy the whole cloth of PBS. Gingrich wanted to know, if Barney toys made so much money, why was the taxpayer supporting PBS at all? Gingrich was seeking to "privatize" the network in the same way that he wanted "privatization" of the NEA. It was too bad that PBS had turned Gingrich down when he was peddling his history series years before; perhaps an acceptance then would have mitigated his later attacks on public television. The American public ultimately saved public television from being privatized, but at a cost. The on-air solicitations increased, as did commercial advertising.

Jim Billington, the librarian of Congress, was lucky. Newt loved books, and the Library was Congress's own, so despite the fact that Billington never had enough money to archive all the library's volumes digitally, he emerged relatively unscathed from the cultural attacks by the 104th Congress.

We who headed the cultural institutions and agencies in D.C. shared a feeling that we were all in this together, as well as a sense of purpose in the need to overcome a common enemy. It really did seem that the barbarians had scaled the castle walls and were inside the gates. They had targeted the Fulbright fellowships, the Pell grants, and the Woodrow Wilson International Center for Scholars for decimation, threatening scholarly study both here and abroad. Newt and the new Congress felt that the marketplace would take care of everything and that the trickle-down from a successful economy would take care of us all. Wasn't this Reagonomics all over again? Hadn't it been tried and failed? Didn't we learn anything at all from our past?

The most interesting man in Gingrich's kitchen cabinet was the budget maestro John Kasich, from Columbus, Ohio. He objected to all government support of the arts on the grounds that our Constitution did not intend such far-reaching government involvement. It was an important argument, and one to which many people had subscribed historically. As a strict constitutionalist, Kasich was in favor of reducing the overall scope of the federal government. I made the argument that the Endowment was not a burden to the taxpayer because it increased revenue at the local level by matching the federal award and helped sustain institutions, increasing employment and hence revenue for the IRS. I said that it existed, like the Small Business Administration, or tax breaks for corporations, or agricultural subsidies, to offer a helping hand to artists and to benefit society at large. Hadn't he ever had a helping hand that pushed him that small bit over the edge to success? I asked. No, he replied, not from the federal government. But I knew that his father had been a post office employee decades before, when the post office was a public entity. His father's government employment had surely helped the Kasich family.

I enjoyed theorizing with Kasich. He thought the federal government was too big, and in many respects I agreed with him. The wheels grind slowly in government. Even the president of the United State is powerless to accomplish all he wishes. He has the bully pulpit, but making his agenda a reality is another thing altogether. The Constitution was fashioned by men wary of putting too much power in the hands of one person or entity. They hadn't escaped the monarchy of George III to be subjugated to another single authority. The checks and balances between the three branches of government—executive, legislative, and judicial—are admirable in concept but nightmarish sometimes in execution. A reporter once asked Al Simpson what he wished he had known on entering the Senate that he knew upon leaving it. He replied, "That it takes twenty years to pass a bill."

The process is decidedly slower in the public sector compared to the private sector. Government has grown exponentially since the Continental Congress in 1782, but there are still only twenty-four hours in a day. According to Kasich, the "Contract with America" was about restoring accountability in Congress, reducing the size of government, and returning more power to the states. The problem with dismantling the behemoth that now existed, however, was that almost every facet of government was the object of someone's vested interest. When the 104th Congress thought, for example, that they could easily eliminate a program like the president's own AmeriCorps, hardly two years old, there were those who stepped forward to save it. The new Congress believed that the NEA was an easy target too. They didn't believe that artists were well organized, that arts advocacy was widespread, or that there was any coherent vested interest in the agency. Besides, the NEA had enemies nationwide in the Christian Right. It is true that the individual visual or literary artist is rarely part of a bargaining collective, but performing artists are well represented by AFL-CIO affiliates—the many unions that represent vast numbers of dancers, actors, musicians, directors, playwrights, and screenwriters. They all weighed in with support for the Endowment, as did arts advocates nationwide. The 104th Congress also boldly sought to rid government of the Departments of Education, Energy, and Commerce, Amtrak, the Legal Services Administration, and the Corporation for Public Broadcasting, along with the Endowments. None of it ultimately happened. Reagan's budget director, David Stockman, wrote in 1986 of his own inability to accomplish a similar agenda: "Sacred cows run in herds—that's the part I didn't understand."

Newt Gingrich and the new revolutionaries in Congress were idealists, but as a historian the speaker could have saved a lot of angst and time, not to mention taxpayer dollars, if he'd read his history more carefully. Nothing much was really going to change. *Plus ça change, plus c'est la même chose*—the more things change, the more they remain the same. His hubris overrode his intellect, a condition that seems to affect most people who rise to power. The American way of politics is entrenched and here to stay. It is both frustrating and satisfying to know that our system is mostly inviolable, warts and all.

Kasich's belief that the arts and humanities should be independent of government subsidy was an argument shared by others, for different reasons. Many contemporary artists thought that the business of art was to challenge the established order of things, and that it should thus remain outside the establishment and independent of authority. They were not interested in biting the hand if that hand also fed them. Some lawyers I spoke with also believed that government subsidy was danger-ous for the same reason. If artists received substantial subsidization they could be mollified over time into withholding a critical voice. One can imagine a situation in which the government is promoting a single viewpoint for its own ends and the writer or theater or art gallery is the last alternative voice to be heard—unless that voice has been easily silenced because it's on the government payroll.

The reach of the National Endowment for the Arts is significant throughout arts institutions in America today. The size of the grants may have diminished in recent years, but 90 percent of the country's art network has received federal, state, or local funds at one time. If an organization is bound to uphold a "decency clause" when accepting government funds, or to restrain in any way the content of the artwork it produces, alternative voices nationwide can be silenced. That is why it is so important to uphold the right of freedom of expression whether government funds are involved or not.

I don't believe that Ron Athey ever imagined he would become a cause célèbre because of a few performances at the Walker Art Center in 1994. Athey's work is not the usual establishment fare, and he knew it. Indeed, it is questionable whether he would ever have been awarded an individual artist grant by a panel of his peers. He had not applied to the Endowment for a grant for himself or his company, but he became embroiled in the controversy anyway because the venue in which he performed was funded by the NEA. He then joined the distinctive group of performers whose work catapulted to fame *because* they had become the newest government poster boy. I don't think that is what Athey had in mind when he created his shows. Nor do I believe he welcomed the contretemps or the criticism. Few artists do. Karen Finley has spoken openly of the emotional turmoil she still is subjected to as a result of her NEA grant and the court case that ensued. In "Art Papers" of January and February 1995 she said:

> Getting a master's degree and going through that system of being with my peers, I saw myself as a professional. What was very difficult or devastating for me in the NEA experience was being looked at as if I were crazy, out of control, or unprofessional. That's what I hate most about the way artists are perceived by most American culture. They are looked at as if they're crazy or don't have any sense of morals, or don't have any sense of responsibility, and that basically they are also thieves, that they are just out to get the most out of things. I found that very difficult.
>
> My reaction was depression. It hurt me so much because I felt that that was my identity. But first I had my public responsibility, which was suing the government, the NEA. Any other artist could have been in my place, too, so I felt that public responsibility. But in my private life, it was very difficult. I was hearing things like, "Oh, aren't you lucky that this is happening to you!" I never wanted to exploit this situation at all, to make a career move out of it. In fact, I turned down anything that had to do with the NEA, which created problems with some of the other plaintiffs. I just could not handle being in the position of having to constantly defend my work.

As a fellow artist I applauded Finley's stand. I was pleased that the California court in June 1993 upheld the NEA Four. I believe that the artist's voice, like that of the journalist, is vital to presenting an alternative viewpoint to established ways of thinking and behaving in our society. But I believe that government subsidy and free expression are *not* mutually exclusive, and that a mature democratic society accepts the full range of artistic endeavor, even when it is outrageous. The first measure of a repressive government is the silencing of alternative voices. Hitler did it. McCarthy did it. And their blasts against gays reminded me of the House Un-American Activities Committee's attacks against members of the Communist Party back in the late 1940s and 1950s. It has never been illegal to be a homosexual or a Communist in the United States of America, but some members of Congress have seemed to want to make it so.

Although the 104th Congress was not jailing people or overtly ruining their economic livelihood, they *were* attempting to make laws that would impose a conservative voice on the nation. Newt's close cadre—his "Gang of Four," as I called them—came at the NEA issue in different ways, depending on the size of their brains. Not all of them were as sharp as John Kasich, who was close to the leader but not a member of the gang. Dick Armey did not think the government should be supporting the arts because art exists whether or not the government pays for it. He spoke sentimentally in testimony before a House committee in 1997 of the piano teacher in his little hometown of Cando, North Dakota, as if she were all that was needed to sustain the world of the arts. Tom DeLay, the majority whip, was a pest exterminator prior to becoming a congressman, and that is what we called him behind the scenes, "the exterminator." His brain could fit in an eggcup as far as I could tell, and he railed routinely against the Endowment for the "obscene" art we supported. Bob Livingston from Louisiana, the new House Appropriations chairman, followed the party line. When Connie Chung showed footage on *CBS News* of some folk arts grantees in Livingston's own district who depended on the NEA, he peevishly accused us of putting her up to it (we did not). John Boehner of Ohio, the chairman of the Republican Conference, was quoted in the *Washington Post* on January 9, 1995: "We are out there living high on the hog, funding all of these activities around the country only to pass the bill on to our kids and grandkids." With regard to the Arts Endowment, this was a statement I could make neither head nor tail of, hog or no hog.

The media were in a feeding frenzy over the NEA and the new Congress. Regulars like George Will and Jonathan Yardley had been writing diatribes against us for years. I had no illusions about changing their minds. I bumped into Will one time coming out of a hotel elevator; he had a cast on his arm. I said, "Hello, George," with a bright, courteous smile, thinking all the while that if he had a cast on the other arm also he might not be able to write. The self-appointed NEA hater Lawrence Jarvik was a perpetual presence at our public meetings; he disseminated his bile in any conservative journal that would have him. Syndicated columnists were most to be feared because their sensationalist language and campaign of misinformation spread nationwide overnight. It was very difficult to countermand. Our most vocal enemies continued to be the religious right organizations, and it was not possible to reach all the citizens they reached through their well-organized mail campaigns. We did continue our strategy of writing op-eds nationwide and were pleased when an editorial came to our defense.

Fortunately the Endowment remained a hot issue for the newspapers, and from November 1994 throughout the winter of 1995 there was hardly a day when an article about the agency did not appear somewhere. If the summer had been about controversial grants and the autumn contretemps had been the elimination of subgranting, the winter brought us reinvigorated defenses of the Endowment. Even when there was a negative piece I felt there was reason to cheer. As long as we were thought about and written about it was possible to "flip the pancake," turning negative thinking into positive. This belief of mine had evolved from years in show business. I'd seen the press adore an actor for years and then do a complete turnabout and write negatively about the same performer, only to build that same actor up a few years later. Elizabeth Taylor was a good case in point: she was loved as a child actress, vilified in her thirties and forties, and then loved again.

When I was a young actress at Arena Stage in the 1960s we did a play called *Sergeant Musgrave's Dance* by the Englishman John Arden. I played the leading female role, and although I received handsome reviews in the local D.C. papers, when the *New York Times* came to review the production my name was not mentioned and my performance was slammed. The Irish actor Jim Kenny, who was a member of our company, was reading the notice, and despite the excellent review for himself and for Ed's production, he kept clucking his teeth and murmuring, "Oh, this is awful." I said, "Yes, isn't it? My first review in the *New York Times,* but thank God they didn't mention my name!" "No, that's just what is so awful," replied Jim. "In time people forget whether a review was good or bad about a performer, but it's the *name* they remember!"

Jim's observation was insightful. The important thing was to be talked about, and so I welcomed all the attention the NEA was getting. It gave us the opportunity to educate the public, and for the public to react in letters to the editors. With headlines like "Save the Rembrandts, Dump 'Piss Christ'" (*Washington Times,* December 1, 1994), "NEA Uses Taxes to Promote Filth Disguised as Art" (*New Haven Register,* November 21, 1994), "America's Art and Soul" (*Boston Globe,* December 17, 1994), and "Arts and the Coming Storm" (*Los Angeles Times,* December 25, 1994), we were pretty sure the public was reading. The television industry was starting to focus on us now too. We were no longer a sound bite about some controversial piece of art, but a national issue. I had a few minutes on the *Today Show,* and the PBS *News Hour* regularly updated the public on our struggle.

By the middle of January—and after my umpteenth visit to the physical therapy clinic, which was also the early morning hangout for several cabinet officials—I was ready for the reauthorization hearing. The Hill was awash with hearings of all kinds. Dick Riley was successfully defending a bid to eliminate the Department of Education. He valiantly spoke of the need for "national priorities," such as the teaching of our youngsters, while the GOP sought ways to save the $32 billion allocated to Education.

All eyes turned on me now, since the NEA was a litmus test for GOP action. The room was packed; about sixteen cameras ringed the floor in front of me, the men and women sprawling for position, their casual dress and posture in brazen contrast to the formality of the senators above them on the dais. Ted Kennedy was there despite the death of his beloved mother Rose two days earlier. What a rock he was! The world touts the accomplishments of his martyred brothers, but for remaining steadfast, overcoming adversity, maintaining grace under pressure, and always being there for his family, his friends, and the public, there is no one more remarkable than Ted Kennedy.

"Today the question before you is whether the agency should continue to exist," I began. "To twist Marc Antony's words, I come not to bury the Endowment but to praise it." I held up an envelope with two first-class stamps on it. "I do not believe that the taxpayers I met in towns and cities, large and small, begrudge the sixty-four cents apiece each year that the Endowment costs them. Sixty-four cents: the price of two postage stamps a year!" Cherie had taught me that a sound bite or a photo-op required a prop. An arts advocate on a Maryland trip had presented me with his homemade NEA stamp pin, and I knew we had a winner. Sure enough, the major photo in the papers the next day was of me holding up the envelope.

There were no hard questions at the hearing despite the presence of one of the agency's most vocal foes, John Ashcroft of Missouri, who would make repeated tries to run for the presidency in the ensuing years. All he said was that ridding the agency of objectionable grants was a "doable thing. It's achievable and ought to be achieved." In handling the Athey performance I simply passed the buck by telling Dan Coats of Indiana: "I think you should know that that grant was passed before I came into office."

I was pleased with myself. I was resorting to tricks, beginning to play the game of politics, and actually liking it when I put one over. The year on the road had helped. I was at ease before the legislators and no longer intimidated by them. I had given two hundred speeches to all kinds of groups, and although I was still unsteady without a script in hand, I was able to field questions without hesitation. And I knew how to deflect. I didn't answer Dan Coats about Ron Athey at all; I just bumped the problem to the previous Republican administration—in effect name-calling, a common mode of operation in D.C. As Sandy and I left the Capitol Building, we passed Gingrich moving quickly through the rotunda with four bodyguards, acting like he was president. It was rumored that he had increased the speaker's office allocation by $600,000.

I called Jeffords and Kassebaum to thank them. Nancy told me that she had been very pleased with the hearing, and that she hadn't dared smile for fear she would betray her excitement. I still didn't believe reauthorization had a chance in hell. And this was worrisome, because Ralph Regula had stated that there would be zero appropriations without reauthorization. The GOP was sticking by the rules.

.   .   .

In March 1995, Melanne finally secured an appointment for me with the president. I wanted to make him aware of the areas in which the Republicans were attacking us, to assure him of our internal direction, and to enlist his overt support. We spoke for about twenty minutes in the Oval Office. Melanne accompanied me. The president was relaxed and even seemed buoyed by the challenges his opponents had presented to his administration. "I just want to beat the crap out of them," he said. I was surprised at the locker-room tone, but having never sat down with a president before, I chalked it up to my inexperience. After all, Nixon was pretty graphic on the tapes of his office conversations, and I had read that LBJ even invited people to talk with him while he was on the toilet.

The first area of attack, I told the president, was federal support of the arts. All great nations subsidize the arts, I said, and the nonprofit arts in America couldn't make it on their own. A second area was the accusation that the NEA was "elitist." "Nothing could be further from the truth," I said, and I mentioned the Delta Cultural Center in his own state of Arkansas as an example. "You went to Helena?" he said, his eyes widening. "Levon Helm and I opened that place." I told him of the thousands of places like that all over the country, many of which made the arts accessible to kids who were often at risk of getting into trouble. "You can't do drugs and art," I said, and then immediately amended the statement, looking at this saxophone-playing president as horn players like Miles Davis popped into mind (not to mention legions of writers from Samuel Taylor Coleridge to Jack Kerouac). "Well," I went on sheepishly, "maybe music, but not drama or dance." I was putting my foot in it. I remembered my colleagues on stage during the 1960s in various stages of inebriation and on acid highs, which seemed to put no severe restriction on their ability to maneuver through a two-hour performance. Most of the time the audience did not know the difference. It was true that in the long term you could not get away with it any more than an athlete could. I had often proclaimed in speeches that if you gave a kid a paintbrush he would be less likely to pick up a needle, and I believed that in most cases it was true. But to continue the argument was self-defeating. Addicts are addicts. Clinton shifted his long legs in the wing chair. "What's the third?" he said.

"The third area of attack is controversial art," I told the president. I mentioned some of our internal procedures, such as interim reports, that allowed the agency and an organization to designate where NEA funds were used in a grant that had been awarded for an entire season of work. The organization continued to present its full season, but the NEA money would be allocated to areas unlikely to cause problems. "That sounds good," the president replied. "They've got to understand the public won't pay for that."

My idealism swept over me suddenly. I wished for a president who would tell me that we had the moral high ground and that in a democracy we embraced the full spectrum of tastes, one that included all kinds of art. And that if we went into battle we would stick together to the bitter end in the name of freedom of expression and the First Amendment. After all, the Democratic platform that the president endorsed prior to his election in 1992 was fully committed to the NEA and the NEH.

But my own idealistic beliefs had been bastardized in the past year. And the wave of idealism I felt sitting four feet from my president left me almost as quickly as it had come. The real world was the political game we were all playing. It was not the pure world of the theater, where I stepped out onstage every night and said the same lines and received the same response from my fellow actors, huddled in the safe cocoon of the playwright's world. It wasn't possible to be in politics and not compromise to within an inch of your life. Perhaps that was the meaning of politics: compromise, finding the middle ground; watering things down to make them the most palatable for the most people; being manipulative when need be to get reelected; and being diplomatic which meant not saying what is really on your mind.

When George Bush reluctantly got rid of John Frohnmayer, he compromised his own belief in the value of the Arts Endowment for the sake of political expediency. His letter to Frohnmayer in June 1990 illustrates the "inevitable tension between art and politics," as Garrison Keillor said:

> I do not want to see censorship, yet I don't believe a dime of tax-payers' money should go into "art" that is clearly and visibly filth. I was shocked by the examples cited in a recent *Washington Times* story. . . . We have to find a way to preserve the independence and creativity of the arts, yet at the same time, see that in egregious cases such as those mentioned above, the taxpayer will not subsidize filth and patently blasphemous material.
>
> You are doing a good job and I support you. Keep it up!

Bill Clinton could not have written a letter like his predecessor's, I was convinced, but he *had* compromised much of what he stood for. I had watched him move to a centrist position, adopting much of the Republican agenda, but with a twist: he refashioned it and made it his own program, often beating them at their own game. I admired his political savvy immensely. He never gave up, and he always played to win. Winning was what it was all about. It was what kept him in the game. I knew he would never desert us because he didn't want to lose the fight and the NEA was a big symbolic battle.

In a political world he was right: "The public won't pay for that." The irony was in how he was conducting his own private life, and in what emerged a few years later in the Monica Lewinsky scandal. The public in the end *did* pay for that. A majority of Americans did not want him removed from office for sexual exploits and moral turpitude that made some of our NEA controversies pale in comparison. In many areas he succeeded brilliantly as our leader, but we ultimately accepted his failures as well. Still, I wanted more from the man in the highest office of government. I wanted him to be not only a skilled politician but also a visionary, with lofty ideals and a devotion to the finest cre-ations of human beings—like the arts.

I was asking more from my president than I was from artists. I knew that in the panoply of arts only a few ever achieve greatness, and I knew that the NEA would be giving grants to artists and arts institutions that would be only mediocre in the larger scheme of things, despite our best efforts. And yet I expected the public to support all manner of arts in the hope that most would be of some value to a community. Why couldn't I accept the weaknesses of my president in the same way? Especially since the majority of the people did? I held on to my ideals, but I tried to cease being judgmental.

It was clear that we needed to make some changes at the Endowment if we were going to survive elimination. The president was encouraging more procedural changes, and Congress was asking us to find ways to privatize the agency. I had an idea, one that would require a trip to the West Coast and meeting with the movie industry's top brass. Influencing Hollywood is a little like herding cats, but I ventured into their territory with a plan for finding new sources of income for the arts in general, and for the NEA in particular.

CHAPTER TWELVE

Hollywood

Flying into Los Angeles is like entering another country. It sprawls like Mexico City in ever-expanding pods of humanity stretching as far as the eye can see. There is "the Valley" to the north, Pasadena, San Bernardino, and the mountains toward the east, the coastal communities jamming into the sand like so many beach umbrellas in the west, and the industrial neighborhoods to the south, belching their pollutants into the overburdened basin. It takes the better part of a day to get from one end to the other.

More than sixty different languages are spoken in the Los Angeles schools, and the city is home to more Spanish-speaking people than those who speak English as their native tongue. The city also hosts Native Americans, Cambodians, Chinese, Thai, Iranians, Irish, and Africans in abundance, all drawn to the land of plenty—plenty of food, plenty of jobs, and plenty of sunshine. There is also plenty of misery: life on choked highways, air that is unfit to breathe, and a stark dichotomy between rich and poor, who share no neighborhoods.

It was impossible in my visits to experience even one-tenth of the diaspora present in this vast area. The arts were everywhere, but the cultures that had brought them to Los Angeles were adapting so quickly to American ways that art forms were being lost daily. The Folk and Traditional Arts Program supported many cultures in and around L.A. The NEA also helped fund the Western European traditions of art, music, and theater housed in the huge museums and the Los Angeles Music Center. Dorothy Parker said of Los Angeles: "There is no there there." I disagree. There is no one "there," as in the old downtown cities of the

East Coast, but there are a multitude of "theres"—more than one person in one lifetime could experience. Los Angeles is not a place you can get your arms around, it is more a place of mind. An architect once said that "place is a space with memory." Memory of place implies history and heritage. Los Angeles *has* history, but its mad dash into the future often obscures its past.

As NEA chairman I visited arts programs in just a few of the eighty-eight satellite cities that make up Los Angeles. I admired Al Nodal, who headed up the L.A. Arts Council, in his efforts to keep up with all that was going on. He had a plan for increasing arts support through partnerships of agencies at the federal, state, and local levels and bringing in the private sector more. It was extremely difficult to accomplish with a fluctuating city and state arts budget, not to mention a declining federal one, but Al was making some headway.

The Hollywood community needed no help from the government, at least not from the National Endowment for the Arts. The commercial arts of film, video, music, and publishing are collectively one of the leading exports from the United States to the world. The powers that rule the studios—the television networks and the pop music world—are adept at lobbying Congress on behalf of their own needs: promoting their industries, seeking corporate advantage, and protecting intellectual property rights. Besides, Hollywood has its own ways of dealing with politics by producing scathing movies on the subject. I was entering an elevator in the Rayburn Building one day to pay a call on one of the new Republican chairmen. For a moment I thought I was back in L.A. on my way to see a movie executive. There was Oliver Stone crammed in the back of the elevator surrounded by blue suits. "Well, hello, Oliver!" I gushed. "What are you doing here?" "Shhh," he whispered as we both ducked out on the third floor. "I'm scouting locations for a film about Nixon," and he strode swiftly down the corridor.

Jack Valenti, the president and CEO of the Motion Picture Association of America (MPAA), is one of the highest-paid lobbyists in Washington. For close to three-quarters of a million dollars a year he does a great job for the movie studios. He had been at his job so long that he knew everyone of importance in D.C., and he courted the newcomers in Congress out of his own pocket, giving a hundred dollars here, a hundred there, to campaigns regardless of party. You got on the wrong side of Valenti at your own peril. Jack Valenti was good to me, and the soul of courtesy always, as were most of the big players in Hollywood, but I wanted more from them than courtesy. I wanted them to give more than just lip service to the nonprofit arts.

I went to Hollywood in February 1995 for two reasons. The stars wanted to know how they could help the NEA in its battle with Gingrich and the 104th Congress, and I wanted the studio bosses to know how they could help the NEA and the nonprofit arts.

Sherry Lansing, the chairman of the Motion Picture Group of Paramount Pictures, and my agent, Joan Hyler, the new president of Women in Film, an organization dedicated to helping female directors and producers advance in film and television, hosted an event for me at Paramount's largest screening room. Sherry was a woman I had known and admired for many years. In 1978, when she was at Columbia Pictures, she was the supervising producer on *Kramer Versus Kramer.* Dustin Hoffman, Meryl Streep, Justin Henry, and I were all nominated for Academy Awards for our roles in the movie, and Dustin and Meryl each went on to win one.

In the 1980s Ed and I spent a great deal of time on the West Coast. He was directing television series and films, and I was a producer as well as an actress. Sherry was always welcoming at Paramount, and even though the studio never produced any of the feature film projects I brought them, I was respectful of her decisions. She and Joan wanted to help the NEA in any way they could.

There was a full audience of three hundred on the night I spoke, including stars like Sally Field, who had just played Tom Hanks's mother in the hit movie *Forrest Gump.* Sally was charming and forthright, suggesting to all assembled that "the trouble with Newt is that he has never been to the theater—I'm going to take him and Mrs. Gingrich, his mother, to dinner and the theater," prompting Joan to say later that it would make a great sound bite: "Mrs. Gump takes the Gingriches."

Faye Dunaway, Annette Bening, Jamie Lee Curtis, and Ted Danson were among those at another event hosted by the talent agency ICM (International Creative Management). So many of us actors had begun in NEA-sponsored nonprofit theaters that it was easy to involve the stars in support of NEA's survival. Faye and I had started our acting careers together at Harvard's Loeb Theater in the summer of 1961. I played Rosalind in *As You Like It,* and Faye played the fickle shepherdess Phoebe. Both she and Annette had performed in NEA nonprofit theaters before they had movie careers. Each spoke of the grounding that theater gave them and the importance of nurturing new talent.

My own remarks centered on the pressures the NEA was under. I entreated all of them to make the connection between the nonprofits and the commercial sector, to remember their own beginnings, to give back, and to mentor. Later I unabashedly asked my old friend Martin Landau to put in a plug for the NEA in his Academy Award acceptance speech. I was sure he would win for his supporting role in *Ed Wood,* and a month later he did, graciously mentioning the Endowment in his remarks. I hoped the Academy of Motion Picture Arts and Sciences would give the Endowment a special award on its thirtieth anniversary, as it had for its twentieth in 1985, but it declined. Arthur Hiller, president of AMPAS, did mention the NEA, however, in his remarks at the televised ceremony. The Academy Awards reach a greater audience worldwide than almost any other televised event. By letting the world know that the United States was backpedaling on federal funding for the arts I hoped to shame Congress into reversing its position. I knew the tactic might backfire, but I thought the chance was worth taking.

Barbra Streisand understood the dilemma of promoting a cause on an awards show. In 1995 she spoke passionately about the arts to Harvard's John F. Kennedy School of Government. She prepared her remarks carefully and wrote them herself. I called to congratulate her after reading her speech. In thinking about accepting a lifetime achievement award on the Grammys, she was wondering about whether to mention the NEA in her remarks. She thought better of it when she realized that the press would probably distract her from the NEA message she wanted to project. Besides, the music world was having its own problems with Congress because of violent and salacious lyrics. It wasn't a good idea to embroil the NEA in that issue as well.

I tried to distance the agency as much as possible from congressional attacks on Hollywood. I did not view the issues of the NEA's controversial grants and Hollywood's controversial movies and lyrics in quite the same light. Movies and commercial music are big business. It seemed disingenuous of Hollywood not to claim some responsibility for the product they were producing, particularly when they carefully targeted their audiences. Sex and violence sold tickets to the young male audience, market research had told them. It also seemed a bald-faced lie when bright studio executives claimed that the images projected on a screen would not influence people's thinking. How could that be when the advertising world banks on the power of images to sell products? Where would advertising be if images did *not* influence people? And why then did advertisers pay so much to have commercials aired on prime-time television?

It's true that art influences us too and can change our perceptions of life. Although there will always be gratuitous sex and violence in the world, and marketing forces will seek to exploit some of the public's demand for it, I never felt that the NEA was promoting or exploiting gratuitous sex or violence. The art the NEA funded may have had some sex and violence in it, but the agency was not selling sex and violence per se to a targeted audience, as some marketed films and lyrics were. Gratuitous sex and violence exist to promote themselves. Pornography promotes sexual feeling, and violent action films feed off the rush of adrenaline that comes to the viewer. These "highs," like those from drugs, can be marketed and sold to the public, as they regularly are. Great works of art can contain sex and violence too, but within a larger context. The film *Saving Private Ryan* depicts an enormous amount of violence, but we view and understand it in the context of a devastating war, just as we understand Picasso's masterpiece "Guernica." The NEA was not awarding arts organizations to promote gratuitous sex and violence; we were attempting to give grants for the best art our nation's creative minds could make.

During the 1995 trip to Hollywood I was also hosted by the Directors' Guild of America. This powerful group and the William Morris Agency gave a breakfast for me that was attended by leading directors, producers, and writers. Angela Lansbury kindly introduced me before leaving to begin her day's work on the set of the TV series *Murder, She*

Wrote. Within minutes after I made my remarks the DGA, the Writers' Guild of America (WGA), and the Screen Actors' Guild (SAG) formed a committee to help the Endowment. Their subsequent contributions included letters to Congress, testimony, and financial help to arts organizations. The leaders of these organizations understood the value of nurturing artists for the future of the film industry.

The nonprofit arts world has a direct impact on many areas of film-making. Movies draw on the talents of designers, musicians, and visual artists as well as writers, directors, and actors, all of whom make their start somewhere else. Some begin in the independent film world, coming out of film schools like AFI, NYU, or USC, while others emerge from theaters across America. Developing talent takes time, and I wanted movie executives to understand that the "farm teams" for their films were usually in the nonprofit sector, and often NEA-sponsored. The film artists, the directors, and the writers freely acknowledged their beginnings, but it was more difficult to impress that fact on studio executives who liked to believe that they "discovered" the talent.

In the days of the studio contract system, talented young players like Judy Garland and Mickey Rooney or budding stars like Loretta Young and Lucille Ball were groomed; the system included acting and voice lessons along with etiquette and other training. But that system had long since been abandoned, and most actors fended for themselves. I thought that if the studios recognized the contribution of the nonprofits to the talent that created their films, they might set aside a portion of their profits to benefit those entities. They might even provide the matching funds to organizations that won NEA grants.

I first visited the king of them all, the grand old man Lew Wasserman. He had been chairman and CEO of MCA-Universal for years and made significant campaign contributions to the Democratic Party. Universal was also the parent company of the series my husband produced, *Law and Order.* Lew welcomed my visit. He recognized the nonprofits as the feeders for the commercial arts but drew the line at creating an independent foundation with MCA-Universal profits that would nurture talent and match NEA grants. He said he had created a number of foundations of his own that gave to many causes already, most of them having to do with health and social issues. I knew that Lew was a generous man, but what I wanted was for the MCA-Universal corporation to dedicate a percentage of its profits annually to an MCA-Universal foundation for nurturing new talent.

It was disappointing not to have the renowned Lew Wasserman showing enthusiasm for my idea. He could pick up the phone and enlist other studio executives for a cause in a flash. His lead would often cause the bosses at Warner Brothers or 20th Century Fox to follow. But the studios were undergoing massive change, and Lew would soon retire. The bosses now were international conglomerates with backing by Japanese corporations or other consortia. There was not a single person who could call a major studio his own anymore, or who would create a foundation for the purposes I envisioned. There *were* foundations; Disney had one, and so did some of the others. But their assets were pitiful compared with the corporation's income. In 1995 the Walt Disney Company Foundation made grants to a variety of causes, most of them not arts-related, totaling $2,687,451. This amount would barely have kept CEO Michael Eisner in office annually.

I spoke casually to a few other studio executives about beginning a foundation but was met with silence or a weak argument that the "government should be taking care of that." The fact was that the government was *not* taking care of it, and the private sector generally contributed a lot more to the arts than the corporate Hollywood community. The Sara Lee Corporation, for example, was a major contributor through its Sara Lee Foundation. CEO John Bryan told me that his mother, the company's founder and namesake, was dedicated from the very beginning to giving back some of the profits the company accrued. There were literally thousands of corporations in the United States that did a better job of giving to the arts than the commercial entertainment entities.

Film preservation was another area I wished to discuss with executives in Hollywood. Since the Endowment was no longer awarding subgrants, organizations like the American Film Institute, which had relied on the NEA subgrants for film preservation, had been caught short. The studios were surprisingly scattershot in their approach to conservation of their product. A dedicated band of directors—Martin Scorsese,

Peter Bogdonavich, Woody Allen, and Steven Spielberg in particular—
had brought the issue to everyone's attention. The Library of Congress
was committed to the cause of film preservation and annually restored a
few movie classics, but there were hundreds and hundreds of films
decomposing on shelves owing to lack of funds. Even the relatively
recent *The Great White Hope,* in which James Earl Jones and I starred in
1970, had lost its original color and taken on a blue tone.

The issue of film preservation was a dire one. I met with Roger
Mayer, president of Turner Entertainment, whom I knew to be a strong
preservationist. He had been instrumental in the preservation of
MGM's films for years and was passionate about the issue. Although
Warner Brothers and some of the other studios were taking care of their
own releases, there were a multitude of "orphan films" that no one was
taking care of. Roger understood the problem and became more
involved.

Steven Spielberg *did* have a foundation, Shoah, dedicated to documenting the stories of living Holocaust victims and other pertinent
Jewish histories. It seemed a natural for Spielberg to pick up the care
and preservation of orphan Jewish films. Marge Tabankin, who ran
both Spielberg's and Streisand's foundations, agreed.

Scorcese was an avid film buff. He and I sat down together in his
offices in New York, a buzzing beehive of activity from development to
editing to conservation. He had helped found the Film Foundation and
was working hard to raise money for it. In 1998 the Endowment gave
the organization a large millennium grant, and Roger Mayer is now the
Foundation's chairman. There is still a long way to go in preserving
films in the United States, but with people like Scorcese, Mayer, and
Librarian of Congress James Billington helping, with grants from the
NEH and NEA, there may be hope for these precious reels of our
national history. Perhaps soon the studios, the networks, and the music
industries can be pressured into giving even more to conserving this
important art form, and to documenting the history of our nation.

Unlike some of the entertainment corporations, celebrities are the
most generous people I know. They give of their time and money for
myriad causes. Ted Danson founded the American Oceans Campaign,
making it one of the leading organizations devoted to the waters of our

world. Not only is Robert Redford extremely active with environmental organizations such as the Natural Resources Defense Council, but he founded the Sundance Institute in Utah to nurture independent film, making it the leading organization of its kind in America today. This could not have been accomplished without Redford's personal contribution of time and money. Richard Dreyfuss traveled the United States on behalf of music education in the schools after he played a music teacher in the film *Mr. Holland's Opus*. And Barbra Streisand has given thousands and thousands of dollars for musical instruments in schools.

The relationship between Hollywood and Congress is schizophrenic and hypocritical. The 104th Congress regarded Hollywood stars as "elitist." And yet, when the opportunity presented itself, the congressmen all scrambled for a photo-op with them. I was not in the Hollywood star category myself, having only limited wattage in the movies, but it amused me to watch the interplay between politicians and movie stars.

Liz Robbins, who was lobbying for an organization with the unwieldy name of the Council of Literary Magazines and Presses/Literary Network, held a reception and dinner one summer night in the garden of her quaint Georgetown home. She invited the playwright Wendy Wasserstein, the actress and director Joanne Woodward, Bill Clinton's favorite mystery writer, Walter Mosley, and the movie star Melanie Griffith. They were to pay calls on the Hill the next day and had graciously made the trip to D.C. to support the Endowment. I knew from watching Wendy as a grant recipient and as an NEA panel chairman that she would be a superb spokesman, and Joanne was quietly articulate too. I did not know Walter or Melanie and decided to introduce myself and thank them for giving their time.

It was a balmy evening, and I looked over at Melanie dressed in a white designer outfit with breezy décolletage, tall as a reed. I introduced myself and told her that I enjoyed her work in films. In her soft kitten voice she gushed a bit about *my* film work and then said, "And what are you doing now?" I dropped her like a hot potato, rushed over to Liz, and whispered forcefully in her ear, "Prep that girl for the Hill!"

My friend Al Simpson was there, chatting with another GOP senator, Hank Brown from Colorado. We spoke business for a few minutes, and then I asked whether they would like to meet Melanie Griffith, knowing full well they were salivating already. They hovered over her as they never hovered over a fellow politician, Al's six-foot-six vantage point being perfect for stargazing.

Wendy later reported to me about the meetings that transpired the following day. NEA Chairman Alexander couldn't get an appointment with Newt Gingrich, but celebrities came and went with relative ease it seemed. Perhaps it was the fact that Newt Gingrich's first novel was being published and he felt he was now in the same league as other writers. In any event he flirted with Melanie and told her there was a good part for her in the film of his book. Wendy managed to steer the conversation to the NEA, telling the speaker that the NEA fellowship she received had helped her write *The Heidi Chronicles,* which won a Pulitzer Prize. Gingrich replied, "Arthur Murray never needed a grant to write a play." Wendy restrained herself from saying that perhaps the famous ballroom dancer should have applied to the dance program. As they were leaving, Gingrich realized his mistake and said, "I'm terribly sorry, I meant Arthur Miller." Wendy replied, "Yes, and he did have a grant. It was called the WPA."

Artists, administrators, celebrities, and politicians were brought together annually in March for Arts Advocacy Day in Washington, D.C. The American Council on the Arts (now called Americans for the Arts) and other arts service groups organized the event, which was successful in putting the NEA in a clear spotlight. The celebrities were briefed on the issues and spoke thoughtfully at a breakfast on the Hill and in private meetings with members of Congress. Michael Greene, the aggressive president of the National Association of Recording Arts and Sciences (NARAS), which produces the Grammys, took it upon himself to support the NEA by getting the commercial music world involved. Like many of the stars, Michael recognized that musicians usually began in school music classes and other nonprofit venues. Michael did a wonderful job of promoting the NEA wherever he or the popular musicians went, particularly on the Grammys, the most watched awards show after the Oscars.

The rhythm-and-blues singer Anita Baker became a regular visitor on Arts Advocacy Day. Her foundation in Chicago contributed to arts education, and Anita made an eloquent case for the arts and underprivileged kids. Wynton Marsalis was a constant supporter of public arts funding, and a few others who made the trip to the Hill during my time at the agency were Michael Bolton, Jon Secada, Kenny G., and Esai Morales.

Kenny G., in a meeting with a Republican congressman, said that his early career was made possible through NEA-sponsored organizations. When the congressman told him that he was going to vote the party line even though he personally believed in government arts support, Kenny looked at him with his big gentle eyes and said, "Well, that's not very courageous, is it?" I loved to hear stories like that. They were my feelings exactly, but I couldn't be so candid. Harry Belafonte came to the Hill, as did the great director Alan Pakula. Billy Taylor, the remarkable jazz pianist, also came, as did the classical music giants Isaac Stern and Yo-Yo Ma, who testified forcefully on more than one occasion.

I was grateful to the celebrities who took the time to stump for the Endowment, but their involvement did have its negative side. Although statistics belied it, many congressmen viewed actors and pop musicians as multimillionaires. A few stars certainly were in the top percentile of wealth, but the vast majority live below the poverty line. Of the 107,000 members of the Screen Actors' Guild, 72 percent earn $5,000 or less as actors. Only 1.4 percent earned more than $200,000 in 1995, and those were the actors the public knows about. The average income for the 36,000 members of the Actors' Equity Association who work in the theater is about $15,000. Dishwashing is a more lucrative occupation.

In the push to privatize the Endowment and other government agencies—in other words, to get them off the public payroll—some senators and congressmen looked to Hollywood to pick up the tab. If the stars loved the NEA so much, why didn't they scrape the money together among themselves and support the entire agency as a private entity? Garth Brooks, the megastar country singer, paid a visit to Gingrich, and the speaker asked him that very question. Brooks reportedly answered swiftly, saying he was doing his part by employing close to four hundred people when he toured and made records. He was also paying the government a sizable income tax, and he wanted some of that money earmarked for arts support.

If Hollywood and Nashville stars paid for the NEA entirely, then it really *would* be elitist. The funds would be raised and distributed by a small group of very wealthy people. All American citizens, rich and poor, own the NEA, and there is great satisfaction for most people in knowing that their measly sixty-four-cent contribution (thirty-eight cents in 1997) is making society a little bit finer. Nevertheless, some in Congress persisted in viewing both the Endowment and Hollywood as elitist, and when celebrities championed the cause of the NEA it only made matters worse for us.

This moniker of "elitism" was bogus. Not only did the Endowment support all kinds of art and arts education in diverse communities nationwide, but the very use of the word smacked of "us versus them." I never knew who the "them" were. The East Coast "establishment" had been on hate lists for as far back as I could remember. Lyndon Johnson, from Texas, would talk about them, and Nixon, from California, became downright paranoid about them. There were a handful of third-generation families who still dominated newspaper corporations, but they were the exception rather than the rule. And the wealthiest people in the United States were no longer from the oldest, "establishment" families. Most New Yorkers I knew came from elsewhere, certainly in the arts world. Merce Cunningham came from the state of Washington, Robert Rauschenberg from Illinois, and James Earl Jones from Michigan. If young painters, writers, actors, dancers, and singers gravitated to New York, it was because New York was the nexus of training and presentation in so many of the art fields. People came together in New York from all over the United States and other countries to learn from each other, to get jobs, and to extend the limits of excellence in their field.

Missouri has more lead mining than any other state, Arkansas has more chicken farms, and the state of Washington grows more apples. As a nation we are proud of each state's distinctive accomplishments. It was irritating to hear New York City maligned for being the cultural capital of the world.

It was also irritating when I was thrown into the "elitist" soup for growing up in Brookline, Massachusetts, and going to private schools. My parents had worked hard to fulfill their American dream. Like so many people in the United States, they came from poor backgrounds and had parents who wanted more for them than they had had themselves. Both my mother and father excelled in public schools, and it was their educations that propelled them into the medical world. To want more for my brother and sister and me than they had had for themselves was hardly an elitist wish; it was simply the fulfillment of the American dream.

The charges of elitism were a red herring thrown to the anti-NEA sharks. The Endowment was in pursuit of "excellence," not "elitism," and excellence could be found anywhere. The Endowment gave more money to New York simply because there was more art in New York and the bulk of applications came from there, not because we were serving the "elite." In any case fully one-third of the grants to New York State were to organizations that toured or otherwise disseminated their art to other states.

The argument was lost, however, on the 104th Congress, which continued to label the NEA and Hollywood "elitist" even though many legislators themselves watched the latest films or followed the current TV series religiously. After a while I stopped asking movie stars to promote the NEA in the media because I knew the effort might backlash, embarrassing them as well as the agency. Some great artists, however, continued to come to Washington on their own.

Isaac Stern hugged me one evening at a reception, deeply distraught by the attacks from Congress. "The child's mind is the wealth of our nation," he said, his chest heaving. Issac was also disappointed that more artists were not outspoken about the situation. I knew otherwise. They were waiting, and they were tired, having been through the culture wars for almost a decade. They also were not invited to testify anymore, as they had been when the Democrats ruled the House and Senate. Unlike Sid Yates, Ralph Regula preferred the conservatives Bill Bennett and Lynne Cheney at his hearings rather than leading artists, who I knew were ready to be mobilized should it be necessary. Arthur

Miller would still write stirring op-eds if called upon, and Beverly Sills would rise to the occasion with ironic and cutting humor when the time came. And there were some, like Christopher Reeve in his official capacity as president of the Creative Coalition in 1994, who continued to be asked to speak and to testify.

Chris and I met with another Creative Coalition member, Steve Collins, at a Greenwich Village restaurant to discuss media appearances and his March 1995 Arts Advocacy Day remarks. He was extremely articulate and an excellent choice to head the Creative Coalition, which was founded in 1989 to educate people in the entertainment world about issues of national importance. I told Chris that it wasn't necessary to make any concessions about the NEA or to make any negative remarks about controversial art—that to get into that arena was to begin the slide down the slippery slope. Chris listened carefully, but I did not know until he spoke to the Arts Advocacy Day crowd just how articulate, as well as passionate, he could be. He spoke of the $37 billion that the nonprofit arts generated in America, the employment given to 1.3 million artists nationwide, and the taxes they paid to the U.S. Treasury. He exhorted our elected officials to place our nation alongside the other leading nations of the world in committing public funds to the arts as we all did to education. Christopher Reeve was an excellent spokesman for the Endowment on the Hill, in the press and on television talk shows. The news of his paralyzing fall from a horse a few months later was deeply distressing. The very qualities of commitment, perseverance, and intelligence that made him a fine leader of the Creative Coalition now serve him well in his new life as champion of medical research for spinal cord injuries. His book *Still Me* proves that he is a Superman for all seasons.

Alec Baldwin succeeded Chris as president of the Creative Coalition. His style was more confrontational, but he too made a strong case in defense of the NEA on television and with Congress, and I enjoyed working with Alec on the issues.

Charlton Heston, one of the few outspoken Republicans of the Hollywood community, paid me a visit, suggesting that I needed to be tougher about controversial grants but that I had his full support. More important, as he was making the rounds of the Hill for the National Rifle Association, of which he was a member, though not yet its president, he said he would speak up for the NEA. Strange bedfellows! But he continued to be supportive of the agency throughout my tenure.

There was no movie star, however, who did more behind the scenes than Paul Newman. The world knows of his contributions to young people with terminal illness through sales of his food products that fund the "Hole in the Wall" camps. But he also closely watches what occurs in politics. He and Joanne Woodward contributed to the NEA in substantial ways. Joanne had been exasperated with the level of discussions that she, Wendy Wasserstein, Walter Mosley, and Melanie Griffith had had with members of Congress when Liz Robbins took them to the Hill. I shared her disappointment. The Newmans wanted to help in other ways, and Joanne took time out of her busy schedule to be a panelist for NEA, while Paul volunteered his services to promote the Endowment for public-service spots on film. Paul also wrote excellent op-eds supporting the agency.

One day the Newmans, along with Liam Neeson, came to Washington with the president and CEO of the Heinz Corporation, Tony O'Reilly. Liz Robbins helped organize the largest corporate gift the NEA had ever received. Tony O'Reilly presented me with a check from the Heinz Corporation for $450,000 for arts education. Paul, Joanne, Liam, and the writer Esmerelda Santiago beamed in the background as photographers recorded the event. When Paul was asked to make a few remarks he said that it was unfair to talk of eliminating the NEA for a few problematic grants; after all, the Defense Department was not closed down when some helicopters were lost in Iraq, and Congress did not close itself down for bad legislating. The supportive audience laughed appreciatively.

Borders Books was another corporation that became actively involved with the Endowment. Both Borders and Heinz were responding to gaps in our funding and to a push by the GOP to privatize us. Their contributions were greatly appreciated, and it was a plus to be associated with a corporation like Borders, which marketed literature.

The Endowment was not used to receiving large gifts to be used directly for arts programs. Large donations were made annually to the

National Medal of Arts dinner at the White House, the Heritage Fellowship awards, and other events the NEA conducted, but contributions to the Endowment itself for its program funds were unusual. The money was welcome but problematic. The agency's grants to arts organizations served as a catalyst for the private sector to match the award in their own community. The system worked very well, the Endowment stimulating private investment in a community's culture. When the federal government gave its "seal of approval" to an arts organization through an Endowment grant it was much easier for the organization to solicit and gain private funds. When the money from a large corporation like Heinz or Borders was given directly to the agency, however, not to match a grant from us at the local level, the arts organization lost out and had to work harder to find the resources elsewhere.

It was a generous gesture on the part of Heinz, Borders, and others at a time when the Endowment had few friends. The positive publicity that ensued was a valuable boost to our credibility, but it reinforced in congressional eyes the possibility of privatizing the agency. I maintained that the NEA was already privatized because we generated so much private money with our public grants. Congress would have none of it. I was urged to find sources of funding for the agency other than the annual congressional appropriation.

The Copyright Act of 1976 was coming before Orrin Hatch's Senate Judiciary Committee. It was about to expire, and some powerful and wealthy people, most of them in Hollywood, were seeking to amend it to their advantage. The Great Billion-Dollar Copyright Heist I called it. Protection of the copyrights of authors and creators began with a congressional act in 1790 that extended copyright protection for fourteen years, with a renewal for a total of twenty-eight years. In 1831 the copyright term was increased to a total of forty-two years. In 1908 it was again extended, to fifty-six years of protection. Beginning in the 1960s, when valuable works of art from the early part of the century were about to pass into the public domain, the act was repeatedly extended until it was overhauled in 1976. The Copyright Act of 1976 gave creators copyright for their lifetime and then, essentially rewarding their heirs, for another fifty years after their death. To those industries, like movies, music, and publishing, that paid writers or composers for their creations through "work for hire" arrangements, the new act allowed a copyright term of seventy-five years from the date of publication or one hundred years from the date of creation of the work, whichever expired first. The same held true with works for which the industries had acquired the copyrights from others.

The intellectual property industries and the heirs of creators were seeking to extend copyright yet another twenty years. They argued that U.S. copyright practice needed to be consistent with that of the European Union, which was seeking a term of life plus seventy years for creators in most of its countries. There was some merit in this argument for creators and their heirs, but since the EU did not recognize "works for hire" in the same way the United States did, the argument of the studios and the music publishers had as many holes in it as a cribbage board.

I first heard about the extension of copyright from Senators Bingaman and Dodd. They believed it might be possible to secure a percentage of funds that would accrue from the twenty-year extension for the NEA and the NEH or another public entity dedicated to the arts and humanities. The idea had been floating around for several years. John Frohnmayer had endorsed it, and the Endowment had done some investigation into its feasibility. Two NEA Council members, George White and Ronald Feldman, spent considerable time and their own private resources in moving the idea forward. They even hired a lawyer to help make it a reality. The forces promoting the extension were too powerful for the NEA to be given much credence, but that did not vitiate the soundness of our proposal.

The leaders of the 104th Congress had been urging the Endowment to find ways to privatize, and the several million dollars that might have accrued annually from a percentage of extending copyright, either through royalties earned by copyright holders or other means, could have been the beginning of a true endowment. Senator Dodd called it "Arts Endowing the Arts." But the movie studios and Jack Valenti, who represented them on the Hill through the Motion Picture Association of America, and the music copyright holders—ASCAP (American

Society of Composers, Authors, and Publishers) and BMI (Broadcast Music, Inc.)—were totally opposed to the idea.

Marilyn Bergman, the president of ASCAP, was opposed on principle. She told the *Los Angeles Times* on March 29, 1996:

> Something that comes from the factory of someone's mind is just as real as something that comes from the factory where people create things with their hands. . . . Somebody made this table and nobody would think of taking this table without paying for it. That's called stealing. But if I write a song, which is no less of a creation than this table . . . and somebody takes it without paying for it, it's very difficult to convince most people that's stealing.

This was the kind of skewed thinking that was making headway on the Hill. Songwriters *do* get paid for their songs, just as a furniture maker gets paid for a table. But the furniture maker does not get paid *again* every time the table is sold, unlike songwriters and others who receive royalties because of the copyright law.

The Constitution of the United States gave copyright protection to authors and inventors "to promote the progress of science and the useful arts . . . for limited times." The question is, how long is a "limited time"? And should the heirs of the creators benefit through more than one successive generation? What actually constitutes a creation? As an actress I have invented all kinds of special business for a character that the playwright never wrote. I have watched as that business was "stolen" by successive actresses in the role on stage or in a film version. Is my inventive business copyrightable? Some directors have been winning lawsuits based on this very premise—that their contribution is owned by them and no one else. It is a fine line. Ideas are *not* subject to copyright, but when does an idea expand to become a creation?

As chairman of the federal culture agency representing the nonprofit arts in America I sought to protect the arts organizations from having to pay additional burdensome royalties and also to protect the public domain. Extending the copyright provision for an additional twenty years robbed the public of works that would go into the public domain.

No studio understood the value of the public domain better than Disney. The folktales on which almost all of its great animated film stories were based came from the public domain: *Snow White, Pinocchio,* and *Beauty and the Beast,* to name three. Now Disney was seeking to protect Walt Disney's own lucrative creation, Mickey Mouse, which was about to enter the public domain.

I could understand the need for balance of trade with Europe by having the length of copyright be nearly equal to the EU standard, but what I couldn't understand was the rampant greed of the copyright holders. By taking works out of the public domain for another twenty years, and by taxing the nonprofits that presented those works, they were making life that much more difficult for the individual artist in America, on whom movies, music, and publishing depend for the stories and songs that keep *them* in business. It was like the goose killing the golden egg. Artists use and reuse the works that precede them. And scholars also need to use the writings of their precursors in their current works. The copyright industries wanted to hold all the cards, to the detriment of coming generations of creators. We could not get them to consider giving even 10 percent of the funds accrued during the twenty-year extension to a fund for living artists and scholars. A true endowment, ultimately worth far more than the annual congressional appropriation, would have been a fitting gift at the millennium from the commercial arts world to the artists of today and those of the new century.

Some authors and playwrights wrote Senator Hatch and the Judiciary Committee urging an amendment to the bill so that living artists might benefit; among those were Edward Albee, William Kennedy, Walter Mosley, and David Henry Hwang. Forty-five copyright law professors wrote the committee urging opposition to the bill because it would harm the public: "This legislation is a bad idea for all but a few copyright owners and must be defeated." The columnist Frank Rich of the *New York Times* exposed the underbelly of Hollywood's greed in an article in January 1996, but no one paid much attention. Either the issue was too complicated for the general public to care about or the corporate forces were too great to combat. Probably it was a little of both.

When I spoke with Hatch by telephone he told me in no uncertain terms not to pursue this for the NEA. He reminded me of how much he did for me and the agency behind the scenes, and I knew that to be true. I hung up the phone despondently. The senator was a new member of ASCAP himself, with a CD of inspirational music to his credit and another in the pipeline. As chairman of the Judiciary Committee and a member of ASCAP, Hatch had a conflict of interest. But he told me to lay off the copyright issue. I knew it was dead then and there. You dare not buck the chairman of a powerful committee. Now I knew how the players in Congress felt; they had to do favors for one another in order to get anything passed. There was no favor I could do for Orrin Hatch. And I couldn't blow the whistle on him without the agency suffering consequences.

It didn't matter. Big business almost always wins in America, and this issue was no exception to the rule. Besides, despite my exhortations to the White House, the administration never stepped in to support our position. The letters and phone calls that streamed into the White House from high-profile members of ASCAP, Hollywood executives, and Jack Valenti, who were all major campaign contributors as well, overrode any real discussion of the consequences of copyright extension.

When the bill came before the Judiciary Committee in July 1996 there was only one strong voice of dissent. Senator Hank Brown of Colorado was to retire from the Senate a few months later; he didn't have to worry about raising campaign funds again from corporate entities. Brown stated bluntly, "Why are we providing such a corporate windfall?" He pointed out that seventy years and more in the future does not reward the original creator, or even his heirs in most cases, but instead rewards those who bought the copyrights, in most cases corporate owners. He went on to say: "The public is clearly benefited by having unrestricted access to previously copyrighted works that are now in the public domain."

The bill finally came to the Senate floor in October 1998. Majority Leader Trent Lott saw that it passed on a voice vote; thus, it wasn't challenged and the senators never even came to the floor to register their vote in roll call. As a result of the Great Billion-Dollar Heist of the public's property, no new works will enter the public domain in the next twenty years, with the exception of historical documents that remain unpublished before 2003. Isn't it lucky that William Shakespeare wrote four hundred years ago, not seventy-five years ago? And that all of his works are in the public domain and not locked up by Disney?

Although I welcomed the support from artists, the talent agencies, and the guilds, I left Hollywood saddened that I could not move our NEA agenda forward with the powers who controlled the purse strings. Privatization did not seem a viable option in any case. The Endowment was a government agency, paid for by the taxpayers of America. Very few private citizens wanted to give additional money to a government entity after they had already given substantially to the IRS. Some cities and states had tried giving their citizens the option of targeting a portion of their taxes to nonprofit organizations in fields of their choice, such as health care, the environment, or the arts. The check-off idea on the tax form seemed to work for a few years, but then the amount of money distributed to each organization dwindled as more and more causes in the city or state wanted to be included. Another idea adopted in some locales was dedicating a percentage of lottery or gambling funds to cultural organizations. This was a sustained source of income, to be sure, but morally reprehensible to some people, myself included. The best way to fund the arts in America, as far as I was concerned, was the way we were doing it. In fact, if each taxpayer gave just a dollar a year to the Endowment, instead of the current thirty-eight cents, the agency would have well in excess of $200 million to award. Giving a dollar a year would not be a burden for anyone in the United States.

It had been a very rough couple of months. Dick and I spent most of the spring and summer of 1995 up on the Hill cajoling, strategizing, and schmoozing. The momentum to eliminate the NEA was overpowering. The danger of severe cuts to legions of other important government programs was so great that it was hard to get the attention of our friends in Congress. But the arts service groups and the lobbyists were in high gear: they had organized a massive letter-writing campaign across the country that was attempting to equal the religious right's negative mail. The Christian Action Network was demanding a "death certificate" for the NEA, calling me its "mother" and Lyndon Baines

Johnson its "father." They were going to have a "funeral" and drag a coffin up to the Hill filled with petitions for our elimination. Did that mean me too, I wondered? Oh, and by the way, they added, send fifty dollars or one hundred dollars, thank you very much.

The House subcommittee under Ralph Regula had given us a 40 percent reduction in appropriations. The hearing itself was comical. The 104th Congress was trying to pass so much legislation in such a short amount of time that everyone was running in and out of the hearing room, including Chairman Regula, because they had other meetings to attend simultaneously. When Gingrich had first become speaker he stated that congressmen would get more time to spend with their families. Hah! Instead, everyone was flying by the seat of his pants. What a way to run the government.

I was starting to lose faith in the process. Congressmen had little time to learn about any of the issues and were depending more and more on their aides, who were often callow youth just out of college and who also had no time to be up on the issues. It was wearing to have to explain again and again what the Arts Endowment did for the country or for a congressional district. I went to dinner with Melanne and told her that maybe I should quit; that as a government official I felt muzzled; that perhaps I would be more help to the artists of America on "the outside," where I could speak freely about freedom of expression and the homophobia on the Hill. I was afraid I would not be able to hold my tongue much longer, and I did not want to embarrass the president. Melanne wisely told me that I could accomplish more with the bully pulpit I had as the NEA's chairman, and that it was better to work from a power base inside. It felt good just to talk about these things with her, and I calmed down.

My brother Tom came to town with his wife Janice, my niece Katherine, and my nephew Daniel. It was the thirtieth anniversary of his service in Vietnam, and he wished to visit "the Wall." The Vietnam War Memorial is the most moving monument in Washington. Young Maya Lin won the award to design it from a jury of panelists convened by the NEA in the 1970s. She built a long black wall of stone, thrust into the earth in a wide "V"; the names of the more than fifty thousand dead are inscribed on its reflective face. People leave flowers and mementos at the base of the Wall for their lost loved ones. I watched my brother search the Wall for the name of his roommate, John Brooks Sherman, who had perished in a bombing raid when he was unable to pull his plane up in time. It was 1966, and John was twenty-six years old. Tom quietly brushed his fingers over the name when he found it, the tears welling in his eyes. The memorial, as Thulani Davis says, "was the act of an artist who understood that every single individual in the society craves the rites of acknowledgment of our heroism, our grief . . . and . . . that there are few moments in this society when someone calls our name." Visiting the memorial with my brother put my struggles in perspective. I was not dealing with a life-and-death situation, but art helped heal our most troubled times as a nation and as individuals. I returned to work with renewed commitment.

The Senate was more approachable, as usual. Slade Gorton even began to come around to our side. When I testified before his subcommittee on appropriations he entered the large chamber and almost did a double take: the room was packed to overflowing with arts advocates and members of the public who had come to see me perform before this tough committee. He thought he had entered the wrong room. He subsequently treated me and the agency with renewed respect, and the hearing went well, all of the senators stating their support for the agency. It didn't mean much: Pete Domenici, the chairman of the Budget Committee, told me privately that our budget could be slashed by as much as 50 percent. But, he added, in conference with the House on the Interior bill we might be traded for "one endangered species." I had to laugh at that. What a compromise!

I birded the hills and forest around my home on the weekends. There was a beautiful spring in 1995, and one May day I counted twenty different kinds of warblers, most of them just passing through on their way north. They were so delicate and vulnerable, their long journeys from South or Central America fraught with peril. And still they made it; they came year after year, but in dwindling numbers, as they lost habitat in their winter homes.

I would fight for their right to survive in our harsh world, and I wouldn't trade one of them for a deal with Congress. It shouldn't have been an either-or question—the arts or endangered species? Or as one member of Congress posited—the NEA or breast cancer research? "Both!" I almost yelled. "We can support *all* good causes in this great nation of ours."

Nancy Kassebaum was still eager to find a way to reauthorize the agency, and together in a motel room in Independence, Kansas, we molded the form of a new Endowment that would make it possible. The senator had asked for my help in securing Arthur Miller as the honoree for the annual Inge Festival in Independence in 1995.

I had met Arthur in the late 1970s when Vanessa Redgrave and I starred in a television movie called *Playing for Time*. The playwright had adapted Fania Fenalon's book about her years with the women's orchestra in Auschwitz. I played the leader of the orchestra, Alma Rose, a fine violinist who was gassed by the Nazi doctor Josef Mengele. Arthur's screenplay was sensitive, and we appreciated the time he spent with us on the set at Fort Indiantown Gap, Pennsylvania, which ironically had been a World War II camp for German POWs. The walls were eerily covered with scribbles in German. *Those* prisoners went home, unlike the Jews in Auschwitz.

Arthur was no particular fan of the late playwright William Inge, but I told him baldly that I would win points with Senator Kassebaum if he said yes. Fortunately the film retrospective on Miller at the festival was outstanding, and he and his wife, Inge Morath, did not regret the trip after all.

At seventy-nine Arthur was a wise old man, although as vigorous and robust as someone half his age. I had been feeling slightly paranoid about some of the GOP leadership, and I asked him whether he thought the United States could ever become a fascist government. He pondered the question and then replied, "No, we don't have the tradition here." No, of course we don't. The United States has a history quite different from that of any other country. We were not subjugated by a monarchy for long, or by a dictator, and created our democracy together out of whole cloth. There was a lot an individual citizen could do. I went hopefully to my meeting with Nancy Kassebaum.

She was extremely well prepared. Stephanie took notes as we explored about a dozen options for a reconfigured NEA, including stronger partnerships with the states without increasing their allocation above its current 44 percent, a reduction in the number of grant categories with a stronger focus on the public and communities, and a requirement that grantees could not receive a second grant until all interim and final reports on a current grant were satisfactorily received.

It wasn't easy for her to back the Endowment when so many of her Kansas constituents were telling her to eliminate it. I had immense respect for the senator and thought she would make a good presidential candidate, like her father, Alf Landon, before her. But there was no chance of that; she didn't have the desire to run, and her fellow Kansan, Bob Dole, had just declared his candidacy. She had been in Topeka when he announced, and there were cheers when he spoke of defunding the Endowment. Would he be obstructionist, I asked? Kassebaum replied that it could be a political tactic for the primaries, but she hoped to have the agency reauthorized before then.

Dole was not obstructionist when the time came. But he did vote with the majority against the agency's reauthorization, despite the best efforts of the Republicans Jeffords, Kassebaum, Hutchison, and Bob Bennett of Utah.

Jesse Helms didn't even raise much of a ruckus on the appropriations bill. He thought a cut of 30 percent was okay and did not call for NEA's elimination. When I visited him in his office he even gave me a gift! It was a glass candy canister complete with a top and engraved with his name. I wondered whether I was tilting to the right without realizing it.

The House waged its own internal war regarding our appropriations. There were about thirty moderate Republicans who supported the Endowment. I spent many hours with Amo Houghton of upstate New York, Marge Roukema of New Jersey, Mike Castle of Delaware, and Mike Forbes and Rick Lazio of Long Island. It took courage for the moderates to buck the leadership, especially on such an unpopular issue. But they also knew that their constituents would not be forgiving if they let the NEA down come the next election. The moderates were blocking their colleagues from eliminating the Endowment altogether.

The House deliberations went late into the night, with Dick Armey, who wasn't even on the appropriations committee, demanding zero funding for the NEA. The moderates held the line. In the final back-room deal it was Newt who saved the day. He prevailed upon the "Gang of Four" and their acolytes to accept a stay of execution for the Endowment of two years, with certain death in 1997. He reasoned that it would be unfair and difficult for arts organizations nationwide to be cut off cold turkey, and that two years would give them time to prepare. It was hard for me to believe that Gingrich had suddenly found com-passion for arts administrators. I suspected instead that some high rollers in the area of Marietta, Georgia, had placed a few phone calls to the speaker telling him to lay off. If that were true then the strategy of Americans United to save the Arts and Humanities, and the one behind my own well-placed calls to Georgia friends, was paying off.

That was how it worked after all. A politician was only as good as his campaign finance war chest. If the money didn't pour in he wasn't going to get elected, and if he wasn't going to get elected he couldn't pass the legislation he dreamed of passing. Two years was a very short time in the life of a representative. He was virtually held hostage by the big campaign contributors. And campaign finance reform was never going to be a reality when each and every member of the House was already running his next race and depended on those large contribu-tions.

Whatever happened to sway Newt at the midnight hour was reason to jump for joy. We had been given a reprieve of two more years—two more years of to engage in intensive persuasion and climb into bed with strange fellows. The major blow we had sustained, however, was the elimination of individual fellowships, with the exception of literature and the honorary Jazz Masters and Heritage fellowships. Liz Robbins's lobbying on behalf of literature had paid off, but the other arts suffered terribly from the loss. The retention of literature fellowships amused me: if individual artists were "the problem," as Ralph Regula and others in Congress maintained, surely writing, which could be readily copied, had the capacity to be more controversial than any other art form. Rev-olutions throughout history were begun through literature. Maybe con-gressmen thought that no one read anymore—or maybe *they* did not read anymore. Writers had lobbied the Hill intensely to preserve the grants, and whatever it was that ultimately saved the literature fellowships was all to the good. It was a sad day when the Endowment no longer gave individual artist grants to choreographers, composers, performing artists, filmmakers, and visual artists.

I didn't know how we could revive the fellowships in the future, but at least the agency was alive. It was on life support, but it could be resuscitated. I said a prayer of thanks for those rich old women in Georgia who loved their symphony and maybe had a museum wing named after them.

CHAPTER THIRTEEN

Backstage

The blizzard raged outside. The six of us who were considered "essential" personnel" hunkered down inside our offices at the Old Post Office Building. It wasn't the snow that kept the Endowment staff from coming into work on that December day in 1995, but the immutability of two warring parties and their leaders, Bill Clinton and Newt Gingrich. The stalemate was ostensibly over the budget that Congress was proposing. The president had vetoed it, and then the Republicans, in a pique, refused to allow a continuing resolution (CR) to keep the money flowing in expectation that a budget would eventually be passed—so the government shut down. Forty-three million Americans were in danger of not getting their Social Security checks, and the government was at risk of going into default.

Everything ground to a halt. Washington was a ghost town, the buildings empty of personnel, the snow-covered streets empty of cars. It was eerie and yet surprisingly peaceful. This was the second shutdown in a month, and those few of us squirreled in our cubbyholes used it as an opportunity to catch up on correspondence, clean out our files, and come together for tea and cookies in the late afternoon.

It all seemed so stupid. Even the American public recognized the "boys will be boys" aspect of the quarrel. Clinton and Gingrich were more alike than they ever suspected. They were both southern boys who had grown up in similar family situations, they were both leaders of political "revolutions," and they both needed to win. They were the two faces of Janus, each looking forward but championing a different party.

Gingrich was losing ground. Like a petulant child, he'd complained that no one paid attention to him on the Air Force One flight home from the funeral of Israeli Prime Minister Yitzhak Rabin, eliciting the *New York Daily News* headline "Cry Baby." Because the shutdown continued through Christmas and into the new year, people were talking about the "Gingrich Who Stole Christmas."

Clinton loved to make him squirm. At the Kennedy Center honors two weeks before the shutdown, Ed and I were again seated in the presidential box. This time I got to see the show—which honored Marilyn Horne, Jacques d'Amboise, B. B. King, Sidney Poitier, and Neil Simon—because I made sure that I was behind Hillary and Ed was behind the president. At intermission we all gathered in the red velvet anteroom of the box for champagne and conversation. The president, weary and exhilarated by a successful Bosnian treaty and a visit to Ireland, slipped out to the foyer for coffee. He returned a few minutes later, nudging a pasty-looking Gingrich before him. This was like throwing wolves to the lions. The president leaned back against the wall, his arms folded, and let Gingrich hang. There were no introductions, but the speaker shook hands with those he knew—Michael Jordan of Westinghouse and CBS, and Jim Wolfensohn, who was about to leave the Kennedy Center to head up the World Bank. The room was quiet as the ten of us gazed at the enemy in our midst. The president's mouth twisted mischievously. He loved this cat and mouse game, the subtle manipulation. I couldn't pass up the opportunity and moved swiftly in front of the First Lady, thrusting out my hand: "Mr. Speaker, I'm Jane Alexander." "Oh, hello," he said unenthusiastically and literally turned a cold shoulder to me. He was saved by the bell calling us back to our seats and beat a hasty retreat.

When about one hundred children from homeless shelters and other underprivileged venues took to the stage in a rousing dance to honor their teacher Jacques D'Amboise, the president said we needed more arts for kids: "You don't read about dancers in jail." Bingo! This was the first time I felt he got it. It was programs like these, I told him, that were going to be eliminated with the NEA. "I know, I'm going to use it against them," he replied with a twinkle of anticipation that told me he had a plan. God, I hoped so.

The final cuts to our budget, after reconciliation of the House and Senate budgets, were as massive as anticipated—amounting to 40 percent. Although the president had not signed off on the final budget for the nation for fiscal year 1996, the White House had told us that there was nothing more they could do for us because the Republican leadership would not negotiate on the NEA. My hardest day at the Endowment came in the autumn of 1995 when I had to tell eighty-nine of the staff that they would be laid off. It didn't matter how good any of them were at their job, or how much I needed them; they were forced out by politics. And the rule for civil servants was "last in, first out." Even if I had wanted to get rid of "deadwood" on the staff, it was not possible if an employee had been in government for a long time. As a result I saw some of the best new people leave. We went from a staff of about 240 to 150 overnight. Our director of human resources, Maxine Jefferson, mitigated some of the distress for those departing. She was a lovely, compassionate person for all of us in those troubling days.

We consolidated offices, giving up entire floors of the Old Post Office Building that the NEA had occupied for years. As the shutdown finally ended in January 1996, the 150 of us left hunkered down to work, reshuffling offices, winnowing file cabinets, and dealing with a new round of applications and panels. The halls were piled high for months with furniture, books, and papers with nowhere to go, adding to the demoralization of the staff. I was grateful when the archivist of the United States offered to relocate our historical files to the Archives in perpetuity.

Because we had anticipated a major budget cut, the entire restructuring of the agency and how it did business had been in the works for most of 1995. Under the leadership of Ana Steele, Scott Sanders, and the program directors, the agency shifted from seventeen programs to essentially four. The time line was very fast for this kind of massive change after thirty years. Many people rightly complained when they were not consulted. I received calls from arts administrators all across the country and told the PDs that I would take the heat when they got the calls.

I *was* responsible for the changes. If we were going to have to shrink programs like Music, Theater, and Visual Arts, and if we escaped the slated elimination in 1997 but might have to endure more budget cuts, then I saw the 1995 restructuring as an opportunity to rethink our entire process of grant-giving. I wanted to create a structure that would still have an impact even though the NEA's budget was radically reduced, a structure that was impervious to future congressional assault. If we continued to give awards in the same way, then the panels and the program directors would be in favor of giving the same number of grants to virtually the same arts organizations year in and year out, thereby reducing the amount annually until it made no significant impact. This had actually been going on for some time as the agency's allocation to each program was decreased with every congressional cut. The grants of $300,000 and $400,000 that used to be given regularly to large and medium-sized museums, theaters, and symphonies were a thing of the past.

I thought I knew how to make the Endowment bulletproof. As long as we gave blanket grants for an entire season of an organization's work without knowing exactly where the money was to be used, Congress, which called this buying "a pig in a poke," would be after us indefinitely. If, however, we gave to an organization for a specific work in progress, or for presentation or conservation of that work, it would be clear where the money went. Organizations would then be able to present what they wished during the rest of their season and not have the feds on their back. The drawback was that a grant for seasonal support usually gave organizations the funds they needed most to take care of basic maintenance and keep the doors open. A grant for project support was easier to come by; foundations and philanthropists liked to endow projects because they were more visible than annual maintenance. A Cezanne exhibit was certainly "sexier" than the heating and air-conditioning system of the exhibiting museum.

In any case the NEA could no longer give significant grants for seasonal support to all the worthy arts institutions nationwide. The Endowment would have needed a budget of at least $350 million per year, not the $99 million that had been appropriated for fiscal year 1996. The NEA could still help in specific circumstances, like the long-term planning and stabilization of an organization, but communities nationwide would now bear the burden of, and the commitment to, their own cultural institutions' maintenance and overall seasonal support.

In redefining how the agency did business it was important to consider the arc of creative work. It always begins with the creator—the writer, the musician, the painter—then proceeds to the presenter—the publisher, the concert hall, the museum or gallery. The arc ends, if the creative work is worthy, in the realm of our heritage—in libraries, archives, and schools. Along the way we must ensure that art has an audience by giving people access to the works of today and education to be the audience of tomorrow. We also must help those organizations that need it through planning and sound management. The categories we came up with were:

- Creation and presentation
- Heritage and preservation
- Education and access
- Planning and stabilization

Our vast and growing arena of partnerships with the states, with other federal entities, and with the private sector was a category all its own but administered along with planning and stabilization.

Our mission was reworded slightly: "To foster the excellence, diversity, and vitality of the arts in the United States, and to broaden public access to the arts."

The NEA's focus was now on the public and the communities they lived in, as well as on the artists. Our critics in Congress liked to accuse us of being "welfare for artists"; they couldn't so easily attack us if we were an "investment in communities."

We also added a special category called leadership initiatives. This was my baby. I wanted to highlight and reward specific arts organizations, or communities, that were good role models in management, in technology, in community outreach, and in projects to celebrate the millennium.

From almost my first days at the Endowment I began to talk about the millennium. How, after all, do we celebrate the accomplishments of a nation except through the arts and the humanities? Even if we are celebrating the accomplishments of science—going to the moon, for example—we do so through literature, the visual arts, and music.

My excitement about preparing for the millennium through the arts was met with blank stares almost everywhere I went. Even my own staff thought I was off base at first, back in 1994 when there were only six years to go until the year 2000. Britain had long been at work on its celebration and had selected one region and one art form to be highlighted each year through 2000 and beyond. Germany was having a worldwide festival in Hanover in 2000. Australia was hosting the Olympics in 2000 and planning a huge cultural component as well.

In the United States there was barely a murmur about the millennium. Apocalyptics were preparing for doomsday, but the U.S. Congress couldn't see beyond the next election. Besides, they were *cutting* the budget, not adding to it. I thought of all the millennium franchised goods that would be sold by Time-Warner, Disney, and the other huge entertainment companies: 2000 T-shirts and cuddly little millennium creatures that wailing children would insist on having—and that would end up in the back of bureau drawers before 2001 was over.

But where was the celebration of who we were as a people? The museum exhibits, the plays, the paintings, the sculpture? Who, at this one-thousand-year turning point, was tracking the diaspora of cultures to America? I remember poring as a child over *Life* magazine's book *The Family of Man,* compiled with such loving care by the great photographer Edward Steichen.

I wanted us to compile a similar photographic history of America's communities at the millennium. Brian O'Doherty, the director of the media program for over two decades, shared some of my excitement about the possibilities and agreed to be the director of millennium projects. Within weeks he was able to launch a project that involved major photographers documenting faces and places at the close of the century. But my own dream, to have all communities in the country taking pictures of themselves, telling the story of who they were, and then showing it and maybe touring the best exhibits, remained unrealized. It was a large idea, unattainable with our limited and decreasing resources. We managed to get barely a dozen projects in play for the year 2000: one with National Public Radio, one with the Whitney Museum, one with choruses nationwide, and one with a Pacific Northwest Indian tribe to re-create the mammoth canoe of their ancestors. But there was so much more that could have been done.

Instead of lofty millennium projects we dealt with the specter of certain death in 1997 and the fallout from our total restructuring. A. B. Spellman, who was in charge of our guideline books for prospective applicants, managed to create a single book to supplant the numerous books we'd had before in each art field. He called it the "One Book," and it looked very snappy. It created consternation, however, for the thousands of applicants who had applied in the past to a single field— Music, Dance, or Expansion Arts. They were now asked to fill out one application only, in just one of the four categories. There was understandable confusion. Where, for example, should a production of an American Chinese opera company apply? In "Creation and Presentation" or in "Heritage and Preservation?" The answer that evolved ultimately was to apply where your chances of receiving a grant were the greatest. Most of the Folk and Traditional Arts Program fell neatly into the "Heritage and Preservation" category.

The new direction was not palatable to many. Change always has its detractors, and I had learned when I cut subgrants just how sensitive these issues were. We did our best at the agency to consult by mail with as many of our "clients" as possible, but it was not the same as sitting down with them over the course of months and hammering out guidelines that pleased everyone. It wouldn't have been possible to please everyone anyway.

The criticism hurt, but as an actress it was not new to me. In fact a negative review of my acting work was much harder to take than the criticism I received in the press regarding the Endowment. A character I created for the stage or on film was somehow the raw truth of me; a decision I came to as the chairman of the NEA involved mitigating circumstances. One was art, and the other was politics. Art hurts; politics pricks.

When artists criticized me it hurt more than the barbs of any columnist or arts administrator. They seemed to be telling me I was no longer one of the club, that I had become one of "them." Fortunately most artists were muted in their discussions of me with the press. In New York I would pick up the phone and ask that they please withhold their criticism publicly until the agency got through its appropriations process. The last thing we needed was dissension in the ranks; it was fodder for those critics who sought to eliminate us. I was thankful to those in the avant-garde in New York. I had reneged on my initial promise to turn it all around in six months, but whatever they thought, they mostly held their tongues.

In my enthusiasm for refashioning the agency I inevitably made a number of errors, but the infeasibility of one process in particular seemed obvious to everyone but me at the time. I wanted to have one super panel for each of the four categories, made up of people who would be capable of choosing the best applicants from among all the art forms. In Creation and Presentation, for example, the super panel would be choosing from among the best applicants in Dance, Music, Theatre, Folk Arts, Opera, and Photography at the same session. My staff tried to talk me out of the idea, pointing out that a panel expert on opera would be the person whom all other panelists would turn to when the opera applications came up, the education expert when arts education came up, and so on. No, I persevered, there would be people who could judge all of the art forms equitably. Why I was so pigheaded about this I will never know. Members of the National Council also tried to talk me out of it. Judith Rubin in particular made a valiant effort, which I responded to by blowing up and storming from the room. It was only the second time I ever let my anger get the better of me in front of staff. I never thought that emotional indulgence was at all valuable for those in leadership positions. I could recall too many leading actors or directors who yelled and swore to get their way, creating only a fearful and unproductive company. The NEA staff had too much stress to deal with already to be loaded down with mine. In this instance my anger served only to give me my own way—and my own way turned out to be the wrong way.

The super panels made it through one season before they were jettisoned. I'll never forget sitting next to the great ballerina Maria Tallchief, who was on the Heritage and Preservation super panel. When the slides of visual arts applicants flashed on the screen I thought she might hyperventilate. The game Tallchief could judge dance with authority, and music with real knowledge, but when it came to certain kinds of painting she was as much a neophyte as I was. The panels reduced themselves, as my staff had warned, to the experts in a certain art form holding forth for the edification of the other panelists. My idea was a lousy one, and I was as glad as anyone when it met its timely end.

The blowup with Judith was a warning sign to me, however. Although I didn't show it overtly, I was extremely angry with Congress. I felt contempt for many of the members and despair over the level to which our federal government had sunk. One night at a dinner for Democratic contributors at Ted Kennedy's home I complained to John Kennedy Jr. "They tell me they're *for* the Endowment when I meet with them in their offices, and then they turn around and vote against us!" John shrugged, his lips curling in a slight grin. He said nothing, but the twinkle in his eye told me that he knew politicians were no better than used-car salesmen and it was time I wised up. He was about to launch *George* magazine, a refreshingly humorous look at a world that, like me, took politics too seriously. I congratulated him and then, catching a glimpse of his gregarious uncle across the room, told him what an incredible supporter Ted was of the NEA and of the arts in America. "Yes," John replied, "now we just have to get him some taste." JFK Jr. had a special knack for bursting pretentious balloons and coaxing a laugh.

There were other respites in those dreary days. One afternoon I was invited at the last minute to dine at the home of Ann and Vernon Jordan, with the First Lady and the Dalai Lama. It was a remarkable evening. Vernon was away, but his lovely wife hosted twelve of us at a candlelit dinner. Meeting the spiritual leader of Tibet was a touchy political situation for the president because of relations with China, but Hillary and Chelsea Clinton were there, as were Tipper Gore, the First Lady's chief of staff, Maggie Williams, and Melanne Verveer and her husband Philip. Harrison Ford and his wife, Melissa Matheson, longtime supporters of the Dalai Lama, were also at the table. Melissa was writing the screenplay *Kundun* about the life of the Dalai Lama, to be directed by Martin Scorcese.

Our son Geoff had become more and more committed to Buddhism and found like-minded friends high in the Rocky Mountains north of Boulder. The religion suited his gentle relationship with the natural world and his love of humanity. He was happy in Colorado and had just opened a restaurant, the Tungsten Grill, where his dream of being a chef was finally realized. Because of his interests, Ed and I were learning more about Buddhism.

It was a great gift meeting the Dalai Lama. After Chelsea excused herself to go back to the White House to do her homework, he and I were left alone for ten minutes. I brought him up to date on my friend Hope Cooke, whom he had known when she was the queen of Sikkim, and told him that my former daughter-in-law, Hope Leezum, was now living there again, running a trekking business in the Himalayas. He asked all about them and wondered whether I knew of anyone passing from Sikkim into Tibet. I didn't, although I knew that Hope Leezum's treks in the world's highest mountains sometimes brought her close to the border.

Despite his political involvement on behalf of the people of Tibet, the deep spiritual calm of the man was palpable. I yearned for it. I longed to be around it. The Dalai Lama's look was so direct and connected that tears came to my eyes. When we spoke his gaze never wandered, and it seemed I was the only person in the world who mattered at that moment. He recounted the last time he saw Lhasa—riding out in the dead of night and then turning in his saddle at dawn to glimpse the great monastery in the early morning light, knowing he might never return. It was a poignant moment for him, but not a sad one. He laughed a lot, and his smile made my petty concerns about politics and politicians seem pretty insignificant.

Tipper Gore was seated at one end of the table, and I was next to her across from Harrison. The conversation naturally gravitated toward the 1996 campaign. One election melded into another in my mind; everyone always seemed to be running for something. I shot my mouth off about congressmen being untrustworthy and then realized I better shut up in this town. Mostly I gazed down to the end of the table where the Dalai Lama glowed in the candlelight as he engaged in quiet conversation with another world-weary soul, Hillary Rodham Clinton. The daily toll of Whitewater drained from her face as she bathed in his concentration.

I was still thinking of the peace of the evening two weeks later when I moved into a new apartment. I was restless but knew that I still had a long row to hoe in the job. I increasingly missed my family and the green haven of my home. Jace's career was taking off, and he was far away in New Zealand directing a few episodes of *Xena: Warrior Princess.* Jon was completing his Ph.D. in neuroscience at Harvard and would soon head to Chicago to earn a medical degree as well. He was already published in medical journals, and his future seemed secure. Tony was moving from film to film as an editor, and Evan was already two. I had spent almost no time at all with them.

Ed's reign at *Law and Order* was making the show an even bigger success with viewers than it had been. It was consistently in the top twenty each week. The salary he commanded had managed to get us out of most of our financial straits. We had only a few more debts to pay off to the Internal Revenue Service, and we were saving enough money to take a trip to Africa. Our time together on the weekends was usually curtailed because we both had so much homework to do, so we were greatly looking forward to visiting Tanzania and Kenya with the Wildlife Conservation Society in the year ahead.

My new next-door neighbor turned out to be Attorney General Janet Reno. I discovered this by peering through my peephole at dawn one morning. My routine was to rise at six, read and write for two hours, exercise, and get to the office by nine-thirty. But someone next door was up and out long before I had drunk my first cup of coffee. Although they were quiet you couldn't miss the sound of several foot-falls on the carpeted hall floor. Through the peephole I glimpsed the attorney general and two bodyguards making their way briskly down the hall to begin her ritual morning walk.

Janet and I became friendly. We had met in her office at the beginning of my tenure to discuss a partnership between the Department of Justice and the NEA on arts programs for at-risk youth. Those programs were now well under way, and the DOJ was monitoring them carefully to see what positive impact they might have. We had also crossed paths at social functions before becoming neighbors.

Janet Reno had more integrity than almost anyone in the administration and was paying for it. The White House was having difficulties with her, and although a staffer had promised to tell me the whole story one day, I never got it.

I had my own disagreements with the Department of Justice. When the California court ruled in favor of the NEA Four in June 1993 I hoped that would be the end of it. The Justice Department, in one of the first decisions made by Reno after she took office, decided to appeal the decision, claiming it was routine to defend a federal agency—in this case, the NEA.

Later, in 1997, when the federal appeals court *also* upheld the NEA Four, I wrote to President Clinton urging that the administration and the DOJ not appeal the case yet again and asserting that another appeal would be a waste of the taxpayers' money. I never received a reply from the White House, but I did engage in lengthy and enlightening conversations with Reno's solicitor general, Walter Dellinger, who, ironically, had been a great litigator for First Amendment issues. The DOJ was pursuing the case *National Endowment for the Arts and Jane Alexander v. Karen Finley et al.,* Walter said, because the department wanted to "keep control" of the case and shepherd it all the way to the Supreme Court if necessary. The thinking behind this strategy was sound: a decision from the highest court in the land on whether Congress had the right to impose content restrictions on a federal agency would be the definitive statement on the issue. Clarity was needed. The NEA and the issue of free speech fell somewhere between two important past decisions. *Rust v. Sullivan* had stated that speech in government health clinics was government speech and disallowed abortion counseling. In *Rosenberger v. University of Virginia* the Court had decided essentially that student groups receiving government funds through the university are protected in their speech by the First Amendment. The Endowment was created by the U.S. Congress; did that mean that all the art it funded was government speech, subjected to decency language and other prohibitions? This was the decision that Walter Dellinger and others at the Department of Justice sought from the Supreme Court. The argument before the justices was still years away.

Although Janet, who was usually at her desk from 7:00 A.M. until 9:00 P.M. every day, was far too busy for us to meet often, we did dine together a few times. She would not discuss business; instead, we shared our mutual love of the outdoors. Whenever she was able to visit her home in Florida the first thing she did was kick off her shoes and walk barefoot in the grass. Her mother had been known to wrestle alligators and had raised some very independent children. Janet had cared for her mother in her last years and chuckled at the orneriness of her charge.

With that in mind, and knowing her love for theater, I invited Janet and her visiting niece, the former model Hunter Reno, to see Albee's latest play, *Three Tall Women,* at the Kennedy Center. Janet was eager to go but refused to be seated in the presidential box, which I had access to most nights because the president rarely used it. Reno did not want any kind of preferential treatment and did not want to draw attention to herself.

Still, at six-foot-three, Janet Reno and her "entourage"—her very tall, slim, blond niece and me—were the focus of attention going down the aisle. As I suspected, Janet loved the play. It was about three generations of women coming together in the last days of an ornery matriarch. We went backstage afterward to congratulate the actresses Marian Seldes and Michael Learned. Edward Albee, who was also the director, greeted us as we three tall women swept through the swinging doors: "Hello!" he said delightedly. "Is this my new cast?"

My new apartment was a duplex. I still dreamed of entertaining, but aside from a few little dinner parties, it never happened. Nevertheless, I loved the spaciousness of the apartment, and especially the view of the Washington Monument, looming like a Ku Klux Klan member with two red flashing eyes in the distance. Unfortunately the apartment also overlooked the ugliest building in Washington, the FBI Building, named for one of the most ugly-spirited men who had inhabited the director's office, J. Edgar Hoover. Janet did not wish to be spied on by those under her command and kept her blinds drawn all the time. I, on the other hand, craved the light and, even knowing there was a surveillance camera on me at all times to protect the attorney general, kept the curtains raised. I hope they have a lot of good tape of me reading stacks of paperwork in my bathrobe early every morning.

I was longing for the perfect world of drama; the messy and repetitive world of politics and the legislative process seemed like purgatory. I missed the stage, although I was doing plenty of acting. Just smiling at some of the fellows on the Hill took real talent. I probably should have done what Janet Reno did with her colleagues at Justice. She loved Shakespeare and gathered her staff around the big conference table one afternoon to read *King Lear.* Janet played Goneril, a role that must have been fun for her, venting rage and spewing bile, especially when she got to say, "The laws are mine, not thine: who can arraign me for't?"

Our nation had been absorbed in its own epic drama for months: the O. J. Simpson trial. It was Shakespearean to me, with overtones of *Othello.* I always believed O. J. was guilty of murdering his former wife, Nicole Brown Simpson, and her friend Ronald Goldman, but it was the reaction of the public that most interested me. I had been delivering the commencement address to the UCLA School of the Arts in June 1994 at the very moment that the cops were chasing O. J.'s white Bronco down the 405 freeway. My voice was unable to push through the microphones because the whirl of helicopters above the stadium made so great a noise. The crowd was totally preoccupied, as was I. Sixteen months later, when the verdict was handed down in October 1995, those closest to me at the Endowment had gathered in my office. Sandy, Noel, Stephanie, LaVerne, and my driver, Larry Manley, watched the TV raptly. We had all been discussing the case daily, but I was completely surprised by the tears of joy that streamed down Larry's face when O. J. was declared "not guilty," and by the whoop of excitement that escaped from LaVerne. The rest of us, who were white, sat in stunned silence. The difference in our feelings was about trust of the police above everything else. Larry and LaVerne did not trust uniformed officials. I had never had a bad experience with the police. But I too was beginning to question authority in ways I hadn't since my teens and twenties. Since I had become successful in my career and was now part of the establishment, was I buying into the big lies of systems that seek to perpetuate themselves at any cost? Was I part of the problem? Should artists be funded by government at all if that government is trying to control content?

I wore black to my third appearance before the House subcommittee on appropriations in March 1996. Yes, it was dramatic, but I was feeling dark. I was forceful but courteous. Even if I felt like shouting, I was not going to reduce myself to the behavior observed of some members of Congress. Sid Yates was great. He tried to push Chairman Regula and the other Republicans on the committee to a more moderate position. Regula replied that the "majority of the majority" wanted us out in September 1997. David Skaggs, a mild-mannered Democrat from Colorado, said that the "majority of the majority" sounded like something from Gilbert and Sullivan, whereupon Yates shot back, "Yes, it reminds me of that song from *Iolanthe*." Then he quoted an entire stanza, ending with: "Got to leave that brain outside, and vote just as their leaders tell them to." It was fabulous. Sid was fond of saying, "Oh, to be eighty again," when something slipped his mind, but here he was at eighty-five with total recall.

Ralph Regula took me aside afterward and confessed to the bind he was in. He said that until the "Contract with America," the Republicans had never been required to vote in a bloc, but now the leadership required allegiance to the Republican agenda. I sympathized but said that I guessed it was then a question of what you turn your back on— the GOP leaders or your conscience. I knew the truth. Ralph would have his chairmanship wrested from him if he didn't vote with the leadership. This was the kind of extortion the Republicans were practicing, and so very few independent voices were being heard. I had renewed respect for the moderates like Rick Lazio, Amo Houghton, Marge Roukema, and Michael Forbes who stood up to Newt and the Gang of Four in support of the Endowment.

The next morning I borrowed Sandy's car and went looking for saw whet owls in Maryland. I was finding ways to keep my sanity. Another day our literature director, Gigi Bradford, took me into the archives of the Folger Library. I touched Queen Elizabeth I's massive, thirty-five-pound Bible, the delicate rag paper so soft yet sturdy. I marveled at a first folio of Shakespeare, one of seventy-nine the library owned, more than any in the world. I could have spent a year down in those vaults, reading and studying, dreaming of the greatest playwright the world has ever seen.

We don't have a Shakespeare today, and maybe we never will again. We don't have the government funds to support large theater companies, and the countries that still do, such as England and Germany, are beginning to cut back. William Shakespeare didn't have an NEA grant, but he did have Queen Elizabeth and other patrons who made it possible for him to write and produce for many actors.

The number of times I mentally composed my letter of resignation to the president was increasing. If he had a plan, as he intimated to me at the Kennedy Center honors, it wasn't surfacing, and he didn't mention it again. I saw the president at a White House event where he signed a proclamation designating Women's History Month. He was circled by over twenty women in government, many of whom, like myself, he had appointed. It was an impressive group, and Health and Human Services Secretary Donna Shalala remarked that for the first time in U.S. history policy could now move *only* through the hands of women before finally reaching his desk. I looked around at Secretary of Energy Hazel O'Leary, Carol Browner, the head of the Environmental Protection Agency, and others, and I felt proud to be among these fine women. Sandra Day O'Connor and Ruth Bader Ginsberg, the two female justices of the Supreme Court, came over to say hello to me. Justice Ginsberg quietly told me how much she had enjoyed *First Monday in October* with Henry Fonda and me in 1978. "She played me!" said Sandra Day O'Connor, even though my role had predated her Supreme Court appointment. "I know," replied Bader Ginsberg. "When are you going to play me?" I was dying to ask them their thoughts about the NEA and content restrictions, but some things are verboten in politics, and asking Supreme Court justices about a case you're involved in is one of them. Maybe they would uphold the First Amendment after all, and we would all be able to breathe a sigh of relief.

I resolved to stay and fight all the harder. There was so much to do, and I wasn't in this war alone. I was just the general, and generals don't quit—they either get fired or fade away or both. The senior staff and others at the agency still made coming to work every day a pleasure. We laughed together, held staff parties, planned the future of the Endowment as if it would survive forever, and came up with new ideas.

Larry Baden, who had managed the agency under Ana Steele's watchful eye, was a devotee of basketball. For years he had imagined an

NEA partnership with the National Basketball Association that would involve jazz ensembles playing at halftime. Thelonius Monk Jr. was doing great things with his late father's foundation. He and his right-hand man, Tom Carter, made it possible for Larry's dream to come true. In partnership with the NEA, the Monk Institute, with a $1 million grant from the Nissan Corporation of America, tipped off "Jazz Sports, L.A." at an NBA game between the Los Angeles Lakers and the Phoenix Suns.

Unfortunately Larry was ill the day we were to fly to L.A., so NEA's own jazz aficionado A. B. Spellman accompanied me instead. On the flight across country we reached into the seat pocket in front of us and got a kick out of seeing the American Airlines magazine with me on the cover. It was a good article, one I hoped the other passengers were reading too. A. B. shared with me his new CDs of Rostropovich playing all of the Beethoven cello concertos as we glided through the clouds, transported by the music.

Even more memorable was the trip down the stadium hall to the locker room and being greeted by seven-foot Kareem Abdul-Jabar, who held out his hand and said to A. B.: "Loved your book on bebop." Kareem, another jazz lover, was on hand to promote the program and get involved with the high school kids who were part of it. Billy Dee Williams and Herbie Hancock were with us too. As we made our way down the tunnel and onto the court I nervously whispered to Kareem that I didn't think the crowd was going to hold still for my explanation of the project and the NEA. "Oh yes they will," he said, firmly but gently nudging me ahead of him to center court. "I'll introduce you." The crowd went wild when Kareem stepped out. He still commanded the love and attention of the fans long after he had left the game. They listened to me respectfully, as Kareem had said they would, and cheered the kids when Herbie led them in the best "Star-Spangled Banner" I had ever heard.

The next day all of us visited several of the schools in Watts and South Central Los Angeles and listened to the jazz they were playing under Herbie's tutelage. I thought one young man was going to burst he was so excited to have Herbie Hancock at the keyboard while he played solo saxophone. The look of adoration and pride, the acceptance of all he could learn under the great musician in the weeks to come, made everything we had been fighting for at the NEA crystal clear to me.

We had more than a year and a half to go before D-day in September 1997, when the House had vowed behind closed doors to end the Endowment. If we were going to avert the leadership's intent, we needed to focus our efforts in several ways. The first was to increase confidence in the agency, a goal I felt we were achieving through the agency's restructuring and our constant attention to educating the public through the media. The second goal was to maintain and increase the support the Republican moderates gave us in Congress, and I felt that we were doing well in that respect through our frequent visits to the Hill. The third effort was to expand advocacy of the arts nationwide by solidifying the network of local, state, and federal arts agencies with citizens and arts organizations across the country.

Several of us on the senior staff began to work on the third issue. We decided to go to six cities in the coming year and hold forums to discuss the arts in order to discover what was working in these communities, what wasn't, and how we might work together to make a difference. We called the initiative "American Canvas." We hired a professional, Val Marmillion, to develop the syllabus and be the moderator in each city. Unlike with ART 21, our 1994 federal conference on the arts, we gave ourselves more than four months to plan. We asked educators, administrators, and artists to advise us on the project, and we hired the writer Gary O. Larsen to write the book of our journey. By involving state and local arts councils in American Canvas, together with their legislators and business leaders, I was hoping to promote a sound future for the arts with or without federal funding. I still, however, envisioned a huge hole should the Endowment be eliminated.

Behind the scenes I engaged a few prominent individuals to discuss creating a nonprofit national arts foundation if the NEA disappeared. It was pulled together in secret because I did not want Congress to think we were privatizing the agency, and I certainly did not want my name involved when I was fighting so desperately for a continuation of federal funding. The NEA was still the single largest funder of the arts in

America. Foundations like Lila Wallace and Pew were closing the gap, but if the economy took a nosedive their giving could be affected as well. Years, maybe decades, would pass before a newly created national art fund would be capable of giving large grants. But I envisioned a foundation that wealthy artists could remember in their wills rather than create their own foundations, and to which the American public could give as well. With the help of some leading Washington lawyers, like Jim Fitzpatrick, who gave of their time pro bono the 501c3 non-profit art fund was created, an empty shell waiting to be filled should the need arise.

It was clear that the arts had to have more clout on the Hill. It wasn't enough to try to convert elected officials to our way of thinking. If money was the overriding influence because of the way campaigns were run, and because special-interest groups contributed, then the arts needed to start backing candidates through campaign contributions. If altruism had ever existed in politics, it didn't seem to be in evidence in the 1990s.

Bob Lynch of NALAA was having similar thoughts. He and I met privately several times to exchange ideas. The American Council on the Arts, which had been founded in the 1970s by the pollster Lou Harris and other concerned arts advocates, needed more networking at the grassroots level. The group decided to join forces with NALAA. The merger of the local arts agencies with the influential men and women who sat on ACA's board, which was chaired by Don Greene of the Coca-Cola Company, seemed a marriage made in heaven. In a short period of time they renamed themselves Americans for the Arts, and with Bob as president and CEO they created a political action committee in order to contribute to campaigns with a strong arts platform. Americans for the Arts became the major clearinghouse for information on the latest congressional actions and held an annual conference that gave important workshops on the arts and advocacy. It also began to award politicians for their pro-arts stance and united with the U.S. Conference of Mayors for an annual gala in Washington, D.C. The mayors were always the savviest elected officials regarding the arts. They knew art was a good thing for their communities, that it revitalized downtown areas, was good for tourism, and made life more livable. The combination of the three groups coming together—the local arts agencies, the influential advocates, and the mayors of cities nationwide—was unbeatable.

One way to get the word out about the agency was through the Internet. Although government bureaucracy and ineptitude had kept the Endowment from being fully "wired" internally, a handful of us had Macs and were online. A diverse group of techno-devotees banded together and created the NEA's web page in record time. Within months "arts.endow.gov" had had a million "hits." The web bunch, led by my speechwriter, Keith Donohue, and our technology director, Arthur Tsuchiya, was one of the most creative and excited group of men and women in the agency. They wrote articles for the page, on a different theme each month, and plugged in audios of blues singers we had awarded, as well as listing all the comprehensive information about the agency. It was a very popular government site, and a lot more fun to visit than the Department of Defense site.

A growing number of people in government knew that technology was where the future lay. Vice President Al Gore was one of them, but I had doubts about the fellows on the Hill. We knew that artists and arts administrators would benefit greatly from being wired, and so we began an NEA partnership with the Benton Foundation to help each state give artists Internet capability. Microsoft joined us in this initiative a while later, and the Open Studio Project continues to train artists and arts administrators in how to use the web for commerce and creativity. With all that we were able to accomplish externally, it was pitiful that we couldn't get e-mail internally for our own employees in the four years I was there. The bureaucratic wheels turn very slowly indeed sometimes.

I took to surfing the Internet when I had a free hour. I could access photographic archives and museum exhibits and see the nascent digital works of online artists. The web took me to the distant shores of Canada and the Caribbean, it compiled the latest migratory bird patterns, and it gave me all of the works of Shakespeare at the touch of a key. It was a miracle, and nothing will ever be quite the same again on our planet for those of us tapping into it.

On May 8, 1996, the NEA's Senate hearing before Slade Gorton's appropriations subcommittee took place. The senators on both sides were complimentary about the procedural changes at the agency, and the sailing seemed smooth until Gorton baited me about the language in his own Helms-Gorton amendment of the year before, which prohibited grants for art that displayed "patently offensive sexual or excretory organs" or "denigrated religion." I replied that the Department of Justice was looking at the language for its constitutionality and that existing prohibitions were sufficient. Gorton then said that my response was "troubling." I knew what he wanted, but I was not going to say it. He wanted to hear me say that Congress had the right to supersede the Constitution by imposing content restrictions on our grantees, and that as chairman of the NEA I was sanguine about the language. I was praying that the Supreme Court would rule in favor of the NEA Four, but it was unlikely that it would even hear the case for another year or two. Meanwhile, the congressional leadership was closing in on me.

The Republicans were getting ugly about the president too in this election year. Arianna Huffington, the new doyenne of the GOP social scene, was a clever speaker and loved telling jokes. At one event she told the audience: "Dick Morris (the president's main adviser in 1996) runs into the Oval Office: 'Mr. President, what should we do about this abortion bill?' The president: 'Pay it.'" For all the Republican attacks, snide and otherwise, the public still rated Bill Clinton's presidency high in the opinion polls. The economy was good, the deficit was down, and no one was terribly enthusiastic about the Republican nominee, Bob Dole.

The House and Senate members who were up for reelection were eager to get home to their districts to campaign in late September 1996, but the new self-appointed prosecutor of the NEA, a representative from Michigan named Peter Hoekstra, who chaired the Oversight and Investigations Subcommittee for the Economic and Educational Opportunities Committee, wanted to punish the Endowment. The interminable GOP sleuthing for dirt on the NEA had turned up a grant to the filmmaker Cheryl Dunye for her movie *Watermelon Woman*. The film had received good reviews and was winning awards at independent film festivals. It was about a group of African American women who were lesbians seeking information about a silent film star called "Watermelon Woman." It contained one tasteful lovemaking scene that was in no way obscene and barely in the same league with what commercial filmmakers in Hollywood routinely presented to the American public.

The issue seemed so overt in its targeting of minorities that I could not believe anyone would take it seriously, but after the *Washington Times* made sure that an article about it appeared shortly before our House debate on appropriations, the controversy threatened to engulf the agency once again. Unfortunately the Endowment did not have one grant in Hoekstra's rural Michigan district, so there were no arts advocates I could call up to lean on him.

In the middle of the *Watermelon Woman* struggle I finally saw Newt Gingrich. The speaker met with me for fifteen minutes—not because he had decided to honor my standing request of a year and a half, and not because Hoekstra was after me. No, it was because my friend and fellow actress, Ceci Hart, had sat next to him at a dinner party at the Library of Congress. Ceci, a little blond spitfire, is one of the more tenacious and outrageous people I know. She is married to my friend James Earl Jones, and they live not far from Ed and me. According to Ceci, the speaker arrived late at the dinner for the Library's advisers, the Madison Council, of which James Earl is one. When Gingrich sat down next to her and they began to chat, she said: "Why haven't you met with my friend Jane Alexander?" The speaker demurred, and she pressed on, urging him to call me and ending with, "You won't get a photo-op with James Earl if you don't." She reported this to me the next day, and Dick called Gingrich's aide immediately. We had our meeting scheduled soon thereafter.

Waiting outside the speaker's capacious offices, one might have thought we were waiting for God. Half a dozen small groups stood or sat and chatted in hushed tones. Five, ten, fifteen minutes went by, and then the man of the hour swept by with his entourage. Dick and I waited for one group to emerge and then were ushered into the inner sanctum. Gingrich was not a bear at all, and not defensive. He sat, on this hot June day, in his shirtsleeves, the bright blue of the cloth contrasting with the red roundness of his face. He called Ceci "very persuasive," and we discussed our mutual love of animals, although he was more fond of dead ones (dinosaurs) than I. He said my friends at the Wildlife Conservation Society had spoken highly of me when they recently took him on an island retreat off the Carolinas. He said that slogging through mud in search of alligators was more his milieu than art. I didn't doubt it.

Then he launched into the NEA: "Ninety percent of your problems are controversial grants." The idea man took over, and he suggested repackaging the NEA with a name like "The Public Trust." We had explored many such ideas at the agency in the past year, including merging with the NEH, changing names, and so on. None of them seemed to work, but I thanked Gingrich for any support he would throw our way, and we departed. As I had suspected for a long time, the Endowment was not terribly important to Gingrich, but it was a pawn in the game and he would use it in any way he needed. If it could be a bone to throw to the rabid young bucks in the House, then so it would be.

When the NEA was brought up on the House floor a month later, Hoekstra offered an amendment to cut our budget by $31,000, the cost of the film.

It was Sheila Jackson Lee, a Democrat and African American from Houston, who saved the day. She spoke eloquently about art being in the eye of the beholder and about the country being vast and diverse. That did it. It was one thing to attack black lesbian culture, and it was quite another to take on a formidable black woman legislator like Sheila Jackson Lee. Hoekstra withdrew his amendment in turn for a formal commitment to eliminate the Endowment a year hence. What had been a late-night backroom deal was now out in the open, and my heart sank when Ralph Regula, chairman of our House subcommittee, publicly agreed to it. It meant that we would receive zero appropriations when the committee next met on our budget, in the spring of 1997. Assuming the House was still controlled by the GOP after the 1996 election, there was nothing our friends like Sid Yates could do.

I went to Nantucket with Ed during the August recess. We swam in the surf, went clamming with my teenage niece Katherine and nephew Daniel, and rejuvenated ourselves for the heavy autumn workload. I had been trading limericks with a friend anonymously since the beginning of my chairmanship. When the going got rough the limericks got rougher. Here's one I penned in the frustration of the summer:

> While sitting in sand on Nantucket
> With water and shovel and bucket
> I'm building my castles
> Without any hassles
> The rest of the world can go . . . on without me.

In November 1996 Bill Clinton was reelected handily despite the crises—Whitewater, Travelgate, Paula Jones—that had overshadowed his first four years. All of us who had been appointed by the administration gathered behind the White House the following day and donned white T-shirts printed in blue and red with "Welcome Home! President and Mrs. Clinton, Vice-President and Mrs. Gore, Nov. 6th 1996." We all looked pretty silly, especially Attorney General Janet Reno, who, unlike the rest of us who wore suit jackets, preferred dresses. The white T-shirt she wore over her dress made her look especially prominent, like the coach of the Davenport, Iowa, junior high school basketball team. The next crisis was brewing there and then as the president hugged the intern Monica Lewinsky in the famous beret photograph that surfaced later, but none of us were aware of it as we waited for our own hug from the boss.

The House and Senate changed very little, the voters seeming to prefer the stasis created by extreme partisanship to new legislation. My own take on it was that with a good economy the public didn't want anyone to "make waves." In addition, with all the squabbling going on between the two parties, people had little respect for politicians and didn't show up at the polls. In my travels I found that people everywhere seemed way ahead of the politicians in their thinking. Life was good, politicians were dumb, and who cared? I didn't disagree. It took so long to get anything accomplished, and the private sector accomplished so much more quickly—why get involved? Still, the United States government was here to stay and was very much needed by all citizens, including the private sector. It needed to be better than it was.

Some of the finest politicians had decided to leave, and I attended an arts reception in their honor with tears in my eyes. Senators Al Simpson, Nancy Kassebaum, Paul Simon, Claiborne Pell, and Mark Hatfield were stepping down. Steve Gunderson and Pat Williams were leaving the House of Representatives. They had become my good friends, and I honestly didn't know who was going to take their place on behalf of the arts. Kennedy was still our champion in the Senate, and Sid Yates in the House, but who else was going to stand up and defend us on the floor as these fine people had? It was sad to say good-bye to friends and worrisome for the agency. I understood why they were leaving; the political game was too hard, and the Washington scene was no fun anymore. The austerity of the new Congress and the low level of civility had made everyone's life miserable. In the old days a great deal had been accomplished over the dinner table, Republicans and Democrats alike leaving their partisanship in the Capitol Building and finding common ground by breaking bread together. But those days were gone.

Dale Bumpers, the Democratic senator from Arkansas and a great statesman, told me he would retire too in 1998. He said that he was weary of the new politicians, and that he missed the days of meaningful debate on the issues. He called the current Congress "troglodytes" and said that the Senate wasn't the place it used to be. I wanted desperately to go out with them all. But there was a year to go in my four-year term, and I wasn't going to quit early, not when the battle for the Endowment's budget was at its most intense. It was important, though, for my own peace of mind to adopt a larger perspective on all that was going on and to not be debilitated by the daily assaults on the agency I loved. The world was a far larger place than Capitol Hill.

CHAPTER FOURTEEN

Curtain Down

The twin engine broke through the fog and rain, scattering a herd of zebra, and landed on a patch of earth on the Serengeti. Nothing in my life experience prepared me for the great plains of East Africa—not all the reading I'd done, not all the pictures I'd pored over, not the hundreds of movies and TV shows I'd seen about wildlife. I stood on that plain that stretched for hundreds of miles—in any direction I turned it just kept going, to the horizon and beyond—and I saw thousands of animals everywhere. There were lions and zebras cheek by jowl, wildebeest, ostrich, buffalo, hyena, and gazelle. Grazing in the branches of nearby acacia were giraffe, and elephants walked in stately procession toward a mud hole. It was the vastness and abundance I could not comprehend. I pinched myself. Was this real?

It came to me that my entire understanding of the Serengeti and East Africa up until that point had been circumscribed by the rectangle of a TV or movie screen, a photo, or a book; my vision had literally been narrowed about three hundred degrees. The experience of being there, in the actual place, awakened in me a spiritual connection I did not even know I'd lost.

I began to think about authentic experience, and about the winnowing of dimension in our world. Real life is in three dimensions, and yet we glue ourselves to one or two for much of our daily life. We talk on the telephone, we surf the net, we listen to the radio, we watch TV.

Back in the late 1940s my family became the first on our block to have a television. My father brought home a little Motorola, and the neighbors left their own homes, their radios, their turntables, and their books to come to ours. The screen was round, a ten-inch diameter. In my child's eye I thought the round screen represented the round ball, the earth, from whence everything came. The next TV we had was a rectangular twelve-inch Zenith; a designer somewhere had changed the shape of television. TV was the eight-hundred-pound gorilla that had come to stay. We forsook our games of backgammon and chess, our knitting or sewing by the radio, and our family songfests gathered around the piano and guitar. All over America families migrated stealthily to the TV corner.

For all that we have gained in information and diversion, what we have lost is incalculable. Our voices have been silenced, quite literally. In the time before TV, earphones, cell phones, and boom boxes people sang or whistled in their homes and on the streets. I remember this dimly from my youth. I remember doing it myself as I walked to the bus for school.

What we don't know we don't miss. Human beings are immensely adaptive. We live everywhere on the planet, in intense cold and in the hottest climates. We live in tiny spaces and on the vast tundra, and we adapt to survive. The great experiences of life, the transformative experiences, could pass us by and we would never know it. Not only that, we wouldn't care. Most of us don't care. We slog through the day and plunk down in a couch potato haze for respite before the grind of the next morning sets in.

The visit to Africa changed things for me. I longed for authentic experience, for beauty, and for spirituality. Ed and I had traveled to many places in the world. We had tramped through rain forests, sailed to watch whales, hiked in the highest mountains, and seen the masterpieces of the great artists. The Serengeti was the culminating experience for me. It coalesced and fulfilled the longing for beauty and sense of spirituality that were so stunted in the world of Washington politics.

When I returned from Africa my tolerance for the congressional situation had severely decreased. Life was too short to be playing these idiotic games about the value of art. There was no question that great art taps into those indefinable places in our souls that transform us; I had felt it, and I had seen it over and over and over again. There were phrases from books and poems that reverberated in my life like mantras, hooking me to the truth when all else seemed false. The light captured on the cheek of one of Vermeer's women had taught me how to look at a friend's face. When a Brahms piano concerto was played with the same unrelenting passion that the composer had felt in writing it, the hair stood up on the back of my neck.

If art were diminished in our culture, we too were diminished. The men in power in the Congress of the United States were men of little minds. They dwelt on their fears of obscenity and perversity, diminishing us all with their myopia. "A foolish consistency is the hobgoblin of little minds," wrote Emerson. They revealed a great deal about themselves through their consistent attacks on art. Believing they were crusaders leading the moralist parade to protect the American public, in fact they thought *less* of human beings than I did, not more. I do not believe that any of us needs to be saved from controversy. I believe we learn from it and reflect on it. We decide for ourselves whether it is art we wish to see or engage in, and we accept others whose opinion differs.

In an exhibit in an Arizona museum the artist had spread the American flag out on the gallery floor. To get to the next point the visitor had to step on the flag. Some congressmen railed about the artist's "unpatriotic" statement, but by forcing visitors to make a decision the artist made each of them consider his own relationship to the flag of our country, and to symbols in general. Most people would not step on the flag, even though it was just strips of red, white, and blue cloth with some stars sewn on it.

We are creatures of symbols: our language, our relationship to history, our rituals are all based on symbols and metaphor that mean something to us individually and as a people. No other animal in the world creates this wealth of symbols. And we manufacture more every day.

What we need to understand is that the corporate world is creating many of them for us today, for its own purposes. The economic engine drives the psyche of modern man. Authentic experience is lost in the white sound of product marketing. It was no wonder that the politicians, entangled as they were with the special interests of big business and needing to court them to be reelected, were sacrificing the heart of what it means to be human, the best part of our brains. But then, they were men of little minds.

If I had thought we might get a respite at the beginning of the new year I had another think coming. Pete Hoekstra was still after us. Whether he was receiving orders from higher up to discredit the Endowment and me at any cost was not clear, but he was out to do us in. As chairman of the Oversights and Investigations Subcommittee he had every right to investigate the agency, but his tactics were scurrilous, and his aide Derrick Max was rude and underhanded in his dealings with those of us at NEA and with the arts administrators he contacted.

Hoekstra asked for material on dozens of grants. NEA employees already overburdened with additional responsibility because of a diminished staff devoted weeks to honoring his request. Just when we thought we had satisfied his demands he would ask for more. This was harassment pure and simple, but there was nowhere to turn to air our grievances, and complaints on our part only added fuel to the fire.

He was targeting grants to homosexuals mostly. *Watermelon Woman* surfaced again, as did a few other films about lesbians. In most cases we had not supported the film directly, but the tangential involvement of the Endowment through its support of film festivals or organizations like Women Make Movies was enough for Hoekstra.

The *Washington Times* reported regularly on the latest contretemps, painting the congressman as something of a hero and publishing our latest correspondence. The *Washington Post* articles on the same issue were slanted in our favor because the reporter Jacqueline Trescott would have rightly heard our side of the story as well. When I finally had a meeting with Hoekstra in my office he asked that the rhetoric in the press be ratcheted down. I told him that I would ask Cherie to do her best but that I could hardly control the media. I said that when I read a letter of his addressed to me in the *Washington Times* before it had even arrived on my desk I thought it was "bad faith" on his part. The congressman blushed. He was a tight and intense figure of a man, but the blush humanized him instantly. He admitted that publication of the letter was in "bad faith" and said that he would not let such a leak happen again. Then he went on to say that if anyone continued to claim that he was targeting minorities he would only increase the number of grants he was reviewing. He had all the power and he knew it.

Another man in Washington who had enormous power was our

newly reelected president. Many of us hoped that Clinton would speak of the arts, and of celebrating the millennium, in his inaugural address, or at least in his State of the Union address a few weeks later. The year 1997 was, after all, the last presidential inaugural address of the century, and the address would have been a fitting way to talk of the value of the arts and humanities. Edward Albee, the screenwriter Fay Kanin, and the actor Roddy McDowall were just a few of many to urge the president to speak of the arts.

After some wrangling I was able to obtain a reserved seat for the inauguration in a section about a football field away from the Capitol steps. The White House had special seating for the cabinet, but those of us who headed up lesser agencies and departments had to scramble just like everyone else. The general public massed behind us on the mall, so far from the platform that the president was indistinguishable from the other politicians in their dark coats. At least it was not too cold. After being sworn in, the president began his address, and I waited in vain for a word about the culture of our nation. The speech was tepid; every time the president reached for poetry he got only as high as platitude. One phrase was rather unfortunate: "Nothing big ever came from being small." While people around me snickered exceptions to that rule, I felt like shouting out, "Except Barbara Mikulski!"—the tiny senator from Maryland who was such a powerhouse. Since the inauguration speech was a disappointment, those in the arts community redoubled their efforts to persuade the president to speak about culture in his State of the Union address in February. They were finally richly rewarded.

President Clinton said:

The enduring worth of our nation lies in our shared values and soaring spirit. So instead of cutting back on our modest efforts to support the arts and humanities, I believe we should stand by them and challenge our artists, musicians, and writers, challenge our museums, libraries, and theaters. We should challenge all Americans in the arts and humanities to join with their fellow citizens to make the year 2000 a national celebration of the American spirit in every community, a celebration of our common culture in the century that is past and in the . . . new millennium so that we can remain the world's beacon not only of liberty but of creativity long after the fireworks have faded.

The president received a rousing standing ovation for this statement, not unusual for remarks in State of the Union speeches, except that this ovation was the longest one of the evening, surprising Bill Clinton as much as the postgame commentators. My colleague Sheldon Hackney of NEH and I were immensely pleased and appreciative.

I had made my internal peace with the president. He was capable of intermittent eloquence like this, but he would never run out in front for the NEA or NEH as long as the agencies remained a political liability. Why should he? He was interested in winning, and the Endowments were not big win issues; there were other areas he cared more about. He had chosen Sheldon and me to carry the ball for our agencies, and we were doing the job. Besides, I think the president's men thought that art was a "soft" issue—leave it to the ladies, and he did. The First Lady *was* out front and did say all the right things. And I believed she was sincere.

Hillary Rodham Clinton was involving herself more and more with the Endowment. She hosted the annual National Heritage Fellowships at the White House, where she publicly thanked such remarkable people as the quiltmaker Nellie Star Boy Menard from Rosebud, South Dakota; the ironmonger Bea Ellis Hensley from Spruce Pine, North Carolina; and the cowboy poet Buck Ramsey from Amarillo, Texas. These ceremonies were the most joyous the Endowment held, and Hillary looked forward to them as much as I did. The twelve honorees, who received $10,000 each, had elevated their craft to fine art and were among the most talented people in America. They were usually poor; many did not know how long they could keep doing their artwork in a world that moved right past them into franchises and reproductions. At the NEA we did our best to see that their art survived and that they taught others how to keep it alive.

The First Lady was a leading proponent of arts education, speaking of its importance whenever she had a platform and visiting schools to reinforce its value. She also began a sculpture garden at the White

House where revolving shows of contemporary work from around the United States were held. She held meetings of the heads of the cultural agencies and leading arts advocates to determine the best course to take in increasing private-sector involvement with the nation's arts and humanities. And she also embraced the ideas we were promoting for the millennium.

In early 1997 Ted Kennedy, Jim Johnson, the new chairman of the Kennedy Center, and I met with the First Lady to encourage administration support of a millennium bill that Ted was going to introduce to raise funds. Hillary decided she would chair a Millennium Council, stressing the themes of heritage and legacy in our monuments, historic properties, and national parks. The coalition of cultural agencies in Washington that I had brought together to explore joint millennium projects now coordinated with the President's Committee on the Arts and the Humanities and the White House to advance our nation's celebration of the millennium. Although Congress never allocated satisfactory funding, the First Lady toured heritage sites all over the country under the auspices of the White House Millennium Initiative, which was run by Ellen Lovell, who moved over from the President's Committee, with aid from my assistant at the Endowment, Stephanie Madden. It was one of the few national efforts marking the year 2000 and the new century.

Several of us on the senior staff were also touring the United States in late 1996 and 1997 on behalf of the NEA's initiative American Canvas. We began the American Canvas dialogue in six cities to encourage new thinking on the issue of arts funding and arts advocacy. I took as our cue the citizens' movement of the late nineteenth and early twentieth centuries that was dedicated to preserving our natural resources and out of which grew our national parks. Today there are forceful environmental groups that are able to effect change at the federal level: the Sierra Club, the National Wildlife Federation, the National Audubon Society, the Natural Resources Defense Council, and the Nature Conservancy, to name just a few. By comparison, we are babies in the effort to preserve our cultural resources. While hundreds of groups are dedicated to the preservation of wildlife and the environment, there are only a handful of national arts advocacy groups. The environment even has its own protection agency, the EPA. Could we imagine an Arts Protection Agency? It seems as important to me to protect the "interior of the mind" as the "interior of the land."

ART 21, the federal conference on the arts that was held during my first year on the job, focused on the artist in relationship to society; American Canvas, my last large-scale federal initiative, focused instead on the value of the arts to communities. We visited Miami, Los Angeles, San Antonio, and Salt Lake City, as well as Charlotte, North Carolina, Rock Hill, South Carolina, and Columbus, Ohio. In each place we brought legislators, businesspeople, and artists together to discuss the role of the arts in the community. We talked about quality of life, economic vitality, and citizen pride, among other things.

The twin cities of Rock Hill, South Carolina, and Charlotte, North Carolina, had both revitalized themselves through investment in culture. William Simms, the president of Transamerica Reinsurance, and an African American, said:

> I'm convinced that the arts are a part of that definition of what makes a city become a rising city. . . . It's that feel-good element that makes people want to be there, makes businesses want to relocate there, encourages businesses to grow. And I'm convinced that it's the absolutely essential part of a city's economic strength and economic vitality.

Simms had been tested in his conviction about the arts just a few months before our arrival in Charlotte. Tony Kushner's Pulitzer Prize–winning play *Angels in America* was picketed by a group of seventy religious right adherents on opening night. They claimed that the seven-second nude scene was the problem. Homosexuality was the problem. The mayor had threatened to close the play down, Simms talked him out of it, and a court order let the play continue. Things had quieted down when we visited Charlotte, but in April 1997 the county commissioners cut $2.5 million from the $11 million budget of the Arts and Science Council and passed a resolution barring public funds to groups that show "perverted forms of sexuality . . . (or) promote, advocate, or endorse behaviors, life styles, and values that seek to undermine

and deviate from the value and societal role of the traditional family."
On April 3 the *Charlotte Observer* had quoted the remark of one of the
commissioners on the play's producer, the Charlotte Repertory Theater:
"If they don't know they're walking dead now, I suggest they get a clue
pretty quick." The nastiness I had been encountering at the federal level
was manifest, regrettably, at the local level as well.

In Miami there was censorship of another kind. Our theme, fit-
tingly, was that the arts ensure equity and access to all citizens and
bridge populations. This was a touchy subject in Miami because some
of the more militant Cuban American citizens had actually stopped
performances that were favorable to Castro's Cuba. The censorship had
been ongoing and was sometimes dangerous to the performing artists
or visual artists involved. All over America there were art controversies
that pointed to the need for a strong defense of the First Amendment
from the highest levels of government. If the Congress of the United
States could censor the National Endowment for the Arts, why couldn't
legislators in communities nationwide follow their example? We
needed to triumph over these bigoted, small-minded politicians.

The book documenting our American Canvas forums was issued by
the Endowment in the autumn of 1997. As a blueprint for the future, it
reports valuable information from communities that have successfully
sustained their arts organizations.

With all that I was doing for arts organizations, I had precious little
time to see what they were presenting in the way of art. My days and
nights were full of NEA business, and I rarely thought of my past life as
an actress. But one day, when I had a few minutes, I indulged in my
favorite in-house activity, visiting a panel. I dropped in on a theater
panel in the Creation and Presentation category one afternoon and listened to the panelists deliberate on some of the hundreds of theaters the
NEA had helped make possible throughout the United States since the
1960s. When they took a break they turned to me, with all the vivacity
that theater people are capable of, and asked when I was going to return
to the stage. When this fight is over, I said—someday soon. They
hugged me, and one of them snapped a picture of all of us together.

When I headed back down the stone corridor to my office I was surprised to find tears streaming down my cheeks. I loved the theater more

than almost anything in life except my family and friends, my home, and the great outdoors. I loved theater people. They were good people with big hearts. Starting rehearsals for a new play was always exhilarating. The schedule was proscribed: four or five weeks to rehearse, several weeks of previews, and then opening night. If the audience responded well the play could run for a year or more, although a few months was the norm. The system was result-oriented, and everyone knew what they had to do. The atmosphere was collaborative and cooperative. There was no wasting time in wrangling over the end result, even though there was plenty of room for airing differences in rehearsal. The open-endedness of the legislative process was tedious and unproductive so much of the time. The tears that sprang to my eyes were for the joy of the theater community. I had not cried for years, and I didn't let these tears linger long in the halls in case one of the staff should see me feeling down.

The theater productions I tried not to miss in Washington, D.C., were those of the Shakespeare Theater. Michael Kahn was masterful at directing the plays and casting fine actors. He and I had worked together in the early 1970s on productions of *The Merry Wives of Windsor* and O'Neill's *Mourning Becomes Electra*.

Michael called me one day to ask for a chairman's "extraordinary action grant" to keep the free Shakespeare performances alive in the summer. I had use of a special fund for grants up to $30,000 that did not need Council approval. Our budget had been slashed so deeply that I had turned over most of the money to our programs to make up the shortfall, and I couldn't oblige him. Fortunately, at the last minute, some donors made it possible for the free performances at the Carter-Barron Theater to continue. The productions were always standing-room-only. Entire families would attend, the elderly would bring friends, and teenagers would come in dating groups. I watched one eleven-year-old girl sit enrapt through an entire production of *Henry V.* She reminded me of myself as a little girl seeing *Copelia* with my dad fifty years before, and of how that one ballet performance had changed my young life. It was incomprehensible to me that our society might lose these treasures, or that governments didn't totally subsidize these productions that the public clearly craved.

I wasn't allowed to act while I was at the helm of the NEA; I wasn't allowed to take remuneration from any other source. My unions had accepted my temporary withdrawal, but one day I received an offer I couldn't refuse: to play myself, in a play called *Inspecting Carol.* Dan Sullivan, who had directed *The Sisters Rosensweig,* had written a piece about a government inspector coming to see a theater production for a prospective grant application. It is a singular romp of a play, and at the end of the farce the inspector, deus ex machina, enters to put everything right. I enjoyed my five minutes onstage as much as the audience enjoyed seeing me in the role I played daily, and I donated my night's salary to the theater.

On another occasion I reprised my portrayal of Eleanor Roosevelt, with Ed Herrmann as FDR at the White House. This time, as the older Eleanor, I didn't need the padding and my hair was graying. I had put on an ungainly twenty pounds since I'd been in Washington, the result of too little exercise and too much food, not an unusual circumstance in the world of politics. The president and the First Lady hosted a fund-raising dinner for the new FDR memorial designed by the former NEA Council member Lawrence Halprin. Ed Herrmann and I were part of the after-dinner entertainment in the East Room. We read from letters, slipping easily into roles and voices we had not used since the *Eleanor and Franklin* miniseries twenty years earlier. The Clintons, especially Hillary, identified with the pressures that Eleanor suffered. While Hillary was being vilified for Whitewater, Travelgate, and the failure of the health care initiative, Eleanor had been ridiculed for her travels nationwide and for her unpopular stances. Hillary Rodham Clinton related one of her favorite Eleanor statements: "Women are like tea bags—put them in hot water and they get stronger."

Despite the constant pressure, I knew *I* was growing stronger; I felt that I could withstand anything that came my way. And one day I had what I regarded as a clear, strong omen that we would prevail. I dreamed of a peregrine falcon, a bird that had once been on the list of endangered species because the pesticide DDT made it impossible to produce viable eggs; once the poison was no longer in use, however, the bird had made an incredible comeback. I dreamed that the falcon flew into my outstretched hand and let me hold it in my palm; that was the extent of the dream. The next morning, as I walked the three blocks down Pennsylvania Avenue to my office in the Old Post Office Building, I chanced to look up, and to my amazement a peregrine falcon was wheeling fifty feet above the rush-hour traffic, chasing a flock of pigeons. I expected the clouds to part and a bright ray of sun to shine down, so vivid was the omen. I skipped the rest of the way to work, quite convinced that the NEA was going to be okay after all.

I also sensed that there was some desperation on the part of the Republicans regarding the Endowment. The agency was not the pushover they had imagined us to be two years earlier. Now it was down to the wire. They had to get rid of us in September as planned. But in their eagerness they were acting stupidly.

One of my favorite sculptures in Washington is a monumental piece by Alexander Calder called "Mountains and Clouds." Every time Dick Woodruff and I visited the Hart Senate Office Building we would spend a few minutes gazing at it. It dominated the entire atrium, with triangles of black iron thrust to the very top of the space, the "mountains," and a black mobile of "clouds" hanging from the ceiling. The piece can be contemplated from the balconies of all the eight stories. It has seriousness and purpose, as if Calder were reminding the senators that theirs is a weighty calling. The stabile and mobile above also have great movement, like the largo of a Beethoven symphony. I loved it, and so did Dick. Together we would inspect it for graffiti or dents, calling Senator John Warner to have it attended to when necessary.

I knew the GOP was in trouble when two aides published a piece in the Hill's newspaper, *Roll Call,* calling for the sculpture's removal. The men worked for Senators Spencer Abraham and Dan Coats, neither of whom had any love for the NEA. "'Mountains and Clouds' is several tons of sheer ugliness," they wrote.

> It is time for people to say what used to be obvious: the purpose of art is not to make people feel uncomfortable or "challenge" them through shallow mockery and/or vulgarity. That undermines art's true calling—to ennoble us and our surroundings. . . . We think this insult to nature should be removed and banished from the light of day.

This diatribe was a little too close to the Senate floor for comfort. It would have been scary—smacking as it did of the Third Reich's attack in the 1930s on modern art as "degenerate"—if it hadn't been so ridiculous.

There was an ominous repetitive pattern as our critics sought to bring us down and we countered every assault with determination. I supposed that the struggle of art and politics would never really end but that it was important to be vigilant. Controversy, after all, was the price paid for democracy, and there were people in the world, ardent Christians among them, who understood that and were as devoted to art as the rest of us. In Bill Moyers's public television interview with Sister Wendy Beckett, the nun whose series on art history was so popular a few years back, she spoke of art as "exercising the muscles of your own individuality" and bid us to look at a painting as a child does, without labels and prejudice. I wished that Sister Wendy could have sat down with members of Congress and calmed them with her reasonableness. The struggle they were engaging in was so insignificant in the larger scheme of things. Why couldn't they just get over it?

The business of the agency continued as usual, with thousands of applications pouring in; there were far too many worthy organizations seeking support, and not enough funds to do the job. I watched as the revision of the programs began to take hold and the applicants and panelists began to feel more comfortable with the direction of the agency. Negative attitudes declined as we all attempted to fix what was not working in the new structure. The staff remained cheerful and committed despite the turmoil.

There are some events in life for which there is no warning, and from which there is no recovery. Such an event occurred to our family on February 4, 1997. Our beloved Geoff died suddenly of a massive heart attack while skiing in Vail. He was thirty-three years old, in good health, and had no previous symptoms of which we were aware. The paramedics did all they could that sunny afternoon high in the snow-covered Rockies, but Geoff left this world within minutes.

He was a golden boy, made for summer sun and a long and happy life. He had many friends and many new acquaintances who congregated in the warmth of his restaurant to be close to him and exult in the meals he loved to prepare.

Nothing is ever the same for those who are left. A light clicks off, and memories cloud the mind. It was hard to concentrate, and anger kept welling in me. I was angry that Geoff had been taken from us and angry at the pettiness of the politicians who were after the NEA. I was having a hard time holding my temper and knew the time had come for me to leave. If I had no more grace to bring to my job, I could serve no one well in Washington. And I needed to be home with my husband at this time.

I told Melanne I had to go. She understood. I said I would stay to shepherd the Endowment through the committee hearings and the markup of our appropriations bills. I thought I might be out by June, but as time went by it was clear that would not be possible: it would be a struggle for the life of the agency to the bitter end.

The desperation on the part of our enemies grew as the months rolled by. They were becoming reckless and looked more and more pitiful in their attacks. One congressman from northern California thought he would receive sympathy from voters and other Republicans in Congress when he circulated the news that "the NEA funds basketmakers." He succeeded only in incurring the wrath of the California Indian Basketweavers Association, which annually congregated for a festival and conference with the help of NEA's $60,000 grant. Ben Nighthorse Campbell, the only Native American senator, and a Republican also, brought antique Indian baskets to the Senate in protest, quickly shaming the poor House member who had brought the issue up in the first place.

I appeared at five committee hearings in the spring of 1997, three in the House and two in the Senate. They were no longer notable. They were repetitious and a waste of everyone's time, most of all the taxpayer's. The Hutchinson brothers from Arkansas, Asa in the House and Tim in the Senate, stepped up their efforts to ridicule us, succeeding only in making themselves look foolish. The whole business reminded me more and more of *Alice In Wonderland*. "Off with her head," I expected someone to shout any minute, while I barely restrained myself from countering with "You're nothing but a pack of cards!" Pete Hoekstra in his Oversights and Investigations Subcommittee hearing, failed to come up with any significant dirt on me or the agency, in spite of massive investigation of dozens of grants and of our administrative costs. The poker game was winding down, but the leadership still had an ace in the hole.

Because the NEA had not been reauthorized since 1990, the House Committee on Rules decided that the Endowment was ineligible for any appropriation at all. Sid Yates rose to the agency's defense once again, as he had year after year, asking that there be a vote on the rule. He knew that we would prevail in any up-and-down vote about whether the agency should exist and receive any funding at all. Louise Slaughter had done a stunning "whip" count of Democrats in support, with only five against, Charlie Stenholm among them. The moderate Republicans Rick Lazio and Amo Houghton had also done a count and expected to have thirty from their party in our favor. When the day for the vote arrived, ironically the only Democrat who did not vote was Louise Slaughter, who unfortunately had experienced a death in her family and returned to upstate New York. The pressure from Gingrich and Armey on their colleagues was enormous; they worked the back of the House chamber demanding the allegiance of the moderates and making promises to them in exchange for their votes. In the final tally only fifteen moderates voted for the NEA. The senior staff and I watched in horror as the numbers flashed up on the TV screen in my office. The final tally was 217–216; we had lost by one vote. For the first time in its thirty-two-year history the NEA had zero appropriations from the House of Representatives.

Congress recessed in August, and our fate still hung in the balance. The Senate was our only hope. I went to Nantucket again and was refreshed as always by daily swims in the Atlantic. Ed joined me on weekends, and we talked about life "A.D." (after duty). In the evening we gazed at the stars and wished we had the time to learn their names and places in the universe.

Earlier, in the spring of 1997, a huge comet had glowed in the northern sky nightly. Hale-Bopp was a rare and bright visitor. One night, while walking my dog in New York City, I was approached by a young man. "Do you know where the comet is?" he said. Thinking he was looking for a nightclub I replied: "No, sorry." "You don't know where the comet is?" he said again, looking puzzled. "Oh, you mean *the* comet!" I replied, finally getting it. "In the northern sky—you'll probably have to go down toward the river to see it." "Yeah, guess so," he said. "It'll probably be about a thousand years before I get another chance." My thoughts exactly on those restful island days in late August.

One morning Caroline Kennedy Schlossberg called and asked me to dinner with the president on the neighboring island of Martha's Vineyard. I didn't know her, but Ted Kennedy wanted me to join them. It was a small gathering, the last I would spend close to the president, and with JFK Jr., who would so tragically die two years later. As I drove the long dirt drive through the scrub oaks to Jackie Kennedy Onassis's summer home nestled in the dunes, I thought of the Kennedys and all they had given to political life. I didn't know how they stood it, but they were the paragon of fortitude and grace under pressure.

There were only twelve of us, and we talked casually of the islands and played a word game after dinner based on quotations from *Bartlett's*. The president loved it, but it was John who kept stumping us with his simple quotes. I looked across the room at the two of them sitting side by side, the leaders of the Western world, one given his power by the people and the other the inheritor of the throne. I had no doubt that John Jr. would be a great political leader one day, but time did not give him the chance.

September was a busy month with numerous arts events, meetings with senators to be assured of their support, and quiet discussions about my departure with Sandy, Cherie, and Scott Sanders, who was to take over the agency when I left. Ed and I were too busy to attend the Emmy Awards in Los Angeles; *Law and Order* had been nominated once again. To our amazement the show won for Best Drama Series. Ed's talents as a director and producer had been honed in NEA-sponsored theaters, but no one mentioned that, of course, when they accepted the award.

When the Interior appropriations bill finally came to the Senate floor on September 16, 1997, it was the Iowa statesman Tom Harkin who defended the agency at the eleventh hour. John Ashcroft of Missouri was grasping at straws. He said the NEA had funded a one-word poem, "Lighght," and that illustrated our misuse of funds. The anthology he unearthed the poem from had received a grant from the Endowment in 1968! Harkin couldn't resist. He gave a brilliant, only slightly patronizing lecture about how writers create and the track of their progress through small presses and workshops, like the one in Iowa, to major publications and sometimes Pulitzer prizes. He made an analogy between the research that the NIH conducts and the help that the NEA gives to artists. The final vote was 61–39 in favor of reappropriating the Endowment at the same level as the year before.

The senators held the line in conference with the House, despite Dick Armey's efforts to cut us well below $100 million, but the two legislative bodies were still unresolved as the negotiating days wore on. Ralph Regula, who was secretly pleased that the NEA was still alive, needed some concession to make to the Gang of Four and sought to eliminate our only existing individual fellowships, the ones in literature. We were sitting in splendid celebration of the National Medal of Arts recipients at a grand luncheon given by the Endowment on September 29 when Ralph told me of his plan. He, Louise Slaughter, and I caucused then and there amid congratulatory speeches from the podium and the main course and dessert. I could not bear to see our last remaining fellowships disappear. It had been bad enough when Congress eliminated the individual artist grants two years before. I had consistently and publicly defended their reinstatement, and now the prestigious literature fellowships were about to go under. Desperate, I pulled Dick aside and told him to slip our millennium book of NEA writers to Ralph's wife Mary at the luncheon table. I knew that Ralph would not have time to look at it, but that if Mary read it she would not be able to help admiring the writing of the fifty former grantees, one from each state. The very next morning Ralph called to tell me I had Mary to thank for saving the fellowships.

The final budget to emerge from the House and Senate conference kept the NEA indubitably alive, with virtually the same budget as the year before. We had triumphed. In the final hour we may have had Mary Regula to thank for saving the literature fellowships, but we had thousands and thousands to thank nationwide for saving the agency.

They wrote letters, they called their congressmen, they gave the Arts Endowment their unfailing support. We had some remarkable members of Congress who never wavered in their commitment to the agency, and ultimately, together, we defeated the most formidable foes the agency had ever faced. The NEA staff never flinched, and now, breathing a sigh of relief, they dug in their heels for the season of work to come. The NEA was now bulletproof; it was here to stay.

The victory was bittersweet for me. I was thrilled that we had overcome those who controlled the 104th and 105th Congresses, but I was left with a residual disappointment. Why all the fuss, all the wrangling, all the jockeying for position and power? There will always be controversy in art, until artists take their last breath of life. But all great nations support their artists.

As long as men of little minds are elected to the highest offices in the land they will continue to dictate what men and women should do or say or see. It is left to us now at the beginning of the new century and the new millennium to ensure that the finest minds of our generation assume the guardianship of the nation. Clearly the best young men and women in America are not being drawn to a life in politics, for many reasons. Getting elected is extremely invasive and costly. Staying elected involves more of the same, as well as separation from loved ones for weeks on end sometimes. The entire process is exhausting for politicians. But one of the biggest changes I've witnessed in my lifetime is in politicians: they don't lead anymore, they follow. They follow the polls and focus groups, thinking that this is what the public wants them to do. If Roosevelt or Churchill had done that during World War II we might all be speaking German today. Not everyone can be a great leader like those two, but our elected officials should be men and women of integrity, honesty, and civility at the very least. I met and worked with many wonderful men and women in Washington; there could be many more. Our political leaders should be the finest in the nation, and we are the ones who are responsible for seeing that they are.

If I had become discouraged about our legislative leaders, I never faltered in my belief about art and the creative minds in America. There is wonderful art to be found all over this great country of ours, art that brings joy, spirituality, ritual, and fun to our lives. Art has the ability at its highest level to reconnect us to places within ourselves that seem to have been slumbering. It doesn't happen often in our lives, but when it does it evokes a clear response in us. As Hank Fonda used to say when he read a great script, "The hairs stand up on the back of my neck." If religion teaches us that love is all-encompassing, art teaches us that anything is possible. We need to safeguard all the possibilities of human experience so that we may chart our map for the future. I believe the National Endowment for the Arts helps keep the possibilities of creativity alive within each one of us, by giving artists time to work, by giving arts organizations places for artists to present their work, and by giving the public the opportunity to see the work. In partnership with private giving, government funding ensures the creation and accessibility of the widest range of art for the most people in America.

The White House had not announced my departure for fear of jeopardizing the Endowment during the budget battle and negotiations. My plans had made it awkward at the agency every day. I could not talk about the future, and I looked with immense fondness on those who had been down in the trenches with me for the past four years. I silently began my good-byes.

I sat with Roger Stevens, now in a wheelchair, shattered and almost mute from a massive stroke he had suffered. We watched young playwrights receive awards under a program that Roger had begun and the NEA aided decades earlier. They would be the playwrights of tomorrow; perhaps there was even a Shakespeare among them. Roger's blue eyes, still dancing despite his travails, glowed with pride. He had begun this great experiment called the National Endowment for the Arts; I had protected it for the future. We had come full circle together.

I packed up my bags, my papers, all the art treasures given to me on the road, and placed calls of thanks to those who had become my comrades in arms. I finally announced my departure to the staff, a day before it appeared in the newspapers. They gave me a rollicking good party, a dozen or more of the women on staff dancing the can-can while the movie in which I played "Calamity Jane" ran on a huge screen above. I like to think they believed I *overcame* calamity, and did not *cause* it. Best of all, they knew of my love for the outdoors and had heard me say that Geoff was going to teach me how to fly-fish. They gave me a gift of fly-fishing lessons and a cap that said: "Gone fishin'."

Ed and I boxed up the things in my apartment and began the drive home. The government had paid to move my belongings to Washington but refused to pay for me to take them home. I guess Washington wanted me to stay. But there were miles to go, and things to do, in the world. It was far bigger and more imaginative a world than the narrow vice of politics would have you believe. As Hamlet says: "There is more in heaven and earth, Horatio, than was ever dream't of in your philosophy."

Epilogue

"Too many pieces of music finish too long after the end." Stravinsky's observation could as well be applied to my time in politics or to this book. I ask the reader's indulgence to bear with me for a few pages more. It may have seemed that I was in a very long run of a bad play when I was in Washington. There were times that this actress wanted nothing more than to break the contract, but there were overriding compensations that made the entire run worthwhile. Public service is a gift to the servant. The opportunity to help people connect with art, and the ability to do so through the people's own agency, was reward in and of itself. I am grateful to have been appointed NEA's sixth chairman by President Bill Clinton. I am grateful, too, for the friendship and support of many fine people in the halls of Congress; and for the enduring relationships I formed with those at the NEA. I was fortunate to be able to witness the cornucopia of art in America at the end of the twentieth century, and to have met extraordinary artists, administrators, educators, and advocates everywhere I went. The abiding virtues of American citizens are their humor, their enthusiasm, and their generosity.

Americans are the most generous people on earth. They give their time to those less fortunate, and they give money to every concievable cause. The individual citizen has sustained the non-profit arts in the United States through personal donations to his or her favorite dance company, museum, or public television affilate. The earned income of non-profit arts organizations nationwide averages only about fifty percent of their budgets. The individual contributor in America makes up the bulk of the shortfall, about thirty-nine percent, corporations and foundations contribute about six percent, and local, state, and federal funds give the remaining five percent.

The National Endowment for the Arts plays a small role financially but it plays a very large role in the pride our nation takes in its artists and audiences. The Endowment, since its founding in 1965, has seeded thousands of arts organizations nationwide, its imprimature acting as a stimulant for matching funds and for community pride. The agency speaks for all artists in America by encouraging them to express who we are as a nation—our individual and collective spirit. Not everyone can be an artist but everyone resonates the art within them because art is what makes us inherently and uniquely human.

As the citizens of our pluralistic society ask to be seen and heard in all the venues that have been dominated by a white Christian male ethic, controversy is bound to erupt again and again. Democracy embraces everyone, not just a privileged few. We might as well get used to the controversy that occurs when cultures collide, and welcome the discussion it engenders rather than repudiate the intrusion. What is most important is the promotion of excellence in whatever art is presented. The recognition of excellence takes time, skill, and education on the part of our artists and citizens, and that is why life-long learning in the arts is vital to our schools and communities.

In June 1998, the Supreme Court handed down its decision in the case of *Karen Finley et al. vs. The National Endowment for the Arts.* The "NEA Four" as Finley and the others were known, had challenged the constitutionality of language that Congress inserted in the Endowment's statute. The legislation states that in awarding grants the agency has to take into "consideration general standards of decency and respect for the diverse beliefs and values of the American public." The court said that Congress and the NEA *did* have the right to include the decency language in considering awardees but that a grantee could not be penalized because the content of their art was offensive to others. This was a muddy decision on the part of the Justices. The inclusion of the decency language surely places a "chill" on applicants to the Endowment. Would a museum submit an application for an exhibit of Picasso's erotic drawings, for example? Sublime as the drawings are, there are people in America who might find them "indecent." Wouldn't the museum rather apply for funding to exhibit the artist's "Blue" period? It is clear that arts organizations in their desire to be awarded will choose the safe path toward funding. It is in decisions such as the Supreme Court's, that liberties in our society are whittled away slowly and incrementally. Doors to diversity and variety silently close.

The Supreme Court *did* uphold the First Amendment, however, by stating that grantees could not be penalized after the fact. This vindicated Karen Finley and the others of the "NEA Four" and will protect artists in the future whose works are attacked by politicians. Mayor Rudolph Giuliani was in clear violation of the court's decision when he threatened to close the Brooklyn Museum in the summer of 1999, because of art he found offensive in an exhibit called "Sensation." The NEA did not fund "Sensation," but the principle of the Mayor's action and the court's decision is the same.

Politicians come and go. Newt Gingrich left Congress, Bill Clinton's term as president is ending. But politics as it is practiced today in the United States is entrenched, and it is deeply in trouble. It is hard to know what a politican believes any more because he is so beholden to the special interests of those who elected him. An elected official has to pay attention to the money in his campaign chest first and foremost. If you are in the House of Representatives you never let it get empty because you have to begin running for the next election just two years hence, almost as soon as you get into office. In the Senate you have a reprieve of six years but you have to raise even more money for your campaign. Corporations spend to the limit, and special interest groups all have their own PACs (Political Action Committees) ready, willing, and eager to give. If all politicians sound alike these days it is because they cannot dare to be different. If all politicians take a poll rather than take a stand, it is because they need to please as many people as possible, and keep the coffers filled. A Congressman is a fool, a lame duck, or a dead duck if he doesn't take all he can get.

The system is so corrupt that it may not ever be fixed. There were campaign finance reforms after Watergate in the 1970s but the loopholes resulted in a massive breakdown of those reforms. Who is going to call a halt to the money pit? Not the Republicans whose party has alwsys prided itself on representing corporate America's special interests; and not the Democrats who need to raise the money for candidates in order to beat the Republicans.

If an organization has no money to give or insufficient money to give it is going to be ignored. And that is exactly what happened with the National Endowment for the Arts. No wonder the 104th and 105th Congress thought that it was a shoe-in for elimination! Who was going to stand up for it? There was no money flooding in from the non-profit arts communities of America as there was from the commercial arts in Hollywood. Even though the non-profit arts in America generated more attendance than all professional sporting events combined, and even though there were more artists in America than there were police and corrections officers, according to Americans for the Arts. Today a few arts organizations have begun PACs to help elect candidates who support government funding of the arts, but the real issue to be addressed is that of campaign finance reform. Until the system is completely overhauled and candidates stand on an equal playing field, it will be nearly impossible for politicians to speak about and support issues like the arts and humanities. It is a testament to the citizens of America who love the arts in their community that the Endowment is alive today. These citizens are a pure force in an impure world and our society needs more of them.

Only through citizen protest will we save the Internet from being inundated totally by corporate entertainment interests. The merger of giants Time-Warner and America Online to be content providers on the Net should be a clarion call to all artists who seek a future home in cyberspace. The commercial arts will be major employers, it is true, but they will also be the piper calling the tune, and they will try to co-opt or discourage competition. Just as the intellectual property industries pressured Congress to rob the American public of twenty years of works in the public domain, so will these same interests try to pressure our legislators to close doors on the Internet for their own benefit.

Meanwhile, I surf the Net along with most of America today and enjoy all the information I receive at my fingertips. Tomorrow, if we are vigilant, our stories will be spun in cyberspace—our literature, our movies, our music and our paintings. Cyberspace art will be its own thing; it will not be a replacement for the authentic three-dimensional worlds of dance, theatre, or sculpture, but it will be art, too. New and exciting ways of making art will be developed and transmitted, but the basic stories of the human condition, of love and longing, will always remain the same.

My family is as glad to have me home again as I am to be home. Jace, Tony and Jon are husbands and fathers now, making Ed and me grandparents of four. I go out birding every day with my dog Cody. Since leaving the Endowment in the fall of 1997, I have performed in two plays, a movie, and a TV series. It is good to be back home.

I remain active on the boards of the Wildlife Conservation Society, helping to preserve the habitat of endangered species, and on the MacDowall Colony, which gives temporary habitat to individual artists so that they may have time to create. I work to reduce the stranglehold of the military-industrial complex on our society, and I dream of the day when our national priorities reduce Pentagon spending and increase federal arts spending. The number of nuclear weapons stockpiled has been reduced, but no comprehensive test ban treaty has been signed. The Pentagon's budget is greater than it has ever been, and it is rising, while that of the Arts Endowment remains stagnant at under 100 million, despite the best efforts of the current chairman, William Ivey. No one will remember or revere the F-22 in a hundred or even twenty years, but Shakespeare is performed all over the world, four hundred years after he began to tell his stories.

We are all storytellers. From time immemorial human beings have invented and reinvented themselves through stories—in song, in fabric and paint, in music, in dance and in drama. We are endlessly fascinated with the predicament of life and what we are doing here. The stories will not end because they give us the possibilities of our existence, and the extension of what it means to be human.

When we teach a child to sing or play the flute, we teach her how to listen. When we teach her to draw, we teach her to see. When we teach a child to dance, we teach him about his body and about space, and when he acts on stage, he learns about character and motivation. When we teach a child design, we reveal the geometry of the world. When we teach children about the folk and traditional arts and the great master-pieces of the world, we teach them to celebrate their roots and find their own place in history.

It is time I made my exit. Everyone needs an exit line, and I always prefer working from a good script. Shakespeare said it best in *The Tempest*, when Prospero, in the epilogue, makes his farewell: "Now I want spirits to enforce, art to enchant. . . ."

Index

PublicAffairs is a new nonfiction publishing house and a tribute to the standards, values, and flair of three persons who have served as mentors to countless reporters, writers, editors, and book people of all kinds, including me.

I.F. Stone, proprietor of *I. F. Stone's Weekly*, combined a commitment to the First Amendment with entrepreneurial zeal and reporting skill and became one of the great independent journalists in American history. At the age of eighty, Izzy published *The Trial of Socrates*, which was a national bestseller. He wrote the book after he taught himself ancient Greek.

Benjamin C. Bradlee was for nearly thirty years the charismatic editorial leader of *The Washington Post*. It was Ben who gave the *Post* the range and courage to pursue such historic issues as Watergate. He supported his reporters with a tenacity that made them fearless, and it is no accident that so many became authors of influential, best-selling books.

Robert L. Bernstein, the chief executive of Random House for more than a quarter century, guided one of the nation's premier publishing houses. Bob was personally responsible for many books of political dissent and argument that challenged tyranny around the globe. He is also the founder and was the longtime chair of Human Rights Watch, one of the most respected human rights organizations in the world.

. . .

For fifty years, the banner of Public Affairs Press was carried by its owner Morris B. Schnapper, who published Gandhi, Nasser, Toynbee, Truman, and about 1,500 other authors. In 1983 Schnapper was described by *The Washington Post* as "a redoubtable gadfly." His legacy will endure in the books to come.

Peter Osnos, *Publisher*